P9-BZE-251

LONE WOLF

LONE WOLF

The Life and Death of U-Boat Ace Werner Henke

TIMOTHY P. MULLIGAN

Westport, Connecticut
London

ISBN 0-275-93677-5

Copyright © 1993 by Timothy P. Mulligan

All rights reserved. No portion of this book may be
reproduced, by any process or technique, without the
express written consent of the publisher.

Praeger Publishers, 88 Post Road West, Westport, CT 06881
An imprint of Greenwood Publishing Group, Inc.

Printed in the United States of America

Copyright Acknowledgments

The author and publisher gratefully acknowledge permission to reprint material from the
following sources:

Timothy P. Mulligan, "German U-boat Crews in World War II: Sociology of an Elite,"
Journal of Military History 56, no. 2 (April 1992), 261–81.

Karl Dönitz, *Memoirs: Ten Years and Twenty Days*, trans. by R. H. Stevens. Reprinted by
permission of George Weldenfeld and Nicolson, Ltd.

Contents

Illustrations

Photographs follow page 126

FIGURE

TABLES

Preface

It has been said that a writer never finishes a book, but merely puts it down and walks away from it for awhile. In the twenty-nine months since *Lone Wolf: The Life and Death of U-Boat Ace Werner Henke* first went to the publisher, new source materials have become available, new books and memoirs have been written, and veterans and other researchers have come forward to correct or supplement issues raised. I myself have begun a new general study of German U-Boat sailors, inspired in part by my work with *U-515*'s crew. The publication of this paperback edition allows me to return to the subject of Werner Henke and discuss the impact of these developments on what I had written.

In reviewing this material, I find nothing that alters my view of Henke's character, career, or fate. Some new information, however, modifies or revises specific details presented in this edition. For the sake of the greatest possible accuracy, I have noted these changes below, together with acknowledgments for the responsible sources.

Among new records, the most significant consist of formerly classified message files of the Atlantic Fleet, recently accessioned from the Navy Department's Operational Archives and now a part of National Archives Record Group (RG) 38, Records of the Chief of Naval Operations. The messages of 4 and 7 April 1944 alerted Capt. Daniel V. Gallery's Task Group 21.12 to the southern movement of three U-boats in his general sector, one of which was Henke's *U-515*. Derived from ULTRA decryptions of U-Boat radio communications prepared by the "Secret Room" of COMINCH (Commander in Chief, U.S. Fleet) Combat Intelligence, Atlantic Section, these messages disprove my claim (p. 193) that ULTRA played no role in Henke's sinking. These message files and their counterparts among British Admiralty records will require careful study by future historians to establish how ULTRA intelligence was used by operational units in the Battle of the Atlantic.

Few German Navy records that identify the officer complements of individual U-Boats survived the war. Ironically, in the course of my new research, I discovered more information on Henke among the handful of extant files. Monthly returns of U-Boat officer assignments for May–Nov. 1941, reproduced as record items PG 36673–674 on T1022 roll 2150, indicate that Henke indeed was advanced to First Watch Officer (I.W.O.) on *U-124* by 1 July 1941; this revises data in E. B. Gasaway's history of that submarine, *Grey Wolf, Grey Sea*.

A simple photograph also forces me to revise the date of Henke's meeting with Adolf Hitler, which I placed on 4 July 1943 (p. 157), when Henke officially received the Oak Leaves to his Knight's Cross of the Iron Cross. As this occurred while Henke was on home leave, I therefore concluded the events had coincided. But another photograph of that meeting (not reproduced in this or the previous edition) includes a similarly decorated U-Boat commander standing next to Henke whom I subsequently identified as *Kaptlt.* Carl Emmermann *(U-172)*. On 4 July 1943 Emmermann and his boat were on operations off the coast of Brazil. By checking the next time that both officers were home on leave, then consulting a summary of Hitler's daily appointments (which identified the attendees only as Knight's Cross recipients), I may now say that Henke's meeting with the Führer took place at 10:30 P.M. on 24 September 1943. (Hitler's appointment book is reproduced on National Archives Microcopy T84, Miscellaneous German Records, roll 387.)

I am indebted to historian and friend Mary Ellen Reese, who has kept me apprised of her research discoveries among the Records of the Provost Marshal General's Office, RG 389. Among these was a War Department memo of 8 August 1942, stating that German prisoners of war held at Ft. Hunt, Virginia, were to be officially considered as internees at Ft. Meade, Maryland. This administrative fiction doubtless furnished the rationale for the Army's false statement that Henke died at Ft. Meade (p. 215).

A review of the Nazi Party membership files of the Berlin Document Center confirmed my beliefs: neither Werner Henke nor any of his family belonged to the Party.

Daniel V. Gallery's personal papers, donated to the U.S. Naval Academy's Nimitz Library in Annapolis, proved a disappointment. Most of the "papers" concerning Henke consisted of clippings of Hans Herlin's serialized feature on Henke in *Der Stern*, 18 Oct.–22 Nov. 1958, accompanied by typed translations which Gallery had annotated with pencil comments in the margin. Particularly enlightening was Gallery's correspondence with the Admiralty, Aug.–Nov. 1955, requesting copies of British official records on the sinking of the *Ceramic*. The questions and replies prove that Gallery's account of the *Ceramic*'s loss in his book, *U-505*, rests more on the author's imagination than on fact.

Nevertheless, the new study by Gaylord T. M. Kelshall, *The U-Boat War in the Caribbean* (Annapolis, 1994), relies exclusively on Gallery in his references to Henke and *U-515*, and thus offers nothing new for my study. The posthumously-published memoirs of Wilhelm Schulz, *Über dem Nassen Abgrund: Als Kommandant und Flotillenchef im U-Boot-Krieg* (Berlin, 1994), furnishes more details on the history of *U-124* but does not even mention Henke. For more detailed information on Allied bombings of Lorient, interested readers should consult the article by Josef W. Konvitz, "Bombs, Cities, and Submarines: Allied Bombing of the French Ports, 1942–43," in the Feb. 1992 issue of *The International History Review*.

Lone Wolf's publication also brought forth new information and memories by German and American veterans. Before May 1993 I did not have the opportunity to interview Hans Schultz, *U-515's* Second Watch Officer at the time of her sinking, as he previously had not attended the crew's reunions. Schultz provided much new information regarding the submarine's last two patrols; especially valuable are his observations of Henke's cold-blooded daring during the engagement with HMS *Chanticleer* on 18 November 1943, when Henke deliberately exposed his periscope to invite an attack by the British sloop. Günther Altenburger, Carl Möller, Hermann Brandt, and Rolf Taubert offered additional comments on the final patrols.

Most illuminating have been my contacts with veterans of Task Group 21.12: Capt. Edwin H. Headlund, former commander of destroyer escort USS *Pope*; Joseph T. Villanella; Frank P. DeNardo; Leon Kresl; and Arthur L. Davis. All of these gentlemen have contributed details to the sinking of *U-515*, the recovery of her survivors, and the treatment of prisoners of war on board the USS *Guadalcanal*. Mr. Kresl in particular recalled an incident when he escorted Henke to the officer's head while anchored off Bermuda: allowed to stop briefly in a passageway near an open hatch, Henke made a move as if to escape, and was stopped only when Kresl audibly removed the safety catch on his pistol. The incident suggests that the beleaguered U-Boat captain already was considering suicide long before his ordeal at Ft. Hunt.

I am also indebted to Eric C. Rust, Gerard E. Hasselwander, Richard Hall, and Fred Geils for their comments and observations; to all those who took the time to express their encouragement; and to my friends and family for their continued support. Sadly I must also note the passing over the last two years of four German veterans who so graciously assisted me: Karl-Friedrich Merten (whose memoirs have been posthumously published by Koehler Verlag as *Nach Kompass: Lebenserinnerungen eines Seeoffiziers*), Peter "Ali" Cremer, Herbert Bölke, and Kurt Lipke. In their memory, I hope to incorporate the above changes and new information in a future edition. Whatever errors or omissions that remain are, of course, the sole responsibility of the author.

TIMOTHY P. MULLIGAN
February 1995

Acknowledgments

In writing a biography, an author is necessarily dependent on many people to share that most personal of possessions, their memories. This writer gratefully acknowledges his debt to so many who allowed a foreigner to partake of their past without reservation or condition.

I am most indebted to Albrecht Henke and his wife Gertrud for their gracious hospitality, time, and endless patience in answering questions and furnishing information. Equally significant has been the kind hospitality and unstinting assistance of Horst Bredow and his wife Annemarie at the U-Boot-Archiv, located on the island of Sylt when this work began but now more accessibly situated at Altenbruch outside Cuxhaven. Without the assistance of these individuals, this project could not have been started.

The veterans of *U–515* deserve a special thanks for sharing their memories of service. In particular, Carl Möller, Günther Altenburger, and Hans Hahn have furnished detailed information on their experiences; the late Günter Eckert, Hermann Brandt, Herbert Bölke, Werner Rasche, Hermann Kaspers, Heinrich Scharnhorst, Kurt Hanisch, and Kurt Lipke and their wives all assisted my efforts and made me feel welcome during reunions at Steinhude am Meer and Lübbenau. Mr. Klaus Schäle greatly assisted my work at Kiel and Cuxhaven.

Among former Kriegsmarine officers, Karl-Friedrich Merten patiently answered detailed questions over an extended period and kindly made his own memoirs available for use. Wilhelm Müller-Arnecke, Peter "Ali" Cremer, and Reinhard Hardegen contributed valuable pieces of a personality puzzle. Despite a terminal illness, Heinrich Niemeyer supplied a detailed account of his long association with Werner Henke.

Eduard Vogt revealed details of U-Boat sailors' training; Mr. Ernie North furnished an account of the damage to HMS *Chanticleer;* Capt. Wyman H. Packard (ret.) clarified an important point regarding the significance of intelligence and its distribution. Mr. Ed Caram kindly assisted in the identification of key photographs. Cdr. C. H. Little (ret.) answered an important question from the Canadian perspective.

Dr. Jürgen Rohwer greatly assisted my research on specific points, while the institution he has directed, the Bibliothek für Zeitgeschichte in Stuttgart, furnished invaluable documentation. Mr. Eberhard Schmidt of the Marineschule Mürwik kindly provided copies of Crew 33 materials. Ms. Terri Sinnott and Mr. Keith Gill of Chicago's Museum of Science and Industry contributed a tour and access to materials regarding the captured Type IXC class submarine *U–505.*

My work benefited from the professional expertise and assistance of numerous staff members at various institutions, especially: Mr. Gus Britton, Royal Navy Submarine Museum, Gosport; Ms. Cathy Lloyd, Operational Archives, U.S. Naval Historical Center, Washington, DC; Dr. A. A. H. Knightbridge, Miss G. L. Beech, and Ms. Sue Edwards, Public Record Office, Kew, England; Mr. R. H. Coppock, Navy Historical Branch, Ministry of Defence, London; Mr. Philip Reed, Imperial War Museum, London; Ms. Terri Hammett and Mr. Fred Pernell, National Archives, Washington, DC; Mr. Pierre Waksman, Service historique de la Marine, Vincennes, France; the reference staff of the Haus des Deutschen Ostens, Düsseldorf; Mr. Glenn Wright, National Archives of Canada, Ottawa; Mr. Walther Kapahnke, Forschungsstelle Ostmitteleuropa-Westpreussische Familienforschung, Bad Salzuflen; and Ms. Janne Julsrud, Royal Norwegian Embassy, Washington, DC.

Jak P. Mallmann Showell kindly reviewed and offered suggestions on part of the manuscript. Drs. Eric Rust, Charles Burdick, and Philip Lundeburg all furnished valuable advice and encouragement.

Ms. Elaine Womack provided the drawing of the Type IXC U-Boat in chapter 6. Mrs. Amy Markon prepared the tables.

Finally, my deepest gratitude to Bonnie, who assisted in the preparation of the index, in countless suggestions, and above all in her acceptance to pay the price of this work.

A Note on Terms and Abbreviations

The sea and the military—each requires a separate vocabulary to express its specialized character. A book that discusses both must therefore provide some guidance to the terminology and expressions commonly used in the text.

All reference points for a ship or vessel are based on the vantage point of someone in the vessel looking toward the front of the vessel, the direction in which the vessel is headed. The left side of the ship is known as port; the right side, as starboard. Both the direction in which the ship is heading, the course or heading, and the direction in which another vessel or object lies from the ship, the bearing, are expressed in the 360 degrees of an imaginary compass surrounding the ship. If a vessel was heading due north, its course would be 0 degrees; another ship that appeared directly opposite her on the eastern horizon would have a relative bearing of 90 degrees; a ship appearing directly behind her on the southern horizon would have a relative bearing of 180 degrees; and so on.

The front part of a vessel is the bow; the rear, the stern. The central segment where the ship attains its greatest width is known as the beam. That section running from the beam back to the stern is known as the port and starboard quarter for the left- and right-hand sides, respectively. Thus, a ship torpedoed at the center on the left side would report a hit on the port beam; a U-Boat spotted ahead and to the right of the ship would be reported as "off the starboard bow."

All distances and speeds are given in nautical miles or knots (roughly 6080 ft.). Figures for tonnage of merchant ships reflect gross registered tons, without regard for weight of cargo. Unless otherwise indicated, all times given are as maintained aboard *U–515*, which held to German time regardless of the time in the operational area.

German naval ranks are reproduced in the original, though translations follows the first use of each specific rank.

The war diary (*Kriegstagebuch*, or KTB) of *U–515*, reproduced as file PG 30553 on roll 3067 of National Archives microcopy T1022, Microfilmed Records of the German Navy, is cited so frequently in footnotes that the standard citation used is "KTB *U–515*." The German term *Fünf-fünfzehn* (Five-fifteen) is also used to identify *U–515*.

Provided below are the abbreviations and acronyms used in the text and footnotes.

ADM: Admiralty (file citation)

Aphrodite: a radar decoy used by German U-Boats

Asdic: British term for sonar, after the Allied Submarine Detection Investigation Committee that invented the device in 1917

B-dienst: Beobachtungsdienst, the German Navy Signal Intelligence Service

BdU: Befehlshaber der Unterseeboote, Commander in Chief of Submarines

Bold: device released by a submerged U-Boat to decoy Allied sonar

DEMS: Defensively Equipped Merchant Ships, British equivalent of Naval Armed Guard aboard merchant vessels

Engima: designation for the cipher machine used by the German armed forces to encode security-classified messages

FAT: *Federapparat Torpedo,* spring-operated torpedo

FuMB: *Funkmess-Beobachtungsgerät,* radar-detection equipment

GHG: *Gruppen-Horch-Gerät,* "group listening apparatus," array of hydrophones installed on a U-Boat's bow

Hedgehog: a mortar-like antisubmarine weapon that fired a pattern of 24 projectiles ahead of a warship, detonating only upon contact with a submerged object

HF/DF: High-frequency/direction-finding ("Huff-duff"), shipborne apparatus for locating a U-Boat by its radio transmissions

Hohentwiel: manufacturer and common name for a type of primitive radar carried aboard U-Boats

HSO: *Handelsschiffsoffizier,* merchant marine officer who entered the German Navy after 1933

I.W.O.: *Erster Wach-Offizier* (colloquially *Eins W.O.*), First Watch Officer (equivalent to U.S. Navy Executive Officer)

II.W.O.: *Zweiter Wach-Offizier*, Second Watch Officer

KTB: *Kriegstagebuch*, war diary

L.I.: *Leitender Ingenieur*, Chief Engineer

Metox: manufacturer and common name of a primitive form of radar detection gear (FuMB) mounted on U-Boats

MGFA: Militärgeschichtliches Forschungsamt, Military History Office

NA: National Archives, Washington, D.C.

Naxos: code name for a type of radar detection gear (FuMB)

ONI: Office of Naval Intelligence, U.S. Navy

OpArchives: Operational Archives, U.S. Naval Historical Center, Washington Navy Yard, Washington, D.C.

Op-16-W: office designation for the Special Warfare Branch within ONI, responsible for psychological warfare

Op-16-Z: office designation for the Special Activities Branch within ONI, responsible for interrogation of prisoners of war and the evaluation of captured equipment

OWI: Office of War Information

Pi–2: *Pistole–2*, German term for a type of magnetic detonator used with torpedo warheads

POW(s): prisoner(s) of war

PRO: Public Record Office, Kew, England

RAF: Royal Air Force

RG: Record Group, used by the National Archives to indicate the records originated by a specific agency or department

SA: Sturmabteilung, Nazi party storm troopers

SS: Schutzstaffel, "Guard Echelon," Nazi party security organization

SX: Abbreviation for old German battleship *Schleswig-Holstein*

T–5: German acoustic torpedo, also known as the *Zaunkönig* (wren) to the Kriegsmarine and as the "gnat" to Allied intelligence

ULTRA: code for Allied interception and decryption of secret German radio communications

USNIP: United States Naval Institute Proceedings

UZO: *Überwasserzieloptik*, device used on U-Boat bridge for surface torpedo firings

Wabos: contraction of *Wasserbomben*, German for "depth-charges"

Wanz or Wanze: contraction of *Wellenanzeiger* ("wave detector"), common name for a type of radar search receiver that replaced the Metox FuMB

Table of Comparative Ranks (World War II)

German Navy	U.S. Navy
Matrose	Apprentice Seaman
Maschinengefreiter	Fireman, 3d Class
Matrosen- or Mechanikergefreiter	Seaman, 3d Class
Maschinenobergefreiter	Fireman, 2d Class
Matrosen- or Mechanikerobergefreiter	Seaman, 1st Class
Funkmaat	Radioman, 3d Class
Mechanikersmaat	Torpedoman's Mate, 3d Class
Maschinistenmaat	Fireman, 1st Class
Bootsmannsmaat	Petty Officer, 3d Class, Coxswain
Oberfunkmaat	Radioman, 2d Class
Obermaschinistenmaat	Machinist's Mate, 2d Class
Obermechanikersmaat	Torpedoman's Mate, 2d Class
Oberbootsmannsmaat	Petty Officer, 2d Class
	Boatswain's Mate, 2d Class
Mechaniker	Torpedoman's Mate, 1st Class
Bootsmann	Petty Officer, 1st Class
	Boatswain's Mate, 1st Class
Maschinist	Machinist's Mate, 1st Class
Oberbootsmann	Chief Petty Officer, Chief Boatswain's Mate

Obermaschinist	Machinist (Warrant officer)
Obersteuermann	Warrant quartermaster
Fähnrich zur See	Midshipman
Oberfähnrich zur See	(Senior Office Candidate)
Leutnant zur See	Ensign
Leutnant (I)	Ensign—Engineering duties
Oberleutnant zur See	Lieutenant (j.g.)
Oberleutnant (I)	Lieutenant (j.g.)—Engineering duties
Kapitänleutnant	Lieutenant
Korvettenkapitän	Lt. Commander
Fregattenkapitän	Commander
Kapitän zur See	Captain
Kommodore	Commodore (courtesy title for Captain holding flag rank)
Konteradmiral	Rear Admiral
Vizeadmiral	Vice Admiral
Admiral	Admiral
Generaladmiral	Admiral (Fleet Commander)
Grossadmiral	Fleet Admiral

Introduction

After fifty years, the image of the World War II German U-Boat commander remains blurred by emotion and controversy on both sides of the Atlantic. The cruel nature of unrestricted submarine warfare and lingering propaganda images have influenced British and American views of the subject. Nicholas Monsarrat in his 1951 novel, *The Cruel Sea*, captured wartime sentiments by describing U-Boat crewmen as "people from another and infinitely abhorrent world—not just Germans, but U-Boat Germans, doubly revolting," whose tall, blond captain possesses "slightly mad eyes, a contempt that twitched his lips and nostrils, and a sneer against life."[1] Writing in the official British history in 1956, naval historian Stephen Roskill writes, "Although we British are notoriously bad haters . . . there is no doubt that the German U-Boats did finally arouse feelings of the strongest loathing," due in part to the "arrogance of the majority of U-Boat officers we rescued." Roskill adds, "It is sheer casuistry for German apologists to claim that their methods of waging war were justifiable."[2]

The strength of these images is evident in the 1977 script changes proposed by American screenwriters for the motion picture *Das Boot*, when German producers approached Hollywood for co-production of the film. Rejecting the character of the first watch officer as drawn in the novel of the same name by Lothar-Günther Buchheim, Hollywood replaced him with a hate-filled fanatic who machine-gunned survivors in the water.[3]

In Germany, the publication of Buchheim's novel in 1973 sparked a major controversy for its realistic depiction of submarine life and its harsh criticism of Grand Admiral Karl Dönitz, commander in chief of

U-Boats (and eventually of the navy as well) for sacrificing his men in a hopeless cause. Previous U-Boat literature featured the heroic exploits of individual aces and submarines at the expense of broader issues. Buchheim's account shifted the focus, though the accompanying debate has shed more heat than light.[4]

Partly in response to the issues raised in this debate, some collective studies have addressed the question of the relative youth of U-Boat officers and crews.[5] Most useful is a group analysis of the careers and attitudes of Crew 34, the class of officer candidates who entered the German Navy in 1934.[6] Others have begun to examine the navy as an institution of the Third Reich, especially in regard to its relationship with National Socialism.[7]

Yet the place of individual U-Boat commanders in the broader context of the war remains to be established. Some recent memoirs furnish invaluable insights,[8] but memoirs can never be written by the vast majority of those who captained Germany's submarines. New biographies incorporate the discussion of broader issues, but largely ignore the personal and institutional backgrounds that provide context.[9] We know who these men are; we do not know what produced them.

This study of the life and career of Werner Henke attempts to redress that imbalance. Henke matches many traditional criteria in studies of U-Boat commanders: he was highly successful, earning the Oak Leaves to the Knight's Cross of the Iron Cross for his sinkings; a professional officer, he served aboard submarines for more than three years of the Battle of the Atlantic; he enjoyed a reputation as a *Draufgänger*, a daredevil; he was strikingly handsome; and he suffered a unique fate, the only U-Boat captain killed while trying to escape as a prisoner of war.

But Werner Henke was much more than all of this. Within the navy, his personality and lack of discipline rendered him an outsider. His character incorporated both traditional and modern elements of German life, reflecting his society as a whole. The history of Germany in the twentieth century represents Henke's own story: born into the Kaiserreich, uprooted by World War I, prosperous under Weimar, devastated by the Great Depression, sent to war by Hitler.

In treating Henke's successful record as a U-Boat commander, a secondary aspect our study examines the crew of *U–515*, Henke's command. Another convention of U-Boat literature is to focus upon the individual captain, with the crew largely irrelevant. Much of Henke's success in fact depended upon a select, veteran crew kept together for a much longer period than usual, and perhaps a much more significant ingredient to success than previously considered.

The question may well be asked: Were Henke and his men typical of the U-Boat service? In two essential aspects they were not: They were successful, and most survived. Whether they were typical in other ways can only be determined by systematic study, using standards that transcend wartime stereotypes.

NOTES

1. Nicholas Monsarrat, *The Cruel Sea* (New York: Alfred Knopf, 1951), 225–26.

2. Stephen W. Roskill, *The War At Sea 1939–1945*, vol. 2 (London: Her Majesty's Stationery Office, 1954–61), 306.

3. Such proposals led to the abandonment of coproduction and the German studio's sole sponsorship of the film. See Wilhelm Bittorf, " 'Das Boot': Als Wahnsinn imponierend," *Der Spiegel* 36, no. 53 (29 December 1980), 81–82.

4. Lothar-Günther Buchheim, *Das Boot* (Munich: R. Piper, 1973), and his subsequent trilogy *U-Boot-Krieg* (Zurich: R. Piper, 1976); *Die U-Boot-Fahrer* (Munich: C. Bertelsmann, 1985); and *Zu Tode Gesiegt: Der Untergang der U-Boote* (Munich: C. Bertelsmann, 1989). The controversy is reviewed in Michael Salewski, *Von der Wirklichkeit des Krieges: Analysen und Kontroversen zu Buchheims 'Boot'* (Munich: Deutscher Taschenbuch, 1976).

5. See Rolf Güth and Jochen Brennecke, "Hier irrte Michael Salewski: Das Trauma vom 'Kinderkreuzzug' der U-Boote," *Schiff und Zeit* 28 (1989), 43–47; and Timothy P. Mulligan, "German U-boat Crews in World War II: Sociology of an Elite," *Journal of Military History* 56, no. 2 (April 1992), 261–81.

6. Eric C. Rust, *Naval Officers Under Hitler: The Story of Crew 34* (New York: Praeger, 1991).

7. For example, Keith W. Bird, *Weimar, The German Naval Officer Corps and the Rise of National Socialism* (Amsterdam: B. R. Grüner, 1977); and Charles S. Thomas, *The German Navy in the Nazi Era* (Annapolis, MD: Naval Institute Press, 1990).

8. Peter Cremer with F. Brustat-Naval, *Ali Cremer: U 333* (Berlin: Ullstein, 1982), trans. by Lawrence Wilson as *U-Boat Commander* (Annapolis, MD: Naval Institute Press, 1984); and Erich Topp's reflective *Fackeln über dem Atlantik. Lebensbericht eines U-Boot-Kommandanten* (Herford, Germany: E. S. Mittler & Sohn, 1990).

9. For example, Jordan Vause, *U-Boat Ace: The Story of Wolfgang Lüth* (Annapolis, MD: Naval Institute Press, 1990).

LONE WOLF

I let go of Fate
I, poor devil, just couldn't hold
That million-ton weight.
    —Joachim Ringelnatz, "Aufgebung"

Prologue

The warm, humid evening of Thursday, 15 June 1944, completed the passage of another day of wartime routine in Washington, DC. The headlines of D-Day, the great invasion of Normandy only nine days earlier, had already given way to news of the landings on Saipan halfway around the globe. Homeward-bound government workers in the overcrowded city scanned the latest bulletins before searching the classifieds for the all-important housing advertisements. After surviving the evening rush hour traffic, Washingtonians could look forward to a quiet summer evening. Of all the wartime capitals, none had escaped war's ravages as had the city on the Potomac River.

On this night, however, the shooting war came to the suburbs of Washington, DC.

Seventeen miles to the south stood Fort Hunt, a former coastal fortification overlooking the Potomac's west bank. Residents of the nearby Virginia communities of Mount Vernon and Alexandria believed that the installation served as some kind of POW (prisoner of war) facility, but only Fort Hunt's personnel knew that they manned a specialized interrogation center for selected German POWs, especially U-Boat sailors. Here prisoners were isolated, interrogated, and monitored for intelligence information before moving on to regular POW camps elsewhere in the country.[1]

In its nearly two years of operations, no one had tried to escape from Fort Hunt. The multiple barbed-wire and cyclone fences, and the squat, circular guard towers combined with the very limited open spaces for prisoners to discourage any effort. That, too, would change this evening.

In a narrow exercise yard, a solitary figure strode purposefully about.

The U.S. Navy fatigues he wore accentuated his sturdy build and striking good looks. Clean-shaven, blond hair neatly parted and combed, the man looked to be someone used to command. Since the beginning of his exercise hour at 6:00 P.M., he maintained a brisk walking pace even as the temperature reached its daytime high of 75 degrees.

At five minutes before 7:00 P.M., the figure stopped in his tracks. He turned and suddenly dashed for the barbed-wire fence at the end of the enclosure. In seconds he scrambled up the ten feet of wire strands and vaulted over the top, landing on the grassless stretch of ground beyond. A couple of strides took him across the six feet to the main barbed-wire barrier that encircled the compound.

"Halt!" The cry came from a surprised guard in the tower at the corner of the compound, mere yards to the right of the escaping prisoner.

The latter made no attempt to stop, but immediately began scaling the second fence.

"HALT!"

Again there was no response. The guard brought his machine gun to bear on the struggling figure. He called once again as the individual, now in his sights, reached the top of the wire. At close range and in full daylight, the guard could not miss.

A brief burst of fire broke the evening stillness. The figure shook momentarily, then collapsed on the top of the fence, spread-eagled and motionless. It took the guards ten minutes to remove the body from the wire.

An examination revealed that bullets had penetrated the prisoner's right thigh and shoulder; a third passed entirely through his right arm, then pierced his right side between the sixth and seventh ribs to enter the lung. The fatal bullet, however, ripped through the upper right temple into the brain.

Korvettenkapitän Werner Henke, age thirty-five, German Navy officer and one of the top U-Boat aces of World War II, was dead.[2]

Who was Werner Henke, and what steps had preceded the suicidal leap onto the fence? Despite the passage of nearly fifty years, the answers have been incomplete at best, distorted at worst. German writers have either lacked access to official sources, or demonstrated more interest in excitement than explanation.[3]

Allied writers have either acted as principals in the Henke story, or are reluctant to shed wartime stereotypes. The senior U.S. Navy officer involved in Henke's capture described his prisoner as "a professional regular navy man . . . a Junker," referring to the aristocracy that had once dominated the principal German state of Prussia; the American later published an imaginative account of one of Henke's sinkings.[4] The navy propagandist who made "the big, blonde bully" Henke the subject of a special radio broadcast later published his own version of the incident.[5] Kenneth Poolman, British writer and Royal Navy veteran, identified Henke as "almost a caricature of the typical clean-cut, arrogant, ruthless Junker who gloried in war . . . a fanatic."[6]

Beyond physical descriptions, none of these characterizations is correct. He was neither a Junker, a fanatic, nor truly a regular navy officer. In many ways Werner Henke embodied the opposite of stereotyped "German" behavior. He was impetuous, ill-disciplined, hot-headed, and outgoing; a daredevil and ladies' man; a U-Boat commander with an extensive collection of American jazz and Cole Porter phonograph records. His indiscretions almost resulted in his discharge from the navy before he became one of its most decorated heroes. It was the fate of this highly idiosyncratic individual to be caught between his enemies' propaganda image of the U-Boat captain and his own navy's image of a decorated line officer. He was indeed a "lone wolf."

But far beyond his submarine career, Henke's life encapsulates Germany's history in the twentieth century. He was born into the kaiser's Germany; endured the First World War and the traumatic upheavals that followed; came into his own during the prosperity of the Weimar Republic; experienced disaster and unemployment with the Great Depression; and entered the service after Adolf Hitler assumed power. He participated in Germany's intervention in the Spanish Civil War; witnessed the first shots of World War II at Danzig; and served aboard U-Boats for three and one-half years of the Battle of the Atlantic.

His spectacular success against one convoy in May 1943 commanded the attention of Winston Churchill and prompted an inquiry by the British War Cabinet. Within one month's time, he was decorated by Hitler and investigated by the Gestapo. And the manner of his death presaged the fiery end of the Third Reich less than a year later.

This is his story.

NOTES

1. On Washington, DC, see David Brinkley, *Washington Goes to War* (New York: Alfred Knopf, 1988); on Fort Hunt, see John H. Moore, *The Faustball Tunnel: German POWs in America and Their Great Escape* (New York: Random House, 1978), 31–54; and the U.S. Army history of the facility, "CPM Branch," among the records of the G–2 Division (MIS-Y Branch), Records of the War Department

General and Special Staffs, Record Group 165, National Archives (hereafter cited in the format RG 165, NA).

2. Weather data from the *Evening Star* newspaper, 14–16 June 1944. Henke's death is described in the report of Col. Francis E. Howard to the State Department's Special War Problems Division, 29 November 1944, formerly classified decimal file 704 General no. 2 (Operations Branch), RG 389, NA; the autopsy report of Lt. Charles H. Reier, 16 June 1944 (copy in the custody of the U-Boot-Archiv, Cuxhaven); and the account of fellow POW Fritz Kuert, who claimed to have witnessed the incident (copy in the U-Boot-Archiv). The references to his death at Fort George G. Meade in Army reports, however, are erroneous and doubtless intended to protect the secrecy of Fort Hunt.

3. An example of the former is Hans Herlin, *Verdammter Atlantik* (Munich: Wilhelm Heyne Verlag, 1982), 115–204, based on extensive interviews with contemporaries; an example of the latter is Karl Alman, "Kapitänleutnant Werner Henke," *Der Landser-Ritterkreuzträger Nr. 2*, Nr. 680 (1971), 11–85.

4. Daniel V. Gallery, *Clear the Decks!* (New York: William Morrow and Company, 1951), 196; and Gallery, *U–505* (New York: Paperback Library, 1967), 194–210. The latter book mixes fictional incidents regarding Henke's sinking of the liner *Ceramic* with factual quotations from Henke's war diary.

5. Ladislas Farago, *The Tenth Fleet* (New York: Paperback Library, 1964), 146–50.

6. Kenneth Poolman, *The Sea Hunters* (London: Sphere Books, 1982), 168–69.

1

Beginnings and an End

In 1909, Imperial Germany stood at the pinnacle of its power. German military and industrial strength knew no equals in Europe. A rich cultural legacy was now supplemented by the highest scientific and technological achievements. The country's relatively backward political structure and the tensions generated by class structure aroused concerns, but even opponents of the regime trusted to an evolutionary solution to these problems. No one imagined the degree to which their world would be destroyed within a few years; none suspected the future that awaited their children.

Reflecting the developments of his lifetime, Werner Henke's hometown was as thoroughly German at the time of his birth as it would be completely Polish after his death. The German city of Thorn, situated on the Vistula River about 110 miles northwest of Warsaw and 100 miles south of Danzig, served as major trade center in the Kingdom of Prussia's province of West Prussia. Today's Polish city of Toruń looks very much the same, except most of the German presence of nearly 700 years is gone. The cataclysmic process that effected this transformation also reserved a special role for the son born to Hugo and Margrete Henke on 13 May 1909.

Fear of the future could not then have been further from the minds of Thorn's inhabitants. The first decade of the twentieth century marked a period of prosperity and growth for the city, as it did for all Wilhelmine Germany. A natural trade center surrounded by farmland, Thorn by 1914 boasted six railway stations and a thriving harbor as the hub of a modern transportation network. Thorn linked the Polish interior with the Baltic and bound East Prussia to the rest of Germany. The meats and produce of the surrounding countryside fed states and provinces throughout eastern Germany. Lumbering grew steadily as a major industry, drawing upon the forests west and south of the city and the miniature islands of bound logs floated downstream from Russian-ruled Poland, a mere seven and one-half miles upriver. The sawmills gave birth to a furniture industry, while machine factories, a chemical plant, and a foundry testified to the overall expansion of the German economy.[1]

Yet this prosperity did not extend to the neighboring farmland, dominated by the vast estates owned and operated by the Junkers, the Prussian landed nobility. The size of these estates and their reliance on seasonal farm workers from Russian Poland discouraged small farming. Throughout the last quarter of the nineteenth century, thousands of young men from the countryside, most of them ethnic Poles, followed Thorn's railways west to seek better jobs in Germany's Ruhr cities.

Others doubtlessly moved into Thorn for the same reason, contributing to a rise in population from 21,000 in 1881 to over 46,000 by 1914. They were joined by numerous immigrants from more distant regions, to whom the city beckoned as a "land of opportunity." A 1905 census counted over 500 inhabitants from other parts of Germany, more than 850 other Europeans (the majority from Russian Poland), 4 Englishmen, and 19 former citizens of the United States.[2] The Lutheran parish to which the Henkes belonged, in the village of Rudak south and east of the city, provided its own index of growth: Granted parish status in 1904, the congregation consecrated its new church building a mere four months after Werner's birth.

The compact city easily combined the styles and structures of several centuries. Dominating the city's center, the fourteenth-century *Rathaus* (town hall) resembled a red-brick castle, unsoftened by restoration work in the seventeenth and eighteenth centuries. Reinforcing this impression were ruins of medieval walls and towers and the massive Gothic cathedral, the Marienkirche (St. Mary's Church). The baroque facade of the Wendish House, built for a wealthy cloth merchant in 1697, housed a soap firm in 1910. The Vistula's great breadth had finally been conquered in 1872 with the 1,000-meter long Railroad Bridge, the longest bridge anywhere over the river. In the newer part of the city, the classical city theater had just been completed in 1904.[3]

Beyond the level of prosperity it shared with the rest of Germany, Thorn enjoyed a special advantage in avoiding many of the problems and social costs that accompanied development and modernization. Young Werner, for example, doubtless quenched his thirst on summer afternoons from the Vistula riverbank, a refreshment impossible along Germany's polluted Rhine and Elbe Rivers.[4] Crime posed little problem, as the theft rates of the depression-era 1880s declined by nearly half in 1914. So stable was the situation that Thorn's police rented out its dogs to private citizens for personal use.[5]

Thorn's history reflected its mixed Polish-German heritage, tracing an independent yet weaving course between two national destinies. Founded as one of a chain of river strong points by the Order of the Teutonic Knights in 1231, the city joined with other Prussian towns in a major revolt against the order's administrative and financial abuses two centuries later. Thereafter Thorn owed allegiance to the king of Poland, while retaining its membership in Europe's great trading alliance, the Hanseatic League. Thorn's German character remained intact, as demonstrated by the community's conversion to the Lutheran faith in 1557. Poland's policy of religious toleration, established at the Confederation of Warsaw in 1573, spared Thorn and her sister cities the bloodshed of the Reformation in the German states. Thorn's advantageous position was best demonstrated during the turbulent mid-seventeenth century, when the German states to the west were ravaged by the Thirty Years' War while Poland waged costly wars with Sweden in the north and Russia to the east. The city remained a part of gradually weakening Poland until 1793, when Prussia and Russia completed partitioning the kingdom between them.[6]

The debit side of this ledger left Thorn in the middle of one of the Reich's chronic political problems, the nationality conflict between Germans and ethnic Poles. The latter constituted a majority of those living in the surrounding countryside and a growing third of the city's population. Concerned by the growth of nationalism and increasing demographic strength of Prussia's Polish population, official policy limited the use of the Polish language in education and supported the expropriation of Polish peasants to the benefit of German farmers.

The neighboring province of Posen (now Poznan), where the Polish population outnumbered the German by nearly two to one, provided the focus of this conflict, but the issue affected all of Germany east of the Oder River. Twenty years of attempted Germanization produced no resolution of the problem, but served only to deepen divisions between Germans and Poles. Election results are not available for the city of Thorn alone, but the 1912 Reichstag (parliamentary) election returns for the Marienwerder electoral district, which included Thorn, reveal that the Polish minority candidates gained a plurality of the votes cast (38.7%), with the German vote largely split between the strongly nationalist Free Conservative party (20.8%) and the more traditional National Liberals (20.7%). The district's isolation from Germany's political mainstream is indicated by the minor support given the stronghold of German labor, the Social Democratic party (3.7%), and the champion of German Catholics, the Center party (8.1%), the chief victors of the 1912 elections with 34.8 percent and 16.4 percent, respectively, of the national vote.

It is in the context of these results, however, that the great flaws of German political structure can be seen. The Reichstag's electoral representation reflected blatant gerrymandering to minimize the impact of city (and socialist) voters and maximize the significance of rural (and conservative) voters. Thus Marienwerder's 960,000 inhabitants sent 8 deputies to the 1912 Reichstag, while Berlin and her 2,009,000 people sent only 6.

Even worse was the three-tiered electoral system in effect in Prussia, where an individual's voting power was weighted according to the taxes he paid, thus giving the wealthy disproportionate political power. In the 1913 elections for the Prussian Landtag (Assembly), for example, the Conservatives and Free Conservatives named 13 of West Prussia's 22 delegates, although those parties represented less than 29 percent of the province's voters. The Polish minority party, on the other hand, garnered more than 37 percent of the total vote but elected only three delegates.[7]

These factors framed the political landscape of Werner Henke's Thorn, with significant consequences over the next decade for all its inhabitants. To account for Henke's presence there, we must consider his family background.

The Henkes' family roots ran deep in the soil of eastern Germany, but they fail to conform to the established image of a region dominated by wealthy Junker landowners and the peasants who worked their fields.[8] The family genealogy, traced back to the late eighteenth century, reveals neither Junkers, peasants, nor professional soldiers, but independent farmers with moderate holdings and considerable freedom of movement in the Prussian provinces east of the Oder. Most were Lutherans, but his mother's ancestors included some Roman Catholics. Werner's paternal grandfather, Gustav Henke, built up a sizable estate near Schneidemühl (now Pila, Poland), which he retained until the end of World War I. Emil Heinsch, the maternal grandfather to Werner, was born in Silesia and came to West Prussia as a head gamekeeper.[9]

Hugo Henke reflected the changing times when he became the first

Henke to choose a career in government service as a state forestry official. This career choice alone reflected the family's relative wealth, as parents or guardians had to pledge financial support for a twenty-two-year-old applicant for the first twelve years of service. The prolonged period included technical academy and university studies, field apprentice-ships, examinations, and temporary appointments while awaiting a per-manent posting. Presumably this wait led to a position outside Thorn; it was not a coincidence that Hugo started his family shortly before his thirty-fourth birthday.

Responsible for a specific forest district south of Thorn (under the jurisdiction of the state rather than the city), his tasks involved managing the cutting of lumber for both firewood and industrial uses, planting replacement trees, reclaiming marshland, and preserving fish and game. All of these aspects had to be delicately balanced, as the state relied upon a high profit yield on lumber sales but did not want to deplete future supplies. Hugo's choice proved a difficult one, for he lacked the ruggedness and stamina the job often demanded, yet he fulfilled his tasks without complaint. He doubtless found satisfaction that his son wished to follow in his footsteps.[10]

Werner little appreciated, however, how much his father defied the traditional model of a Prussian bureaucrat. Sensitive and somewhat me-lancholic, Hugo Henke held to liberal political views despite a ministry policy of weeding out progressives and liberals from the civil service. Eventually he would join the German Democratic party (Deutsche De-mokratische Partei), which committed itself to the Weimar Republic and the social reconciliation of all classes. Hugo apparently shared little en-thusiasm for the army, where—like all Prussian males—he had served two years of active duty at age twenty and continuous service thereafter in the reserves. The most positive impression he retained was a fondness for a rousing Prussian march.[11]

Hugo's wife, Margrete, combined a quiet disposition with a strong constitution and robust health. Though only of average build, she did not shrink from the most difficult physical work in maintaining the household. If Werner inherited his father's independence of thought and spirit, he also received his mother's seemingly inexhaustible re-sources of strength and health.

The young Henke settled into the routine of a comfortable middle-class existence. Though most of his time was spent at home in Rudak, Werner would have become acquainted with Thorn on weekends and holidays. The ritual of a Sunday afternoon *Spaziergang*, the custom of a long walk as widely observed then as now in Germany, doubtless brought the Henkes across the river into town on a weekly basis. Clad in a pinstripe sailor's suit so fashionable for boys at the time—and so prophetic for himself—Werner accompanied his parents to attend afternoon concerts in front of the *Rathaus* or in the nearby Ziegelei Park. Tuesdays and Fridays he probably joined his mother in trips to the old city marketplace. Later, Werner may have seen his first motion picture in the cinema "Metropol," a movie house just converted from a former riding academy and horse market. During the intervals between features, ushers would spray perfume to disguise the lingering odor of the stalls.

At Christmas and Easter the Henkes probably worshipped at the Marienkirche, which had served as a Lutheran church since 1558. Christmas also introduced Werner to the joys of *Thorner Kathrinchen*, the gingerbread figures so popular throughout eastern Germany. The 1853 monument in the town square dedicated to Thorn's most famous son, Nicolaus Copernicus, provided the scene of a gaslight celebration every 19 February, the anniversary of the astronomer's birth.

More popular for the young men and boys of Thorn was the celebration of Kaiser Wilhelm II's birthday, 27 January, which actually began the preceding evening with military concerts and torchlight arrangements in the figures of the Imperial Crown and "W II." The next day at noon, all the army units stationed in Thorn paraded before the garrison church. The multiple names of the formations combined modern nomenclature with personal and regional identities: Infantry Regiment von der Marwitz (8th Pomeranian) no. 61, Uhlan Regiment von Schmidt (1st Pomeranian) no. 4. If weather permitted, the Zeppelin detachment stationed in the northwestern corner of the city provided an aerial accompaniment. None attending this celebration in 1914 imagined that it would prove to be the last, or that in six months the troops would march in earnest.[12]

With the assassination of the Austrian Archduke Franz Ferdinand and his wife at Sarajevo on 28 June 1914, the world into which Werner Henke was born began to change. The succession of ultimatums, pledges of support, mobilizations, and declarations of war of the European powers followed at dizzying speed. Thorn's inhabitants, like those of Berlin, Paris, and London, greeted the war enthusiastically, cheering on its freshly uniformed sons as they marched to war. Men of the Thorn garrison serving in the 35th Reserve Division moved north into East Prussia, where they participated in the great victory over the Russians at Tannenberg in August 1914. Thorn's railway stations quickly filled with field-gray uniforms as German units shuttled between the northern and southern wings of the eastern front. Because of its proximity to hostile Russia, Thorn was the most heavily fortified strong point on Germany's eastern frontier, yet the city was threatened only briefly in November 1914, before the advance of a Siberian infantry corps was beaten back.[13]

Hugo Henke, nearly thirty-nine years of age when war broke out, was called up for duty and served on the eastern front. At some point, possibly during the major German offensives in 1915 that drove the Russians from Poland, Henke was struck in the head by shell fragments and temporarily blinded. He returned home for recovery and was spared further combat.[14]

The year 1915 also marked Werner's entry into elementary school. Over the next three years he received the standard instruction in reading, writing, and arithmetic, doubtless administered with a strong dose of patriotism, as experienced by schoolchildren all over Europe. For Werner and his classmates, however, events soon overtook classroom lessons.

Through 1917 at least, the city of Thorn avoided serious wartime economic disruption by careful management of its finances. The effects of the Allied blockade on imported foodstuffs could not be so managed. By June 1915 bread began to be rationed throughout Germany. The failure of the 1916 potato crop and consequent potato famine in 1917 accelerated the sharp decline in the average German diet, as did another cut in the bread ration in 1917. Because Thorn was a small city surrounded by farmland, its population probably suffered less than Berlin's or those of other industrial cities that depended on the shipment of food supplies from other parts of the country, but malnutrition and hunger assumed a growing significance in the daily lives of every citizen. Mortality rates rose alarmingly throughout the war, less from outright starvation than from the diseases (especially tuberculosis) that thrived in an undernourished population. Hardest hit were the elderly and children between the ages of five and fifteen, whose resistance was most weakened by malnutrition.

The addition of the United States to the war on the side of the Allies in 1917 tipped the final balance against the German-led Central Powers. Domestic political concerns continually influenced Germany's conduct of the war, in negotiating political reform in return for popular support, and in the debate of a compromise settlement versus an annexationist peace. The reforms finally enacted in 1918 came too late, and the divisions within German society culminated in November 1918 with mutinies, the overthrow of the monarchy, and revolution.

Germany's agreement to the armistice that month did not end the ordeal of the civilian population, for the Allied blockade continued and expanded into the Baltic to ensure German compliance with specific Allied capitulation terms. The blockade of foodstuffs remained in effect until March 1919, leaving an estimated 763,000 civilian dead and a source of bitterness as its legacy.[15]

Nine-year-old Werner Henke could not have grasped the significance of Germany's surrender; that would come later. Gradually, he became aware of the change of his diet to boiled turnips, cabbage, and a bread substitute (*Kriegsbrot*); of the unexplained loss of schoolmates, friends and neighbors; of the lack of new clothes and shoes to replace the worn items he put on every day; and of the general unhappiness all about him. For his parents, even the otherwise joyful occasion of the birth of another son, Albrecht, in November 1916, would have been mixed with concern for the infant's health under wartime conditions. (Albrecht in fact survived this and another world war and lives today in Lüneburg.)

The final blow fell on 20 January 1920 when the newly established state of Poland assumed formal possession of Thorn in accordance with the terms of the Treaty of Versailles. Thorn and much of West Prussia now became part of the Polish "corridor" to the Baltic, a source of continual dispute for the next 20 years. Offered the choice of remaining in Polish Toruń or emigrating to Germany, the Henkes joined 27,000 of the 30,000 German inhabitants of the city, and nearly 500,000 other Germans from Posen and West Prussia, in seeking a new life in the west.

The choice cost the family more than its memories, for the compensation received for their land from Polish authorities fell far short of what they considered its fair value. Beyond that, a secure and comfortable prewar existence suddenly evaporated. Hugo Henke, in his mid-forties, had to start over again. Werner, at age ten, was a refugee.[16]

In retrospect, the fate of Thorn/Toruń held true to its history. The pendulum had again swung back to Poland where, except for a brief return to Germany during the period 1939–44, it has since remained. The old town hall, the cathedrals, even the ruins of the Teutonic Knights' castle have changed little since Werner Henke's day. For the German inhabitants of 1920, however, the world had turned upside down, and a prosperous past had been irretrievably lost. That they had at least avoided the pitched battles common to other German cities between armed left- and right-wing groups brought them little solace.

There was another legacy of World War I which, while not yet known to Werner Henke, would play a decisive role in his life. Germany's adoption of unrestricted submarine warfare to break the blockade and sever England's supply lines provided Allied propaganda with one of its most effective themes, the cruelty of U-Boat warfare. The sinking of the passenger liner *Lusitania*, accompanied by the heavy loss of civilian life, outraged neutral public opinion and paved the way for American entry into the war. The image of the pitiless U-Boat commander who torpedoed helpless merchant ships without warning, sometimes even killing the survivors, proved an effective tool in mobilizing British and American societies for total war. The power of that image faded with the end of the war, but did not die.

NOTES

1. Franz Pierburg, "Thorn—wie es um 1910 war," in Horst Ernst Krüger, ed., *Thorn—Stadt und Land. Geschichte, Geschichten, Namen, Erinnerungen, 1231–1981* (Lüneberg: privately published, 1981), 17–25; Great Britain, Foreign Office, *Handbook on Prussian Poland* (London: His Majesty's Stationery Office, 1920; republished Wilmington, DE: Scholarly Resources, Inc., 1973).

2. Stefan Hartmann, "Untersuchungen zum Thorner Finanzwesen im Ersten Weltkrieg im Spiegel der Haushaltspläne," in Bernhart Jähnig and Peter Letkemann, *Thorn: Königin der Weichsel 1231–1981* (Göttingen: Vandenhoeck & Ruprecht, 1981), 395.

3. Jähnig and Letkemann, *Thorn*, 375; Franz Feining and Friedrich Prowe, *Thorn in alten Ansichten* (Zaltbommel, NL: Europäische Bibliothek, 1981).

4. Pierburg, "Thorn," 22.

5. Eric A. Johnson, "The Crime Rate: Longitudinal and Periodic Trends in Nineteenth- and Twentieth-Century German Criminality, from Vormärz to Late Weimar," in Richard J. Evans, ed., *The German Underworld: Deviants and Outcasts in German History* (New York: Routledge, 1988), 179; Hartmann, "Untersuchungen," 401.

6. A survey of Thorn's history is provided by Reinhold Heuer, *Siebenhundert Jahre Thorn 1231–1931* (Danzig: W. F. Burau, 1931); for the latest research on Thorn's and other Prussian cities' relations with the Teutonic Knights, see Michael Burleigh, *Prussian Society and the German Order: An Aristocratic Corporation in Crisis c. 1410–1466* (New York: Cambridge University Press, 1984).

7. See William W. Hagen, *Germans, Poles, and Jews: The Nationality Conflict in the Prussian East, 1772–1914* (Chicago: University of Chicago Press, 1980), 180ff., including data on the westward emigration; electoral statistics are taken from Gerhard A. Ritter in collaboration with M. Niehuss, *Wahlgeschichtliches Arbeits-*

buch: Materialien zur Statistik des Kaiserreichs 1871–1918 (Munich: C. H. Beck, 1980), 42, 68–69, 132–49; the ratio of Polish to German population in Thorn appears in Heuer, *Thorn*, 66.

8. This image is discussed and disputed in David Blackbourn and Geoff Eley, *The Peculiarities of German History: Bourgeois Society and Politics in Nineteenth-Century Germany* (Oxford: Oxford University Press, 1984), 20, 128ff., 273–75.

9. Henke family papers in the custody of Albrecht Henke, Lüneburg; letter from Albrecht Henke to author, 20 June 1990.

10. On forestry, see Frederic C. Howe, *Socialized Germany* (New York: Charles Scribner's Sons, 1917), 148–50; and Ethlyn T. Clough, ed., *German Life* (Detroit: Bay View, 1913), 59–64; family data from Albrecht Henke (interviews and correspondence, 1989–90).

11. The German Democratic party is described in Thomas Childers, *The Nazi Voter: The Social Foundations of Fascism in Germany, 1919–1933* (Chapel Hill: University of North Carolina Press, 1983), 37–39; information on German military service is provided in the *German Army Handbook April 1918*, intro. by David Nash (New York: Hippocrene Books, Inc., 1977), 9–13; and interview with Albrecht Henke, Lüneburg, 5 September 1989.

12. Information from Pierburg, "Thorn," 22–25; and Hermann Trenkel, "Die Thorner Schulstrasse," *Westpreussen-Jahrbuch 1958* (Leer, Ostf.: Verlag Gerhard Rautenberg, 1958), 93–98; army data from *Rangliste der Königlich Preussischen Armee für 1914*.

13. See General Erich Ludendorff, *My War Memories 1914–1918* vol. 1 (London: Hutchinson & Co., 1920), 41ff.

14. Interview with Albrecht Henke, Lüneburg, 5 September 1989.

15. See C. Paul Vincent, *The Politics of Hunger: The Allied Blockade of Germany, 1915–1919* (Athens, OH: Ohio University Press, 1985), 20ff., 124ff.; and Gordon Craig, *Germany 1866–1945* (New York: Oxford University Press, 1978), 386–402.

16. Heuer, *Thorn*, 66: Heinz Rogmann, *Die Bevölkerungsentwicklung im preussischen Osten in den letzten hundert Jahren* (Berlin: Volk und Reich, 1937), 107–8; and Werner Henke's interrogation by U.S. Army intelligence officers, 14 May 1944, in Records of the G-2 (Intelligence) Division (MIS-Y Branch), War Department General Staff, Record Group 165, National Archives, Washington, DC.

2

A Sailor's Life

Most of the German emigres from Poland did not move very far, settling in the provinces that bordered their former homeland. But the Henkes, dependent upon the availability of suitable positions in the Prussian civil service, had to journey over 340 miles to reach the place of Hugo's new appointment, the town of Celle in the state of Hanover.[1]

Celle, onetime residence of the duke of Brunswick and Lüneburg, lay at the southern fringe of the famous Lüneburg Heath. The raw natural beauty of the heath, with its rich growth of heather and juniper, had increasingly attracted vacationers from the nearby cities of Hamburg and Hannover since the turn of the century. Henke's predecessors had already reclaimed much of the moorland for a growing number of small farms. In 1921, a year after Hugo Henke resumed his forestry duties, the Lüneburg Heath Nature Reserve opened as Germany's first nature park. Tending the heath would occupy Hugo for the remainder of his career.

Within three years, however, the family was rocked again by another aftershock of the war—the great inflation of 1923. As the real value of the mark collapsed, savings were wiped out, and real income dropped. Civil servants like Hugo were less severely affected by inflation than by the government's austerity measures to meet the crisis. The Reich, state, and local authorities cut costs by dismissing nearly 750,000 employees, principally at the lower and middle levels. This loss of jobs, the atmosphere of insecurity, and the loss in purchasing power embittered many civil servants against the Weimar government, a resentment successfully exploited by the up-and-coming National Socialist German Labor party, better known as the Nazis.[2]

Hugo Henke proved more fortunate than others in retaining his position. The crisis probably wiped out the family savings, however, resulting in another move in 1924 to the opposite side of the heath, in the vicinity of Lüneburg. For Werner and his family, this would remain home for the rest of their lives.

Lüneburg's Hanseatic past and character invited comparison with Thorn, as did its population of just over 31,000. The city that once supplied salt to all Europe had experienced just enough industrialization to maintain a stable and relatively prosperous economy. As they had in Rudak, the Henkes settled outside the city, in the small village of Kirchgellersen, a community of 515 inhabitants in 1930, 5 miles from Lüneburg.[3]

In the area of politics, Lüneburg belonged more to the mainstream than had prewar Thorn, but the city still retained a particularist character. Local results in the December 1924 Reichstag elections generally followed national trends as the inflation crisis receded. The Social Democratic party (SPD) garnered the largest number of votes, with opposition votes divided between the two rightist parties, the German National Peoples' party (DNVP) and the German Peoples' party (DVP). Lüneburg's particularist tradition could be seen in the strong support given the German-Hanoverian party (DHP), dedicated to the restoration of Hanover's independence from Prussia. For Hugo Henke's party of choice, the German Democratic party (DDP), the liberal appeal to all classes found as limited a response in Lüneburg (less than 9% of the votes cast) as it had in Germany as a whole. Finally, local support for the Nazi party fell below even the 3 percent registered at the national level.[4]

Such matters probably held little interest for the adolescent Werner Henke, who completed his schooling in 1925. The certificate of *Mittlere Reife* he received would not qualify him for entrance to a university, but it sufficed to begin a career in business or government. His final grades from the *Mittelschule* in Lüneburg were not particularly remarkable: Marks of "very good" in English, French, and writing were balanced against "satisfactory" grades in religion, literature, and natural sciences. The last boded ill for his plans to follow in his father's footsteps as a forester, particularly as competition in this field was fierce. At the time of his graduation, the waiting list for appointments to the forestry service—considered one of the more secure government positions—stood at three years.[5]

But Werner had begun to develop a new interest, the sea. Precisely what stirred this interest can never be fully known. The proximity of the great seaport of Hamburg, only thirty-one miles to the north, undoubtedly contributed. Most appealing, perhaps, was the opportunity of employment and travel. Rising from the devastation it had suffered in the world war, the German merchant marine rapidly resumed a position of prominence in world trade. Throughout the 1920s the two principal steamship lines, Hamburg-American (or Hapag) and North German Lloyd, built new passenger liners and expanded their commercial networks. The need for crewmen to man these ships offered a new generation the chance to see the world while learning a trade.

Henke's nautical interest was also fueled by the writings of his favorite author. "Joachim Ringelnatz" served as the pen name of Hans Bötticher, a combination of satirist, poet, artist, merchant seaman, and former navy officer. He gained a popular following in the early 1920s with the publication of his witty rhymes that ridiculed gymnastic clubs and recounted the misadventures of the sailor "Kuttel Daddeldu." Later in the decade he published additional short stories and reminiscences regarding service at sea, including wartime writings initially banned by navy censors.[6] Ringelnatz's critique of the Imperial Navy, *Als Mariner im Krieg* (published in 1928 under another pseudonym), became recommended reading for World War II navy officers as a guide to mistakes and failures of leadership.[7]

Reingelnatz's style of humor—clever, ironic, often sardonic—exactly matched Henke's own. Perhaps the writer's humorous but realistic portrayal of a sailor's life encouraged the forester's son in choosing his calling; certainly it fortified him through subsequent difficult passages. But whenever Henke read his first Ringelnatz verse, he could not have imagined how closely his own life would parallel his favorite author's career from a simple seaman to a wartime navy officer. That some of Ringelnatz's naval characters died heroic romanticized deaths probably left an impression, but not forebodings.[8]

His decision made, Werner Henke entered the merchant marine before the end of 1925. He began as a *Schiffsjunge* (cabin boy) aboard the square-rigged sailing ship *Grossherzogin Elisabeth*. Service aboard a training sailing ship marked the obligatory first step toward the mate's certificate (*Steuermannspatent*). Any romantic illusions the youth may have entertained were quickly disspelled by the physical trials of basic training, combined with the merciless treatment dished out by the older hands. For example, he experienced a common winter exercise once described by Ringelnatz that required the youths to climb the icy rigging from the deck to the mast top and back again ten times.[9]

Another young sailor who preceded Henke by less than a year was Günther Prien, whose path to fame as a U-Boat ace also began with cleaning toilets, serving food, and mending sails at a height of 160 feet above deck.[10] Those who endured this year of travail, however, emerged with a solid knowledge of seamanship and the sea. Werner Henke also carried away a sense of strong shipboard discipline that would accompany him throughout his career.

Now promoted to the rank of ordinary seaman, Henke remained aboard the *Grossherzogin Elisabeth* during her winter cruise of 1926–27 to South America. One of the apprentice seamen he met during the voyage, Heinrich Niemeyer, would later serve under him as a watch officer on *U–515*. Henke remained aboard only as far as Bahia on the Brazilian coast, where he and several others disembarked to join the crew of a German steamer en route back to Hamburg. Hardly had he arrived home before he immediately shipped out aboard a cargo ship bound for Chile.[11]

Such was the pattern of Werner Henke's life for the next several years. Although no exact record of his voyages is available,[12] it is certain that he visited North and South America, Africa, and Asia. He became familiar with the shipping lanes and maritime conditions throughout the Western Hemisphere. At some point he crossed the equator and was duly "baptized" in the ritual of humor and humiliation that has marked a rite-of-passage for all sailors since time immemorial.

During this period, Henke's tastes and interests assumed their final forms. Though not a drinker, he acquired tastes for cognac and Scotch; cigars and Russian tea relaxed him. His travels broadened his perspective and interests, leading to an appreciation of contemporary American music from Cole Porter ("Begin the Beguine" became his favorite melody) to the new sound known as jazz. Henke's reputation as a good dancer reflected not only this interest, but his popularity with the opposite sex. Granted his good looks, impeccable appearance, and outgoing nature, he never lacked for companionship while on shore leave.

By the summer of 1930, he had logged nearly fifty months at sea. At that point he enrolled for a year's study in a training school in the Altona district of Hamburg to prepare for the examinations required for the coveted *Steuermannspatent*, the qualification for advancement as a merchant marine officer. In July 1931, he passed his tests and received his certificate.[13]

But for Henke and his family, there was little cause for celebration. The Great Depression triggered by the crash of the stock market on Wall Street in October 1929 had begun to strike Germany. Trade was especially hard hit, as German exports declined from a value of 12,035.6 million marks in 1930 to 9,591.8 million in 1931, then plunged to only 5,741.1 million in 1932. The two principal shipping lines, Hapag and North German Lloyd, began to pool their resources and costs to meet the crisis, but in 1932 they still acknowledged a net loss of over 13 million marks. The two lines cut back on services, sold or scrapped vessels (amounting to nearly 264,000 tons of shipping in 1932–33 alone), booked fewer voyages, and reduced their payrolls.

For Henke, the effects were devastating. Though he now qualified for promotion and status, Henke found it virtually impossible to sign onto a ship in any capacity. Penniless, he returned home to Lüneburg while continuing to look for work. "Werner would regularly make the trip from Kirchgellersen to Hamburg to apply for work," his brother, Albrecht, later recalled, "but always without success. After returning home empty-handed one evening, he just laid his head down on the dining table and wept bitterly."[14]

Henke's dilemma and frustration mirrored that in many German households. Unemployment rose from 1.9 million employable workers in 1929 to over 4.5 million in 1931, and to over 5.6 million a year later. Small shopkeepers and meat and dairy farmers, especially hard hit by the financial crisis, began to listen to the promises of the Nazi party and its leader, Adolf Hitler.

Lüneburg provides an interesting case study in National Socialism's rise to power. In 1926, the Nazi party did not register a single party member in the city; during the Reichstag elections of May 1928, only 187 out of 16,275 voters cast their ballots for Nazi delegates. But by the time of the next Reichstag elections in September 1930, support for Hitler had risen to 2,870 out of nearly 17,000 votes. The elections of July 1932 crowned the Nazi party's success: 7,141 out of 18,120 votes cast (39.4%) gave the Nazis a plurality among the city electorate. Though his party never won a majority in any national election, Hitler's popular support led to his appointment as chancellor of Germany on 30 January 1933. On 9 March, city officials raised the swastika flag over the town hall of Lüneburg.[15]

Hugo Henke's party of choice, the German Democratic party (DDP), fell out as an early casualty of the political crisis. A left liberal association that probably included the largest Jewish participation of any German political party, the DDP lacked cohesion and lost many of its members to the Social Democrats. The remainder, including Hugo Henke, reorganized themselves on a more nationalist basis as the German State party (Staatspartei) in July 1930. But as German voters grew more radical, the continued perception of the State party as moderate doomed it to irrelevance. In the Reichstag elections of November 1932, Hugo was one of only 240 district voters who backed the Staatspartei. Whether Werner followed his father's example, or voted at all, is unknown.[16]

For Werner, the fateful launching of the Third Reich brought no break in his trips to the Hamburg docks seeking work. Yet it was at the time of Hitler's takeover a new career possibility opened before him. In a major change in personnel policy, the German Navy had begun to take in such qualified merchant marine officers as Günther Prien. Henke and others in his situation naturally had an interest in a chance for employment in a closely related field with a guaranteed income and a gain in social status.

Another incentive subsequently cited by merchant marine officers was the growing influence of the SA, the Sturmabteilung (stormtroopers), affiliated with the Nazi party, especially aboard the large passenger liners. Hardly motivated by ideology, SA membership in the merchant marine had become a way of safeguarding one's job. Who would dare release an SA member with Hitler in power? Merchant officers who tardily joined the SA would find themselves subordinate to ordinary seamen and stewards with longer tenure in the organization. Confronted by this option and unemployment, the navy offered a preferable third alternative. Given the nature of Henke's later relation with Nazi party functionaries, this probably provided additional motivation. Sometime during the spring of 1933, Henke formally applied to the Reichsmarine.[17]

After applying, Henke reported with several other candidates to the Kiel-Wik naval barracks outside of Kiel for three days of tests. Under the direction of trained psychologists, these included written and oral examinations and physical tests. The latter included the *Mutprobe* (Test of Courage), in which each candidate lifted a heavy metal bar while an electric current passed through it. The oral examinations were conducted with the entire group of candidates to identify individual leadership. Upon conclusion, the psychologists prepared detailed character assessments for each applicant and submitted their recommendations to the navy. Prior to 1935, only one applicant in twenty was accepted.[18]

Henke must have excelled at these tests to win recommendation. He lacked the *Abitur* (the educational certificate necessary for enrollment in college) that most other officer applicants possessed, and had only average grades for the education he did have. Moreover, he had no family connections with the navy or army. What he did possess was experience, a good record as a seaman, and what can only have been impressive test scores.

During the protracted evaluation of his application, however, Henke continued to seek work in the merchant marine. On 13 July 1933, his persistence paid off. The great Hapag passenger liner, SS *Resolute*, signed him on as an ordinary seaman for a voyage to the United States. After lengthy preparations, the 20,000-ton liner departed Hamburg on 22 August and, following stops in Cherbourg and Southampton to pick up passengers, arrived in New York on 31 August. The next day the vessel departed for the Bahamas, returning to New York again on the morning of 6 September. There, Henke was mustered out with the rest of the crew and transferred to the homeward-bound liner SS *Milwaukee*. Henke enjoyed a 48-hour leave before his new ship weighed anchor for Hamburg, arriving there 20 September. For the month, he received 105 marks (about $26). He would not see the United States again for another 11 years, and then under very different circumstances.[19]

More significantly, the voyage marked the end of Henke's merchant marine career. Further trips to Hamburg yielded no more jobs because the situation of the German shipping lines remained precarious: In 1935, Hapag would be forced to sell *Resolute* to Italy to raise cash. But by then, Henke had changed his uniform.

At the beginning of April 1934, the long-awaited letter arrived at the Henke household: Werner had been accepted! The pride and happiness felt by everyone in the family could easily be recalled by his brother fifty-seven years later. In accordance with his instructions, Henke reported to the naval station at Stralsund on 6 April for his final physical examination. Two days later he signed the enlistment papers that committed him to twelve years of naval service.[20]

What kind of man was Werner Henke at this critical point in his life?

Now nearly 25, he stood at the peak of physical condition, with a fully formed personality. His piercing blue eyes, handsome face, and sturdy build were the first things one noticed about him. The 175 pounds packed onto his frame of 5 feet 9 inches (average for the time) betrayed neither fat nor a willingness to back down in a dispute. In many ways he embodied contradictions: quick to laugh, perhaps quicker to anger. Vain, ambitious, and obstinate, he was also charming, courageous, and self-reliant. In his tastes for an active social life, dancing, and American jazz, he anticipated the openness of later German society—yet his preference for a Wagnerian opera over a motion picture, his fondness for Ringelnatz, and his idealization of Bismarck all marked him as a product of Imperial Germany. Though likely never conscious of it, Henke straddled the Germanies of the past and the future.[21]

Of more immediate concern was the question of whether a temperamental, worldly, and independent man like Henke could adjust to the values, strictures, and discipline of the navy. The search for an answer was about to begin.

NOTES

1. For specific data on the emigration of Germans from areas ceded to Poland, see Heinz Rogmann, *Die Bevölkerungsentwicklung im preussischen Osten in den letzten hundert Jahren* (Berlin: Volk und Reich, 1937), 107ff.

2. See Thomas Childers, *The Nazi Voter: The Social Foundations of Fascism in Germany, 1919–1933* (Chapel Hill: University of North Carolina Press, 1983), 91–101.

3. Population data taken from *Einwohner-Buch 1930 für den Stadt-und Landkreis Lüneburg* (Lüneburg: Stadtamt Lüneburg, 1930), 634–36.

4. Election data taken from Uta Reinhardt, "Lüneburg zwischen Ersten Weltkrieg und Drittem Reich," *Niedersächsisches Jahrbuch für Landesgeschichte*, bd. 54 (1982), 107–8, 121–22. For the national context of this election, see Childers, *Nazi Voter*, 50ff.; and Richard F. Hamilton, *Who Voted for Hitler?* (Princeton, NJ: Princeton University Press, 1982), 9ff.

5. "Schlusszeugnis Werner Henke (I. Klasse, Mittleschule Lüneburg), Ostern 1925," in Henke family papers; interview with Albrecht Henke, 5 September 1989.

6. For an assessment of Ringelnatz's writings and life, see Walter Pape, *Joachim Ringelnatz: Parodie und Selbstparodie in Leben und Werk* (Berlin: Walter de Gruyter, 1974); a good collection of his writings is reproduced in Daniel Keel, ed., *Das Ringelnatz Lesebuch* (Zürich: Diogenes, 1984).

7. Charles S. Thomas, *The German Navy in the Nazi Era* (Annapolis, MD: Naval Institute, 1990), 209.

8. Interview with Albrecht Henke, 19 September 1987, and Pape, *Ringelnatz*, 131–37.

9. See Ringelnatz's description in "Den Neulingen gegenüber," in *Lesebuch*, 114–16.

10. See Günther Prien, *Mein Weg nach Scapa Flow* (Berlin: Deutscher Verlag, 1940), 12ff. It is possible that Prien and Henke were acquaintances.

11. Letter of Heinrich Niemeyer to author, 16 December 1990.

12. A search of the few personnel records that survived the war failed to reveal any information regarding Henke (letter of Paul-Fr. Schulz, Hapag-Lloyd Aktiengesellschaft, to author, 5 December 1990).

13. Seefahrtschule Altona, "Zeugnis über die Prüfung zum Steuermann auf grosser Fahrt," 1 July 1931, in Henke family papers. Additional data on Henke's characteristics taken from author's interviews with Albrecht Henke, 19 September 1987 and 29 November 1990, and letter to author, 7 November 1989.

14. Letter, Albrecht Henke to author, 22 June 1989; statistical data on trade and unemployment taken from D. Petzina, W. Abelshauser, and A. Faust, *Sozialgeschichtliches Arbeitsbuch III: Materialien zur Statistik des Deutschen Reiches 1914–1945* (Munich: C. H. Beck, 1978), 75–76, 119–20; information on German shipping lines from *New York Times* news articles of 9 July 1933 and 27 July 1933.

15. See Reinhardt, "Lüneburg," 109–27; and Jeremy Noakes, *The Nazi Party in Lower Saxony 1921–33* (Oxford: Oxford University Press, 1971), 91–92, 154. The electoral data given applies only to Stadt Lüneburg and omits the outlying rural districts of Landkreis Lüneburg.

16. Hamilton, *Who Voted*, 245–52, 627–28, for information on the DDP; Reinhardt, "Lüneburg," 126; and interview with Albrecht Henke, Lüneburg, 5 September 1989, for the rest.

17. See Eric Rust's excellent *Naval Officers Under Hitler: The Story of Crew 34* (New York: Praeger, 1991), 32–33, 53–54.

18. Lt. Cdr. William A. Wiedersheim, III, "Officer Personnel Selection in the German Navy, 1925–1945," *United States Naval Institute Proceedings* (hereafter *USNIP*), 73, no. 4 (April 1947), 445–49.

19. Data on Henke's employment taken from the standard form prepared by incoming ships, "List or Manifest of Aliens Employed on the Vessel 'SS *Resolute'* as a Member of the Crew," vol. 11597 of Passenger and Crew Lists of Vessels Arriving at New York, 1897–1942, Records of the Immigration and Naturalization Service, National Archives microcopy M–175, roll 5384; additional information from the announcement of ship arrivals and sailings in the *New York Times*, 31 August–9 September 1933. Henke's wage statement is included among his family papers.

20. Interview with Albrecht Henke, Lüneburg, 29 May 1991; Henke family papers.

21. A copy of Henke's medical examination, 6 April 1934, is located in his personnel record (courtesy of the Henke family); data on Henke's tastes from author's correspondence with Albrecht Henke, 7 November 1989, 8 August 1990, and 8 November 1990.

3

A Zigzag Course

Once again, a key moment in Werner Henke's life reflected a critical turn in German history. With Adolf Hitler's accession to power, the German military cast off the shackles of the Versailles Treaty and prepared to rebuild its strength. But expansion raised anew the issues that had plagued German civil-military relations for decades: the composition of the officer corps, the integration of the armed forces within society, and the precise authority to whom the military owed its allegiance. None of the services shouldered a greater burden in this regard than the navy.

Between 1890 and 1914, the Imperial German Navy grew from a small coastal force to a modern fleet second in size (among European powers) only to that of Great Britain. Five years later the toll of battle, the scuttling of the fleet at Scapa Flow, and the terms of the peace settlement had returned Germany to its former status, with a total establishment of 1,500 officers, 15,000 men, and no modern warship larger than a light cruiser. Even more significant was the legacy of the 1917–18 naval mutinies that had triggered Germany's political upheavals and the overthrow of the monarchy in November 1918. These traumatic events left deep psychological scars for the officers who steered the navy through the Weimar period and the rise of National Socialism.[1]

In late 1932, when Grand Admiral Erich Raeder and the Navy High Command drew up plans for an expansion of its forces, the concomitant question of enlarging the officer corps received careful attention. The situation became more acute with the loss of 36 first-year naval officer cadets aboard the training bark *Niobe*, lost in a storm at sea in July 1932. Even the small size mandated by the Versailles Treaty was never attained, as the Reichsmarine counted only 1,100 officers in November 1932.

The advantage for the Weimar navy meant that the officer corps represented a true elite, whose exclusivity was evident in the 1931 officer selection—only 2.3 percent of nearly 2,500 applicants met the qualifications. To preserve these high standards in the face of expansion, naval planners proposed to add 50 more cadets to the 1933 class of officer candidates, and to enroll 20 former merchant marine officers as well. Such a measure marked a significant change in recruitment policy, but it was not nearly enough. In early 1934, with an avowed goal of attaining naval parity with France and Italy, the navy conceded additional cuts in qualifications to obtain officers. These measures included the promotion of noncommissioned officers from the ranks, the reduction of 10 months from the four-and-a-half-year training program for midshipmen, the reactivation of retired officers, and the enrollment of 30 more merchant marine officers.[2]

Such were the changing conditions that brought Werner Henke into the Reichsmarine (it would not change its name to the Kriegsmarine until May 1935) as an officer cadet in April 1934. Henke's swearing-in ceremony marked another significant moment in history. On 1 May 1934, Henke gave his oath to "loyally and honestly serve my people (*Volk*) and my country," a wording introduced only in December 1933 by the Nazi regime to replace the 1919 oath of loyalty to the German Constitution. Just three months later, Henke and all other personnel in the armed forces were made to swear a new oath, one with fateful consequences for all Europe: "I swear by Almighty God this sacred oath: I will render unconditional obedience to the Führer of the German Reich and people, Adolf Hitler, Supreme Commander of the Wehrmacht, and, as a brave soldier, I will be ready at any time to stake my life for this oath."[3]

Though entering the navy on the same day as Crew 34, the class of officer cadets just beginning their careers, Henke and the other twenty-seven merchant marine officers were retroactively assigned to Crew 33. The differences that marked their training against that of their American counterparts at Annapolis extended far beyond the reversal of entry and graduation class dates. Where the U.S. Navy midshipman spent all of his first four years at the naval academy, the German *Seekadett* experienced a more varied training period that emphasized practical skills. The cadet's program included six months of basic infantry training, three and one-half months aboard a sailing ship, a fourteen-month voyage aboard a cruiser, one year's academic instruction at the naval school in Flensburg-Mürwik, six months of special instruction in ordnance and communications, and twelve months of duty on board warships in positions of increasing responsibility. Around the midpoint of his training, a cadet faced a major examination that qualified him as a midshipman (*Fähnrich zur See*); at the completion of his final training, the officers under whom he had served voted in secret as to the cadet's performance and suitability. Only after passing these tests did the cadet finally receive his commission as *Leutnant zur See* (Ensign).[4]

Because of their prior maritime experience, Henke and his fellow merchant marine officers—known collectively as HSOs, after the German term for their profession (*Handelsschiffsoffiziere*)—followed a somewhat different training regimen. The navy eliminated their sailing-ship training and the extended cruise as unnecessary, and considerably reduced their basic infantry training. This effectively integrated the HSOs with crew 33's regular cadets in time for the academic instruction term at the naval school—which was reduced to nine months as an additional concession to the accelerated training schedule.

More than their different paths into the navy divided the two groups. The average age of the 123 regular cadets was less than 20; nearly all came to the navy directly from university-preparatory schools, with only 12 listing any work experience, and most of that for one year or less. The 28 merchant marine officers, by contrast, averaged 24.4 years in age (Henke was only a month shy of 25 when he enlisted), with 6.5 years of nautical experience. Yet the backgrounds of the groups were not dissimilar. The percentage of regular cadets with fathers in military or naval service was only slightly higher than that of the HSOs (26% versus 21%); a marked preponderance of state officials and professionals among fathers of the remainder characterized both groups; and the majority of each group was born in northern Germany. In all these characteristics, Crew 33 closely resembled its much larger (349 cadets) successor, Crew 34. Many former merchant marine officers became thoroughly integrated within their class, attaining rank and honors entirely on the basis of individual performance. Six HSOs ranked among the top thirty graduates of the class.[5]

For Werner Henke, however, integration and acceptance would prove difficult to achieve.

Having completed two months of boot camp amid the sand dunes and lakes of Stralsund on the Baltic coast, followed by a month's training at the Navy Gunnery School in Kiel, Henke arrived at the *Marineschule*

Mürwik on 12 July 1934. The sight of the red-brick Gothic tower and the high roofs of red tiles must have sparked memories of the Marien-kirche in his native Thorn. Consciously modeled after the castles of the Teutonic Knights when it was built in 1910, the naval school was known both then and today to cadets as "The Red Cloister by the Bay" or, more simply, "The Castle." As the school's appearance reminded him of his childhood, so too did the carefully preserved heritage of Kaiser Wilhelm II and the Imperial period which gave birth to the navy. The omnipresent motif of the Hohenzollern eagle (still evident today) and the portraits and busts of the kaiser and Grand Admiral Alfred von Tirpitz, founders of the modern German Navy, doubtless stirred memories of that era for Henke that were beyond the recall of his younger colleagues.

As with all classes, Crew 33 was divided between executive officers, the vast majority of cadets who expected to hold command positions in the future navy, and such technical specialists as engineering (20), med-icine (9), naval construction (5), and administration (5). (The separate category of "weapons officers" was not added until Crew 34.) Each of the latter took some specialized classes, but shared the basic courses that formed the executive officers' curriculum. Henke's comrades in-cluded several officers destined for fame in the war: Wolfgang Lüth, who sank more Allied tonnage than any other U-Boat commander except Otto Kretschmer, only to die at war's end from the bullet of a too-conscientious German sentry; Reinhard Hardegen, an historian's son, who wrought havoc off the Atlantic coast of North America in 1942; and Gerd Suhren, older brother of U-Boat ace Reinhard ("Teddy") Suhren and the first engineering officer to earn the Knight's Cross of the Iron Cross. Henke studied, ate, and lived with them all.[6]

At the academy, Henke and three other cadets shared a two-room apartment. In accordance with the wishes of Kaiser Wilhelm, the win-dows of all midshipman quarters fronted on the narrow inlet of water that connected Flensburg with the Baltic Sea, so that the future officers would always awaken with a view of water. Henke's daily routine began at 0700 (7:00 A.M.) with fifteen minutes of calisthenics or an outdoor run around the campus. After washing, shaving, and eating a quick break-fast, the cadets attended classes that began at 0800 and continued until nearly 1300. The midday supper brought together all midshipmen, of-ficers, and civilian instructors in the mess hall for the principal meal of the day, generally soup, meat, potatoes, and one vegetable, followed by coffee and cigars. Instructions resumed at 1500 and continued until

1800, usually involving physical training, navigation lab exercises, and boat drills. The evenings were free for study, though midshipmen were neither restricted to quarters nor monitored until "lights out" at midnight. When U.S. Navy observers later commented on the relative freedom afforded German cadets both in the classroom and in the evening compared with Annapolis midshipmen, their hosts replied that this served as a form of selection: Those who abused their freedom and did not keep up their studies would necessarily fall by the wayside.

Henke successfully resisted temptation, at least to the degree of avoiding this fate. The course load of forty-six hours of instruction per week doubtless kept him occupied. Classes in navigation, engineering, foreign languages, naval history, tactics, and ordnance required his full attention; instruction in sailing, fencing, gymnastics, field hockey, horsemanship, and boxing drained whatever remained of his energy. After nine months of study, Henke and his colleagues underwent their final examinations in all subjects. Henke, never a scholar, passed with a "satisfactory" grade that trailed the "excellent" or "good" earned by the majority of his comrades. Ironically, his poorest grades came in the area of physical conditioning, rather than an academic discipline. In the subsequent ranking after graduation, Henke placed 99th among 112 executive officer cadets.[7]

But the education of a navy officer was not simply a matter of courses and examinations. In his integration into the officer corps, his acceptance by his peers, and his incorporation of the prescribed values and traditions, the officer candidate might face his most difficult test. Such was the case with Werner Henke.

One source of difficulty doubtless concerned the minutely detailed standards of social conduct. Under Raeder, officers were not to be seen in public carrying briefcases, smoking pipes, or wearing raincoats in anything less than a downpour. Music and dancing, among Henke's favorite diversions, increasingly became objects of navy commentary and regulation, extending in 1939 to the prohibition of dancing the popular "Lambeth Walk." These strictures invited clashes with a personality like Henke's, independent in taste and accustomed to his pleasures.

The assimilation of naval traditions, however, posed even greater problems for Henke. The navy's responsibility for the mutinies that led to the monarchy's collapse—the "trauma of 1918"—cast a giant shadow over the teachings and attitudes passed on to new officers. Insecurity over their own history led the naval leadership to an uncritical acceptance of Tirpitz's belief in a global naval strength, an exaggerated sense of honor, and a "faithful unto death" credo for future actions. The scuttling of the fleet at Scapa Flow, for example, was elevated by Grand Admiral Erich Raeder from a gratifying but near-suicidal gesture of defiance to the level of a great victory, and the foundation of the new German Navy.

Moreover, the navy of the late 1930s consciously strove to place its officers within a protective cocoon, self-contained and self-directed. Raeder generally eschewed matters of national policy and emphasized instead the navy's need to look to its own concerns. Loyalty to the navy and to the state were the only "politics" needed. National Socialism exerted little influence within the navy during this period, and indeed provided a refuge for those officer candidates who considered the navy the branch of service least exposed to Nazi influence. Yet these attitudes permitted National Socialism free rein, as master of the state, to determine the ends for which this self-directed officer corps would be used.[8]

These values clashed with Werner Henke's background and experience. As we have seen, he was not raised in an environment of unconditional obedience to military authority. More importantly, the Henke family, like many other Germans, had learned to roll with the punches dealt them by postwar problems. When their homeland was turned over to Poland, they moved and started over. When Werner could not be a forester, he turned to a brand new career in the merchant marine. When the Great Depression took away his job, he began anew in the navy. The Henkes were realists, adapting to circumstances instead of defying them. The differing attitudes Henke encountered at Mürwik left their mark, however, and held fateful consequences for the young officer.

Henke's relative acceptance among his classmates raised a more immediate question. Crew 33 was the last of the intimate classes, the final time that as few as 150 *Crewkameraden* would share nine months together at the academy. Everyone knew everyone else, in a manner that later classes could not match. In this situation, Henke's older age, broader range of life experiences, lesser degree of formal education, and lack of a military or naval background had already set him apart; his personality merely reinforced his separation.

The available evidence suggests that "der schöne Henke"—Handsome Henke—did not enjoy the esteem of his classmates. "Henke was the opposite of the silent but energetic [U-Boat ace Otto] Kretschmer," recalled one of his comrades from Mürwik, who added, "[Henke] was very vain but possessed only middling intelligence and was not very well liked." Another comrade compared Henke to a "flashy tennis star" of 1990.[9] In its doggerel-verse observations on each crew member's shortcomings, the crew newsletter issued on the eve of graduation said of Henke:

> Of handsome Werner, we know it's true
> He'll do anything just to flash his smile, the fool.[10]

It was obvious that Henke stood apart from the Prussian military tradition of *mehr sein als scheinen*—be much, display little. In time, he would have the opportunity to allow his actions to speak louder than his words. For the moment, however, Henke was happy and proud to have qualified as a naval officer.

Crew 33 dispersed to their final training assignments and the beginnings of careers cut short by the outbreak of World War II. During the war, nearly half (74) would serve aboard U-Boats, at least 33 of whom would die with their submarines. Twenty-eight others would lose their lives aboard surface vessels or in aircraft for a total loss of over 40 percent of the class, a casualty rate almost identical to that of their successor, Crew 34. (By contrast, the U.S. Naval Academy's class of 1937 would lose only 13 percent of its 323 graduates during World War II.) Crew 33 distinguished itself not only by its losses, but also by its accomplishments: Fifteen members earned the coveted Knight's Cross of the Iron Cross, and three of its graduates ended among the top twenty U-Boat commanders in total tonnage sunk. Werner Henke belonged in both categories.[11]

For the next eight months Henke attended a variety of training courses on naval ordnance and communications. These included six weeks of exercises with torpedoes and one week in submarine warfare—the only specific training Henke received aboard a U-Boat in his first six years with the navy. His longest stint of nearly three months came at the naval gunnery school in Kiel. This was standard, as anyone who expected to command at sea had to first demonstrate his ability as a gunnery officer. The future opportunities for command were enhanced by the most exciting development in June 1935, the conclusion of the Anglo-German Naval Treaty. The British, concerned over the failure of general disarmament negotiations and hopeful of setting some limits to Hitler's announced rearmament, agreed to an expansion of the German fleet to 35 percent of the total tonnage of the Royal Navy (for submarines, 45%). This recognition of the death and burial of the Versailles Treaty first of all represented a tremendous propaganda victory for Hitler, but for the navy it carried the special significance of guaranteed promotion in the expanded Kriegsmarine of the near future—even though Raeder acknowledged that it would take ten years just to build and man enough ships to match the approved tonnage.[12]

After the Naval Gunnery School, Henke received his first detail to a warship, *panzerschiff* (Armored Ship, but more generally known by the designation "pocket battleship") *Admiral Scheer*. Commissioned only in November 1934, *Scheer* represented a new warship design that employed powerful diesel engines for a cruiser's speed and massive 28cm (11-inch) guns for a battleship's punch. Henke remained aboard *Scheer* from December 1935 to March 1936 as a training assignment, then returned to her after a two-month detail to antiaircraft gunnery school.

From May 1936 through April 1937 Henke served as a regular officer on Germany's most modern warship. He arrived just in time to participate in the review of the fleet by Hitler at the end of May 1936, and the accompanying dedication of the gigantic Navy Memorial which still stands at Laboe, outside Kiel. Throughout this period, Henke seemingly met all expectations. Promoted to *Oberfähnrich zur See* (roughly senior officer candidate, though no comparable grade exists in the U.S. Navy) in April 1936, then to *Leutnant zur See* (ensign) six months later, he advanced in class ranking from ninety-ninth to eighty-eighth in 1936 and to eighty-third the next year. Henke's return to *Admiral Scheer* indicates that he had impressed the ship's officers during his training stint aboard. Yet, with time, this favorable situation began to change.[13]

The evidence of this change can be seen in Henke's participation in another significant moment in history. On 24 July 1936, after a night of feverish preparations, *Scheer* sailed with her sister ship *Deutschland* from Wilhelmshaven for Spain, where several months of political unrest had culminated in an attempt by right-wing forces to overthrow the Republican government. The warship's mission involved only the protection and, if necessary, the rescue and evacuation of German nationals in areas particularly threatened by violence. None aboard knew that on the very evening of their departure, emissaries of General Francisco Franco arrived in Berlin to plead for assistance from Hitler, which the führer duly granted on 26 July. Unaware of the future German role in the Spanish Civil War, *Scheer*'s captain carried out his operation without any show of support for Franco, always working closely with British naval forces engaged in similar tasks and even meeting with Spanish Republican officials when the occasion warranted.

After aiding in the evacuation of thousands of Germans and other nationals from Spain's Mediterranean ports, *Scheer* returned to Germany on 28 August. During her several subsequent trips to Spanish waters, however, the *panzerschiff*'s activities conformed to Hitler's policy. Ostensibly as part of an international neutrality patrol, *Scheer* and other German ships in reality facilitated the shipment of arms to Franco and denied the same to the Republicans.[14]

This first taste of action apparently aroused little enthusiasm in Henke. During the first voyage, he confided to his mother: "For myself, I have gained little from this entire operation, and I would be happy if we could return home soon." During the later trips Henke at least found some release in coordinating the air evacuation of German refugees from the airfield at Alicante to Germany. Sometime in November 1936 he again wrote his mother: "The Lufthansa transport pilots have become my best friends, I should later fly to Germany with them—they've even offered to fly me tomorrow on the 'express' to Munich, but I know the Commander would not permit it."[15] It is entirely possible that Henke made the trip anyway, but what is more important is the reference to his "best friends," the Lufthansa pilots—an indication that after nearly nine months of duty aboard *Admiral Scheer*, Henke had formed few relationships with his fellow officers, five of whom were classmates from Crew 33.

Sometime in April 1937, Henke returned to Germany from his last cruise aboard *Scheer*. Ironically, he departed just as the pocket battleship embarked upon her most serious action off Spain: On 31 May, in retaliation for a Republican air attack on the *Deutschland* that inflicted over 100 casualties, *Scheer* bombarded the Republican port of Almeria, killing 19 inhabitants. By then Henke had begun a new assignment with the 5th Naval Artillery Detachment at Pillau, on the Gulf of Danzig.

The transfer was a routine matter—all six Crew 33 graduates left *Scheer* in 1937, most for shore-based units. Yet for Henke, the nearly two years spent at Pillau (now Baltiysk in Poland) probably seemed a punishment. He had joined the navy to stay at sea, yet he would continue to pass most of his early career ashore. The small Baltic port offered few distractions, especially for a man unpopular with his comrades. It was only a matter of time before he suffered his first disciplinary action.

Visiting a girlfriend in Leipzig, Henke overstayed a leave by three days. When he returned, his commander, *Fregattenkapitän* Wilhelm Matthies, had him arrested and punished with ten days of confinement to quarters. This incident represented only the first of many such disciplinary issues to dog Henke throughout his career.[16]

What likely sustained him through this period was the continued expansion of the navy and the future prospects for command at sea. In May 1938, one month before Henke's promotion to *Oberleutnant zur See* (Lieutenant, j.g.), Hitler authorized an accelerated naval-building program to complement his preparations for a possible war over Czechoslovakia. With the increased possibility of British intervention, but assured by the führer that war with Britain would not occur for several years, the Naval High Command developed a large-scale expansion program that was finalized in January 1939. Intended for completion by 1948 at the latest, the "Z-Plan" envisaged the creation of a fleet of 10 battleships, 15 "pocket battleships," 5 heavy and 24 light cruisers, 4 aircraft carriers, 68 destroyers, 90 torpedo boats, and 249 submarines. This balanced fleet would enable Germany to openly challenge British control of the sea lanes, if not coerce Britain into acceptance of German demands. In such a large navy, Henke would have been on track for his own command.[17]

It is instructive that, in his five-year naval career up to summer 1939, Henke had received a total of only one week's training in U-Boat warfare. At the time of his instruction in late August 1935, Germany possessed a total of just six submarines, and *Kapitän zur See* (Captain) Karl Dönitz had just assumed direction of the U-Boot-Waffe.[18]

Henke's limited exposure to the U-Boat, typical for his class of naval officer cadets, serves as an index of the relative status of the submarine in the German Navy during the interwar period. The Naval High Command, like their counterparts in the Royal Navy, believed that the development of sonar (or Asdic, as the British termed it, after the organization that developed the instrument, the Allied Submarine Detection Investigation Committee) rendered the submarine obsolete as a combat weapon. The unrestricted submarine warfare that had led to American entry into World War I "could no longer be considered," stated one directive of October 1936. Future commerce warfare would be waged primarily by surface units, with submarines limited to operations off enemy harbors or to such fleet auxiliary missions as reconnaissance. Those officers who favored the expansion of the U-Boat arm proposed their own version of the "Z-Plan," with a larger number of submarines and fewer battleships; they lost, however, to the visionary program approved in January 1939.[19]

The submarine faction had recognized a fundamental problem with this grandiose plan: Could war with Britain be averted until the paper fleet could be built? The answer would come sooner than even they thought.

NOTES

1. For general studies of these developments, see Holger H. Herwig, "Luxury" Fleet: The Imperial German Navy 1888–1918 (London: Allen & Unwin, 1980); Keith W. Bird, Weimar, The German Naval Officer Corps and the Rise of National Socialism (Amsterdam: B. R. Grüner, 1977); and Werner Rahn, Reichsmarine und Landesverteidigung 1919–1928 (Munich: Bernard & Graefe Verlag, 1976).

2. See Charles S. Thomas, The German Navy in the Nazi Era (Annapolis, MD: Naval Institute Press, 1990), 111–23; and Wilhelm Deist, "Die Aufrüstung der Wehrmachtteile 1933–39," in Militärgeschichtliches Forschungsamt (hereafter MGFA), Das Deutsche Reich und der Zweite Weltkrieg, bd. I (Stuttgart: Deutsche Verlags-Anstalt, 1979), 449–54.

3. The oaths and their significance for the navy are discussed in Karl Peter, Acht Glas (Ende der Wache). Erinnerungen eines Offiziers der Crew 38 (Reutlingen: Preussischer Militär-Verlag, 1989), 32–37; the dates of Henke's oaths appear in his service record.

4. Thomas, German Navy, 112–14.

5. Crew data is based on the biographical entries in Crew-Buch der Marine-Offiziers-Crew 1933), in the custody of the Wehrgeschichtliches Ausbildungszentrum, Marineschule Mürwik; see also Eric C. Rust, Naval Officers Under Hitler: The Story of Crew 34 (New York: Praeger, 1991), 19–22, 63. Class rankings are taken from the Rangliste der Deutschen Kriegsmarine nach dem Stande vom 1. November 1935 (Berlin: E. S. Mittler & Sohn, 1935), 87–89 (hereafter cited as 1935 Rangliste).

6. Crew data taken from the Crew Buch; for more information on the individuals named, see Jordan Vause, U-Boat Ace: The Story of Wolfgang Lüth (Annapolis, MD: Naval Institute Press, 1990); Michael Gannon, Operation Drumbeat. The Dramatic True Story of Germany's First U-Boat Attacks Along the American Coast in World War II (New York: Harper & Row, 1990); and Fritz Brustat-Naval and Teddy Suhren, Nasses Eichenlaub. Als Kommandant und F.d.U. im U-Boot-Krieg (Herford: Koehler, 1985).

7. Data on the naval school's courses and routine taken from C.R.W. Thomas, "Making Naval Officers in Germany," USNIP, 64, no. 1 (January 1938), 39–56; Karl-Friedrich Merten's unpublished memoirs, "Traum und Wirklichkeit eines Berufes. Lebenserinnerungen," Teil II, buch 4, 1–7; Deutsches Marine Institut, ed., Marineschule Mürwik (Herford: E. S. Mittler & Sohn, 1985), 122–39; and Rust, Crew 34, 54–56. Henke's examination scores are taken from his personnel record; his ranking is given in the 1935 Rangliste, 87–89.

8. See the discussions in Rust, Crew 34, 10–14, 70–72; and Michael Salewski, "Das Offizierkorps der Reichs- und Kriegsmarine," in Hanns H. Hoffmann, ed., Das deutsche Offizierkorps 1860–1960 (Boppard, R.: Harald Boldt, 1980), 211–29. For a contrasting view of Nazi influence in the navy, see Thomas, German Navy,

141ff. Examples of those who entered the navy as the "lesser evil" include an unidentified Austrian officer captured in December 1943 (ONI spot item no. 286, Op-16-Z subject files, RG 38, NA); and Lt. Oskar Kusch, whose case is discussed in chapter 14.

9. Letter, Wilhelm Müller-Arnecke to the author, 25 January 1988; interview with Reinhard Hardegen, Washington, D.C., 7 June 1990.

10. "Crew Zeitung Nr. 4, Crew 33, Flensburg-Mürwik," 17 April 1935, in the custody of the Marineschule Mürwik. The German original of the quote:

> Der schöne Werner bringt sich um,
> Lächelnd zu glänzen—ach wie dumm!

11. Data from *Crew-Buch* supplemented by information provided by Horst Bredow, U-Boot-Archiv; Rust, *Crew 34*, 80–82; and Franz Kurowski, *Die Träger des Ritterkreuzes des Eisernen Kreuzes der U-Bootwaffe 1939–1945* (Bad Nauheim: Podzun, 1987).

12. See Jost Dülffer, *Weimar, Hitler, und die Marine. Reichspolitik und Flottenbau 1920–1939* (Düsseldorf: Droste Verlag, 1973), 279ff.; and Thomas, *German Navy*, 95–99.

13. Henke's personnel record, Henke family papers; 1936 *Rangliste*; and Thomas, *Navy*, 147–48, for the Kiel review.

14. *Kriegstagebuch (KTB) Admiral Scheer*, 23 July–28 August 1936, file PG 80613, reproduced on National Archives microcopy T1022, Records of the German Navy 1850–1945, roll 3443 (hereafter cited in the format T1022/roll number/PG file number). For general information on German intervention in Spain, see Gerhard L. Weinberg, *The Foreign Policy of Hitler's Germany: Diplomatic Revolution in Europe, 1933–36* (Chicago: University of Chicago Press, 1970), 284–99; for additional data on the *Kriegsmarine*'s role, see Axel Schimpf, "Der Einsatz von Kriegsmarineeinheiten im Rahmen der Verwicklungen des spanischen Bürgerkrieges 1936 bis 1939," in Deutsche Marine Institut, ed., *Der Einsatz von Seestreitkräften im Dienst der auswärtigen Politik* (Herford, Germany: E. S. Mittler & Sohn, 1983), 76–103.

15. Letters of Werner Henke to his mother, 28 July 1936 and undated (but after 8 November 1936), Henke family papers.

16. Incident described in letter from Albrecht Henke to author, 6 May 1988. Henke names the officer involved as "Stange," but this does not match the data provided in the 1937 *Kriegsmarine Rangliste*; I have relied on the latter for the commander's identity.

17. Henke's personnel data taken from the 1936 and 1937 *Ranglisten* and his service record; Spanish war data from Schimpf, "Einsatz," 96–99. On the "Z-Plan" and its background, see Dülffer, *Weimar*, 471ff.; and Michael Salewski, *Die deutsche Seekriegsleitung 1935–1945, Bd. 1: 1935–1941* (Frankfurt am Main: Bernard & Graefe Verlag, 1970), 51ff.

18. See Karl Dönitz, *Memoirs. Ten Years and Twenty Days*, intro. by Jürgen Rohwer, trans. by R. H. Stevens (Annapolis: Naval Institute Press, 1990), 7–12.

19. See Salewski, *Seekriegsleitung*, I, 21–28; and Dülffer, *Weimar*, 386–91, 531–34.

4

War and Disgrace

Events moved rapidly in 1939 for the German Navy. The "Z-Plan" effectively ended the Anglo-German Naval Agreement, formally abrogated by Hitler on 28 April. Even before this date, Hitler had ordered the Wehrmacht to prepare for war with Poland. The Navy High Command, taking at face value Hitler's assurance that France and Britain would not intervene, cobbled together a plan for the concentration of its still-meager forces in the Baltic. Yet well into the summer of 1939, German warships and personnel continued their routine training duties as if nothing was out of the ordinary.[1]

Lt. z. S. Werner Henke departed Pillau in late March 1939 for his next assignment aboard the predeadnought battleship *Schleswig-Holstein* in Kiel. This venerable veteran of the Battle of Jutland, known to her crew simply as *SX*, now served only as a gunnery training ship. Henke commanded one of the crew divisions, probably that for the 88mm antiaircraft artillery. On 1 July the ship received 300 cadets of Crew 38 from Mürwik, all of whom were looking forward to the routine summer training cruise they believed was about to begin.

The senior training officer for the cadets was Kaptlt. Karl-Friedrich Merten, a member of Crew 26 and destined to be one of the top U-Boat aces of the war. In handling his charges Merten noticed that one of the antiaircraft officers was very lax in his behavior, setting a poor example to the cadets assigned him. It was, of course, Henke. Merten called him aside to reproach him for his lack of self-discipline, though he doubted it would do any good. Merten was surprised, however, to see that Henke took the advice to heart and thereafter conducted himself correctly. The two became and remained friends from that point on.[2]

There followed two brief training exercises in the Baltic, after which the cadets set off to enjoy their first shore leave in Kiel. The new ship's captain, *Kapitän zur See* Gustav Kleikamp, meanwhile departed to Berlin for sealed orders. He could not know that the papers awaiting him would start World War II.

In the German plans for the attack on Poland, the free city of Danzig (now Gdansk) provided the pretext for intervention. Formally administered by the League of Nations, Danzig and its largely German population—dominated politically by the Nazi party—became the focus of Polish-German tensions over conflicting rights. Once war had been decided, Danzig's "liberation" had propaganda value for Germany but little military significance. Yet Hitler took a direct interest in the issue, and had raised the possible use of naval forces in a discussion with Raeder in June. The Danzig German militia, augmented by German troops smuggled in from East Prussia, could seize key posts in the city; but to challenge the Polish fortified depot at Westerplatte, the strategic spit of land that controlled the canal linking the Vistula River with the Baltic, the Germans needed heavy artillery. Only the Kriegsmarine could provide this.

Original plans called for the light cruiser *Königsberg* to provide the needed support, but surface forces were spread too thinly to spare her. Thus, on 16 August, Kleikamp learned from his superiors that it might be necessary for *Schleswig-Holstein* to carry out the mission. The orders were confirmed in writing the next week: "Y-Day" was set for dawn on 26 August. *SX* departed Kiel for Swinemünde, where the ship took on additional antiaircraft guns and their crews. On the afternoon of 24 August, as the ship steamed toward Danzig, Henke and the rest of the crew assembled on the main deck aft to listen to Kleikamp explain their mission. "It is to be expected," he told them, "that during our stay at Danzig the question of the city's fate will be decided, and that this could lead to a resolution by force of arms. Our ship has the mission to participate in the defense of Danzig with all available means. . . . This task must fill us with pride, the more so as the Führer has personally approved and ordered our vessel's action." Kleikamp closed with the salutation, "Adolf Hitler—Sieg Heil!"[3]

The crew's enthusiastic response contrasted greatly with the manner in which Hitler committed them to action. On 22 August, after Hitler lectured his senior commanders at Berchtesgaden on Germany's war aims, Grand Admiral Raeder approached the führer to express his concern over risking such an old and slow training ship as the *Schleswig-*

Holstein in combat. "Well, if the old barge goes down, it's no great loss," Hitler replied. When Raeder pointed out that the possible deaths of 300 officer cadets would constitute a severe blow to the navy, Hitler merely dismissed him with a wave of his hand.[4]

While en route to Danzig, *SX* rendezvoused with a minesweeper flotilla that transferred 225 members of a special naval landing force, the equivalent of marines, to assist in the land fighting. This brought the total personnel aboard to nearly 1,200—twice the normal crew. The overaged and overcrowded ship put into Danzig on the morning of 25 August. Strict adherence to peacetime protocol created an eerie situation when the Polish Commissioner General Marian Chodacki paid a courtesy call that afternoon; he received the salute of a naval honor guard and drank tea with the captain while the marines cleaned their rifles on the deck below.

The strained atmosphere grew worse that night. As the marines prepared to disembark to take up position, word suddenly arrived that the attack was postponed. For five days Henke and his 1,200 comrades waited tensely while diplomacy worked its final course. At last, on the evening of 31 August, a radio message ordered *SX* to commence operations at 0445 on 1 September. At 2300 (11:00 P.M.), Henke joined with all other officers in Kleikamp's briefing for the next morning's action.[5]

At 0430, all hands reported to battle stations as the ship slipped down the canal and swung around to bring her starboard broadside to bear on the red-walled fort and its accompanying installations, less than 500 meters distant. At 0447, Kleikamp gave the order: "Open Fire!" The Second World War had begun.

The two 11-inch gun turrets, accompanied by the secondary 6-inch guns and the 20mm pom-pom guns that could be brought to bear, blasted the stillness of the gray morning and twenty years of peace into oblivion. Henke and the 88mm antiaircraft guns did not join in, guarding against a possible Polish air attack. Instead he had a first-hand view of the cannonade: Around the ship a cloud of dark-brown smoke grew, periodically pierced by three-foot tongues of red and yellow flame, all of which was reflected in the mirror of the water below. A few hundred yards away, black smoke and fires marked the shellfire's effects. In the confined space, the shock waves of the gun blasts alone knocked down some buildings and blew the roof shingles from others. Deafening as it was to those on deck, the bombardment seemed to last an hour—but when Kleikamp ordered cease fire, only seven minutes had passed. The marines, who had landed the previous night to take up positions, dashed forward to seize the battered fortifications—only to encounter heavy and disciplined fire that decimated their ranks and drove them back.

At 0740 *Schleswig-Holstein* resumed her bombardment, this time in earnest and with all available guns. For the first time, Werner Henke fired a shot in war, and with effect. Using timed fuses, the 88mm guns concentrated their fire on the lone 75mm Polish artillery piece in the fort and silenced her. Yet the infantry assault that followed the hour-long shelling again failed, as did the next. Not until 7 September would the Polish garrison finally yield, after continued bombardment by *SX* and other vessels, Stuka air raids, and reinforced infantry attack. In sharp contrast to the brutal nature of occupation that would follow, German soldiers and sailors presented arms in salute when the defenders of Westerplatte marched out.[6]

The Polish defense at the canal had not been the only surprise to the Kriegsmarine. On 3 September, Great Britain honored her treaty with Poland and declared war on Germany. Whether they were prepared or not, senior officers acknowledged the almost impossible odds against them. Instead of the great fleet promised by the "Z-Plan," the German Navy confronted war against Britain with only 2 modern battleships, 3 "pocket battleships," one heavy and 6 light cruisers, 21 destroyers, and 57 submarines; against them the Royal Navy counted 15 battleships and battlecruisers, 7 aircraft carriers, 15 heavy cruisers, 49 light cruisers, 192 destroyers, and 62 submarines. In a supplement to the Naval Operations Staff's war diary for 3 September, Grand Admiral Raeder commented: "[Our] U-Boats are still far too few, however, to have any decisive effect on war. The surface forces, moreover, are so inferior in number and strength to those of the British fleet that, even at full strength, they can do no more than show that they know how to die with dignity."[7]

Younger naval officers, inexperienced in war and ignorant of the full meaning of that disparity, did not view the conflict with such pessimism. Many perceived war with the British as described by one Crew 34 officer: "At the outset of the war we saw it mainly as an athletics contest." Henke may or may not have shared this attitude. As a West Prussian, he doubtless held the common view that the war with Poland was justified, the final step in the burial of the Versailles Treaty. Yet according to his brother, he disliked the English far more than he did Poles, Russians, or Americans—whether this derived from his earlier experiences in the merchant marine, his memories of the World War I blockade, or a combination of factors, is not known.[8]

In any case, Henke enjoyed the distinction of being one of the few navy officers to see action in the war's early days. Departing Westerplatte on 8 September, *Schleswig-Holstein* steamed northwest across the Danzig Bay (now Gdansk Bay) to bombard Polish coastal fortifications along the western coast and on the Hel peninsula. These operations lasted until 2 October, and were not without cost: On 27 September, a Polish battery scored a hit on *SX*, wounding seven crewmen, two mortally. As an artillery officer, Henke participated in all of these actions. Together with the other ship's officers, he received the Iron Cross (2d class), among the first combat decorations awarded in the Kriegsmarine.[9]

But war could not long delay Werner's pursuit of other interests. At midday on 2 October, the final Polish garrison at Hela capitulated to German forces. By 6:30 P.M. that evening, Henke was in the company of an attractive young woman in front of the Deutsches Haus Hotel in the old part of Danzig. Their plans for the evening, however, were interrupted by a minor incident that introduced Henke to the SS (Schutz-staffel, literally "Guard Echelon," reflecting its initial role as a bodyguard to Hitler), and also revealed much of Henke's character and something of the character of Nazi Germany.

As the couple stood facing the hotel, a somewhat inebriated member of the local SS approached Henke: "You, Navy Lieutenant, do not seem to be aware of the need to salute a Captain!" Recognizing the man's attempt to establish his supremacy of rank, Henke did not back down: "I was not aware that I was required to salute an SS *Sturmführer*." The SS officer flashed his own Iron Cross to prove his bravery, disparaged all navy men as "a shameless lot," and demanded that Henke accompany him to headquarters. Unfazed, Henke replied: "Stop making accusations and go home, a man in uniform should conduct himself more appropriately." The naval officer and his date tried to leave, but the SS officer continued to harass them. After being called a "coward" and a "swine," Henke simply turned on the man and dropped him with two punches.

Henke attempted to have his antagonist taken into custody, but the latter fled to his car and drove away. Henke himself reported the incident to SS headquarters, where the *Hauptsturmführer's* superior expressed his regrets and promised to clear up the matter with Kleikamp the next morning. Even the SS officer in question later offered his apologies to Henke by telephone, though the latter insisted upon a written note for the record.[10]

Petty brawls among military personnel of rival services were neither uncommon nor unique to Germany during World War II, but blows exchanged between navy and SS officers at the beginning of the war were rare. The serious clashes that had marked relations between the two branches in 1934 had been smoothed over with time,[11] and no one in higher authority wished to reopen old wounds at a time that demanded national unity. Most important, the SS had not attained in 1939 the supremacy of authority it would acquire as the war went on, when Henke would again encounter it with more ominous results.

At the same time, the incident confirmed Henke's hotheaded and impetuous nature to his superiors; though he had not been at fault, his action might have placed the navy at risk in defending him. He was not disciplined, but he had not improved his standing as an officer. For the next six months he remained aboard *SX* during various cruises in the Baltic for training, icebreaking duties, and occasionally intercepting neutral vessels bound for Britain.[12]

Elsewhere in the navy the "dying with dignity" had begun. In December 1939, Panzerschiff *Admiral Graf Spee* adhered to Raeder's vision of an honorable suicide when she scuttled herself in Montevideo harbor, Uruguay, after which her captain shot himself. The loss rate among U-Boats was as bad as any period in the war: During the first seven months of World War II, Admiral Karl Dönitz lost seventeen of his fifty-one front-line boats. Yet the submarine also provided the Kriegsmarine with its first great victory on 13 October, when the former HSO Günther Prien penetrated the British fleet anchorage at Scapa Flow and sank the battleship *Royal Oak*. As the warship least costly to construct and most capable of striking at England, the U-Boats represented the only part of the "Z-Plan" ship-building program still in effect. The expanded construction schedules established in March 1940 anticipated the addition of 300 U-Boats by the beginning of 1942.[13]

To man this fleet, of course, required first of all officers qualified to command it. There was never a shortage of volunteers, but more sweeping measures were necessary to match production plans. Although exact details are lacking, it appears that regional navy commands—using their own criteria—were ordered to supply specific quotas of officers. One command selected all lieutenants whose personnel evaluations included the rating of "suited for small vessels," an indication of leadership capabilities with small groups of individuals. No one, however, was transferred against his will, and the appeal of U-Boat service (and prospects for promotion and independent command) more than compensated for the risks. Thus it was that in late March 1940, Werner Henke received notice that he had been transferred to the U-Boat service, and was to report to the submarine school on 2 April.[14]

Like many other officers, Henke had received only cursory training aboard U-Boats, a single six-day course in Kiel nearly five years before this transfer. At the U-Schule, located at Neustadt on Lübeck Bay, Henke and his fellow candidates would begin a sixteen-week course learning the basics of submarine warfare. As had Prien and the other aces who preceded them, the trainees received instruction in such fields as the characteristics and use of torpedoes, submerging and trimming a U-Boat, the use of periscopes and sighting devices, general technical data, Allied antisubmarine tactics and weapons, and the unique qualities of leadership necessary for a submarine. They also learned the significance of patience and coordination of effort in convoy attacks, the keys to success in Dönitz's wolf-pack tactics.

The elaborate training facilities included a full-sized conning tower suspended over a sheet of water; officer trainees peered through the binoculars or periscope at miniature ships in convoy formations, which were manipulated by means of metal rods to simulate varying speeds and courses. The operator who controlled these movements—a civilian named Barkow—also reproduced various weather and visibility conditions. Each prospective U-Boat commander was expected to make fifteen successful convoy attacks on this trainer before graduation. Those who emerged from the U-Schule would later claim, "I completed my first patrol under Barkow."[15]

Werner Henke, however, was not among them. One of his escapades during this training period nearly ended his career.

Neustadt's location placed the small town within the range of Royal Air Force (RAF) bombers. In April 1940, when German forces launched their invasion of Denmark and Norway, the RAF's coastal and bomber commands began a systematic mine-laying campaign against German harbors and waterways. The Naval High Command therefore decided to move the submarine school beyond the reach of British aircraft to Pillau, East Prussia.[16]

The move took place in early May. Standard procedure for this kind of transfer involved travel aboard military trains at a specific level of priority, which would normally require a journey of three or four days to reach Pillau. Acting on this supposition, Henke decided to take a detour to visit a girlfriend in Berlin. He believed he could spend at least an evening with her, perhaps a little more, then travel on to the Baltic port in time to meet his comrades. Not until after he finally arrived at Pillau did he realize that his class' transfer had received a higher priority, and that for the last two days he had been "Absent Without Leave" (AWOL).

Henke need not have been court-martialed; commanding officers always had the option of settling a disciplinary problem within a unit, to minimize the damage to the offender's career. Henke's superiors, however, threw the book at him. He was charged with desertion, found guilty, and sentenced to two or three months of duty with a punishment unit. That he received such a harsh punishment provides an indication of his previous disciplinary offenses and incidents, the full list of which is unknown. He began to serve his sentence on 8 May, two days before the German offensive in France and the Low Countries began. While Germany accomplished and celebrated its greatest victory of the war in the summer of 1940, a disgraced Henke languished in a forgotten post.

He at least retained enough friends at the submarine school to accomplish one piece of subterfuge. Knowing how great the shock and disappointment might be for his mother, Henke arranged to send his letters to her through his friends at the U-Schule, there to be stamped with the same navy post office number as before. When his mother replied to the Pillau address, his comrades forwarded the letters to Henke's actual location. Until her death in 1953, Margrete Henke never learned of her son's misdemeanors.[17]

Henke served out his term and was assigned to the First U-Boat Flotilla in Kiel, where he served his probation as the first watch officer aboard the submarine tender *Lech*. Finally, in mid-November 1940, he received orders to report to Lorient as a watch officer aboard *U–124*. Yet even after he had begun rehabilitating his career, his past overtook him. In February 1941, he learned that, officially, he had been kicked out of the navy.

In all probability, Henke's accumulated offenses had convinced navy authorities of the need to release him. Fortunately for him, Dönitz and his organizational specialist, Admiral Hans-Georg von Friedeburg, recognized the need for such mavericks as submarine commanders. Together they worked out a compromise solution to keep Henke in the navy. Oblt.z.S. Werner Henke would, on 28 February 1941, be released from active duty in the Kriegsmarine, with the proviso that on 1 March 1941 he would return to duty with the identical acting rank. Henke was meanwhile advised that, if he "kept his nose clean" and proved himself in action, his personnel record would be wiped clean and his full rank restored. His career as a regular navy officer all but destroyed, Henke could at least make a fresh start as a wartime submarine commander.[18]

Nevertheless, when Henke began his combat career aboard *U-124*, he had no legal standing as a career officer; his name disappeared from the seniority lists; and had he become a casualty, his mother would have learned the truth of her son's status in the worst possible way. And as events would prove, that likelihood was increasing every day.

NOTES

1. Michael Salewski, *Die deutsche Seekriegsleitung 1935-1945, Bd. 1, 1935-41* (Frankfurt/M: Bernard & Graefe Verlag, 1970), 91-92; Charles S. Thomas, *The Germany Navy in the Nazi Era* (Annapolis, MD: Naval Institute Press, 1990), 181.

2. Letter of Karl-Friedrich Merten to author, 31 May 1987, and interview with author, Waldshut, 13 September 1989.

3. On the background to the Danzig crisis, see Gerhard Weinberg, *The Foreign Policy of Hitler's Germany: Starting World War II, 1937-1939* (Chicago: University of Chicago, 1980), 193-201, 583-84; on the commitment of *Schleswig-Holstein*, see Bertil Stjernfelt and Klaus-Richard Böhme, *Westerplatte 1939* (Freiburg: Rombach Verlag, 1979), 39-42; and esp. Willi Schultz, *Linienschiff Schleswig-Holstein* (Herford, Germany: Koehler, 1991), 162-67.

4. See Winfried Baumgart, "Zur Ansprache Hitlers vor den Führern der Wehrmacht am 22 August 1939," *Vierteljahreshefte für Zeitgeschichte*, 16, no. 2 (April 1968), 147.

5. Schultz, *Schleswig-Holstein*, 171-85; Stjernfelt and Böhme, *Westerplatte*, 68-77.

6. KTB *Schleswig-Holstein*, 31 August-7 September 1939, T1022/2734/PG 48503; Fritz O. Busch, *Akten des Seekrieges* (Berlin: Brunnen Verlag, 1940), 24-26, for a vivid physical description of the scene; and Stjernfelt, *Westerplatte*, 78ff.

7. The comparison of warship data appears in MGFA, *Deutsche Reich*, I, 162; Raeder's comment is published in *Fuehrer Conferences on Naval Affairs 1939-1945*, intro. by Jak P. Mallmann Showell (Annapolis, MD: Naval Institute Press, 1990), 37-38.

8. Eric C. Rust, *Naval Officers Under Hitler: The Story of Crew 34* (New York: Praeger, 1991), 110-12; interview with Albrecht Henke, Lüneburg, 18 September 1987.

9. KTB *Schleswig-Holstein*, 15 September—2 October 1939, T1022/2946/PG 48505-06; Henke personnel record, Henke family papers.

10. Henke's account of the incident was given in a report to the Commander of *Schleswig-Holstein*, 2 October 1939, in Henke family papers.

11. See Thomas, *Navy*, 91-94, 142-44.

12. Henke's personnel record; KTB *Schleswig-Holstein*, October 1939-March 1940, T1022/2946/PG 48509-518.

13. See the data in V. E. Tarrant, *The U-Boat Offensive 1914-1945* (Annapolis, MD: Naval Institute Press, 1989), 83-88; and the construction data in Eberhard

Rössler, *The U-Boat. The Evolution and Technical History of German Submarines* (Annapolis, MD: Naval Institute Press, 1981), 122–26.

14. See Gottfried Hoch, "Zur Problematik der Menschenführung im Kriege," in *Die Deutsche Marine*, comp. by Deutsches Marine Institut/Deutsche Marine Akademie (Herford: E. S. Mittler & Sohn, 1983), 195–97; and letter of Karl-Friedrich Merten to author, 2 November 1991; that Henke did not volunteer for submarine service is confirmed by his brother (letter, Albrecht Henke to author, 22 February 1989).

15. The "Barkow" trainer is described in the British report, "U–593, Interrogation of Survivors," February 1943, in ONI Monograph files (Germany 915–510), RG 38, NA.

16. Denis Richards, *Royal Air Force 1939–45, Vol. 1: The Fight at Odds* (London: Her Majesty's Stationery Office, 1974), 88–89; interview with Wilhelm Müller-Arnecke, Bremen-Leesum, 22 September 1987.

17. Müller-Arnecke interview, 22 September 1987, supplemented by Henke's personnel record. Müller-Arnecke, a fellow member of Crew 33, worked in the personnel department of the U-Boat service during this period. Details of Henke's earlier offenses were apparently erased when his success as a U-Boat commander led to a "purge" of his file and the restoration of his former status.

18. Data taken from Henke's personnel record. The author infers that Henke was previously informed of the eventual "correction" of his service record.

5

Rehabilitation

As Werner Henke served out his period of probation, the submarine campaign against Great Britain hit full stride. The fall of France allowed Dönitz to transfer his operational bases to the French Atlantic ports, and in August 1940 Hitler lifted the last restrictions against merchant vessels approaching British ports. Aided by the Royal Navy's lack of sufficient convoy escorts and the excellent cryptanalysis of British communications furnished by their own B-Dienst (for Beobachtungsdienst, Navy Signal Intelligence Service), German submariners described this period simply as "the Happy Time."

At last Dönitz could make use of the *Rudeltaktik*, or "wolf pack" tactics, that traced their origins to World War I. A U-Boat patrol line would be deployed across the path of an approaching convoy, each submarine sweeping a designated area until one sighted the prey. This boat then shadowed the convoy, reporting its course and speed by radio while Dönitz concentrated the remaining submarines for a simultaneous attack at night on the surface. British sonar equipment was useless against surfaced submarines, whose low silhouettes rendered them almost invisible at night. These methods worked to perfection in the devastation of two convoys and the mauling of a third northwest of the British isles between late September and the end of October 1940. Dönitz's statistical yardstick of success—the average tonnage of merchant shipping sunk each day by each U-Boat at sea—reached 920 tons in October, a figure never to be repeated.[1]

The immediate problem for the Commander in Chief of Submarines (or BdU, Befehlshaber der Unterseeboote) lay in the shortage of U-Boats to maintain operations. Instead of the 300 boats he considered necessary to blockade Britain, Dönitz could count on only 5 to 7 submarines available for operations at any given moment. Even this number was attained only by using large Type IX U-Boats, intended for independent use on long-range patrols, for patrol lines and convoy operations for which they were less suited. Through the winter of 1940–41, the lack of boats and bad weather precluded a repetition of the autumn's successes.[2]

It was to one of the returning Type *IXB* boats that Lt. (provisional) Werner Henke reported at Lorient, France, on 15 November 1940. *U–124*, commanded by *Kapitänleutnant* Georg Wilhelm Schulz, had just returned from her second war patrol in North Atlantic, during which she had sunk five merchant ships to raise her total to seven, with an eighth damaged. During the next month Henke familiarized himself with the submarine, her instruments, and weapons. He would serve as the second watch officer (*Zweiter Wach-Offizier*, usually shortened to II.W.O.), which entailed responsibility for such administrative tasks as food and supplies, and for the operation of the deck and antiaircraft (flak) guns.

First he became acquainted with the other officers of the boat. His commander, Schulz, shared with him a background in the merchant marine prior to naval service. One of the "Old Guard," Schulz had served with the U-Boot-Waffe since 1935. Now aged thirty-four, he was as competent a sailor as he was a father to his men. Prior to this boat, Schulz had commanded *U–64* on her only cruise in support of the invasion of Norway. Bombed and sunk by British aircraft off Narvik on 13 April 1940, Schulz and the survivors were rescued by German mountain troops who had captured the key port only days before. When they received a new submarine upon their return to Germany, Schulz and his men saluted their rescuers by adopting the unit symbol of the mountain troops, the edelweiss, as their boat's emblem.

As first watch officer (IWO), Johannes (Jochen) Mohr, was seven years Henke's junior and destined to become, in 1941, Germany's youngest submarine commander. Henke and Mohr would serve nearly a year together aboard the *Edelweissboot*, forming a very effective combination of mutual respect and cordial relations. Finally, Rolf Brinker served as the chief engineer (*Leitender Ingenieur*, or L.I.), responsible for the maintenance of the submarine as a seagoing vessel. From each of these men, Henke learned his new trade.[3]

The mere experience of U-Boat service also conveyed knowledge that could never be taught in a classroom: the idiosyncrasies of each boat's mechanical and technical systems; the adaptation to a daily routine in a cramped, sunless world of dripping pipes and foul odors; and above all, the problems of leadership for a crew of fifty men who had to be appreciated as specialists, but understood as youths just leaving their teens.

Such issues—together with stories of operations at sea—also provided topics of discussion among U-Boat officers during the evenings in the *Prefecture*, the officers' quarters in the former French naval base in Lorient. Kaptlt. Karl-Friedrich Merten, then commanding *U–68* and Henke's former superior aboard *Schleswig-Holstein*, recalls "repeated discussions" with his younger colleague during this period. Wolfgang Lüth, a fellow member of Crew 33, was also stationed in Lorient at this time and probably discussed with Henke his views on leadership and morale, views subsequently disseminated throughout the navy.[4]

But above all, Henke would learn the realities of a U-Boat and its crew from combat experience. The education began on 16 December 1940, when *U–124* departed on her third operational cruise for the North Atlantic. The patrol proved to be one of the worst Henke and his comrades endured. Operating in the convoy lanes west of the Hebrides, the U-Boat was tossed about by week-long winter storms while fruitlessly searching for targets. Scanning the horizon for four hours out of every twelve, Henke and his watch lashed themselves to the conning tower against gale-force winds and crashing waves up to thirty feet in height. Off-duty time below brought little relief, for the violent tossing of the boat inhibited rest or any activity below decks. As the cook could not prepare warm meals, crewmen munched cold sandwiches; all suffered considerable weight loss.

Battered physically by the sea and psychologically by the lack of success, crew morale plummeted. The attempt to celebrate Christmas on board, with a home-made tree and ornaments, failed to relieve the irritability and frustration shared by all. The sinking of a solitary British steamer on 6 January 1941 marked the only victory of the patrol, which finally ended sixteen days later with an inglorious return to Lorient.[5]

More than bad weather contributed to this failure. Following the devastation of one convoy by six U-Boats in early December, the British Admiralty rerouted its convoys further north only four days after *U–124* left port. More convoy escorts and supporting aircraft had also become available.[6] Above all, the period demonstrated an institutional flaw in the German conduct of the naval war, inadequate air support. The Kriegsmarine possessed only a token air arm whose few reconnaissance planes could only cover a small part of the ocean expanses traversed by convoys. Dönitz's efforts in January 1941 to obtain a firm commitment from Hermann Göring's Luftwaffe yielded only one squadron of *Focke-Wulf* 200 Condors, which could perform both reconnaissance and bombing missions. Göring opposed even this, and the net result never met the U-Boats' needs.[7]

Nevertheless, when *U–124* departed on her next patrol on 23 February 1941, Germany had moved closer to an all-out naval war against Britain. Earlier in the month, such major surface forces as heavy cruiser *Hipper* and battleships *Scharnhorst* and *Gneisenau* joined individual commerce raiders in the hunt for British convoys in the Atlantic. The first fruits of *Luftwaffe* and U-Boat cooperation could be seen and although the total number of front-line submarines stood at only twenty-one, over eighty were in training or undergoing sea trials in the Baltic. Given these circumstances and the decreased opportunities northwest of Britain, Dönitz and his operational chief, *Konteradmiral* (Rear Admiral) Eberhard Godt, yielded to pressure from the Naval High Command to divert boats to the south. Thus *U–124* and two other Type IX boats were released from convoy duties to the missions for which they were more suited, long-range patrols in more vulnerable areas, to stretch British defenses to the limit.[8]

Schulz's orders directed him to the shipping lanes off Freetown, Sierra Leone, an area Henke would come to know very well. During this patrol, all aboard could at last feel that they were part of a larger effort. On 4 March, *U–124* rendezvoused secretly with the German tanker *Corrientes* in Las Palmas harbor in the Canary Islands for refueling and supplies. Three days later, Henke's bridge watch sighted two capital ships on the moonlit horizon which, after a hurried radio exchange with headquarters, proved to be *Scharnhorst* and *Gneisenau*. Later in the day, *U–124* came alongside the latter battleship to exchange greetings: The unlikely meeting of David and Goliath so far from home brought crews from both ships onto their decks in joyous curiosity. Less than two weeks later, the submarine linked up with commerce raider *Kormoran*, for additional torpedoes and supplies, and with Henke's old ship, *Admiral Scheer*. To the pocket battleship Schulz delivered a vital package of crystal replacement parts necessary for the ship's radar, and in return received thousands of fresh eggs captured from an English merchant vessel.

U–124's earlier meeting with *Scharnhorst* and *Gneisenau* also produced the rare phenomenon of a battleship-submarine convoy operation. Shortly after the rendezvous on 7 March, the German capital ships spotted a convoy from Freetown bound for Britain and, using their radio link to France, relayed the information to the U-Boats in the area (naval radio communications did not yet allow ship-to-ship exchanges). Schulz diverted to intercept, and in a night attack on the surface sank four freighters in fifteen minutes. In diving to avoid the escorts, *U–124* was almost struck by one of her victims as the latter plummeted to her grave, the noise of her bursting bulkheads echoing loudly about them. Thereafter the submarine operated as a lone wolf, sinking seven independent steamers in the Freetown area before returning home on 1 May 1941.

Henke learned much on this sixty-seven-day voyage. The night surface attack devastatingly demonstrated a submarine's effectiveness when it could slip into the middle of a convoy. As II.W.O., he himself could claim one ship with artillery fire, the small (1,756 tons) *Portadoc*, when a defective torpedo failed to detonate against her hull. Schulz also demonstrated to him that unrestricted submarine warfare did not necessarily require abandoning the laws of the sea: Whenever possible, survivors of sunken ships received water, provisions, cigarettes, and directions to the nearest land. In one case, *U–124*'s doctor treated and set the broken leg and dislocated shoulder of a badly wounded merchant officer who might not have otherwise survived.

Another incident taught Henke the importance of the chief engineer on a U-Boat. Commanding the bridge watch when a British plane appeared, Henke believed it too late to submerge and was about to order the flak guns manned when the last lookout pulled him down through the hatch. Lieutenant Brinker, without waiting for Henke's decision, had begun to crash dive. On this same trip Brinker performed a major repair of the diesel engines at sea, masterfully improvising replacement ball bearings out of the thin metal foil found in cigarette packages. Henke thus learned that the chief engineer enjoyed a wide latitude in handling the boat and her engines, but a lesson not without its disadvantages, as Henke would discover aboard his own submarine.[9]

As the *Edelweiss* tied up at Lorient and her crew began to enjoy a two-month layover, the first signs of a significant change in the sea war became evident. News of the loss in March of three of the top U-Boat aces, Günther Prien (*U–47*), Joachim Schepke (*U–100*), and Otto Kretschmer (*U–99*) spread quickly.[10] On 27 May came news of the loss of the great battleship *Bismarck*, and with it, the end of the use of German capital ships as commerce raiders. *U–124*'s experience with *Scharnhorst* and *Gneisenau* would not be repeated, and the U-Boats would, henceforth, carry virtually the entire load of the naval war. The most fateful news, however, came while Henke was home in Lüneberg on leave.

On Sunday morning, 22 June, the radio triumphantly announced the Wehrmacht's attack on the Soviet Union. His brother, Albrecht—by now serving in the army and also on furlough at the time—recalled that Werner was "shocked and disappointed" at the news of the invasion, as he had always been favorably disposed toward the Russian people. All present realized the war was becoming a more serious and fundamental struggle than before.[11]

Henke could not know that another development during his furlough posed a more immediate peril to all of the U-Boat service. In early May, *U–110* was lost while attacking a convoy south of Greenland. Before she sank, however, a British boarding party recovered her Enigma cipher machine intact, together with many of the accompanying materials and documents. This priceless haul, supplemented by cipher materials seized aboard one of the German tankers intended to refuel *Bismarck*, at last gave Britain the edge in communications intelligence. From the beginning of June, the British Admiralty's Operational Intelligence Centre could read German naval messages shortly after their transmission, allowing Allied convoys to be routed around U-Boat patrol lines and escorts to be shifted to danger points.[12]

The changed circumstances in the war at sea were disguised as "bad luck" in *U–124*'s next patrol. Delayed by engine trouble, the submarine finally sortied from Lorient on 15 July bound for the Freetown area that had proven so fruitful earlier. Two weeks and over 2,000 miles later, Schulz received orders to put about and head north: Dönitz had determined from reports relayed by other U-Boats that the traffic lanes out of Freetown had shifted, leaving too few targets to justify the effort. *U–124* and three other boats previously destined for African waters headed instead for the convoy approaches west of Gibraltar, where the narrow entrance to the Mediterranean created a bottleneck for convoys carrying troops and supplies to the British forces battling Rommel. Yet the two weeks of searching produced only an abortive attack on a solo steamer at long range, and a brief glimpse of a convoy before a destroyer drove the U-Boat off. British air cover during this period forced several crash dives, during one of which a crewman suffered a crushed finger. On 25 August the boat completed her return voyage, having exhausted all her fuel but only two torpedoes.[13]

This was Schulz's last patrol as the veteran skipper advanced to a submarine training command. Newly promoted Jochen Mohr now took over *U–124* as the youngest *Kapitänleutnant* (age 25) in the Kriegsmarine. Henke assumed the duties as first watch officer, the equivalent in the

U.S. Navy of the executive officer. Werner's provisional status had not changed, but the promotion was real enough in command responsibility for the torpedoes and their firing systems. Henke would also carry out all surface torpedo attacks, under the *Kommandant*'s general supervision.

For this, Henke was indebted to Mohr. When Mohr left for the U-Boat commanders' school during the last patrol, Schulz passed over Henke to bring in a new man, Heinz Eck, as I.W.O.[14] At a time when men ten years his junior were commanding U-Boats, and even Dönitz complained that three weeks of tactical training for new commanders could not match the prewar standards of two years,[15] Henke could not help but recognize that nine months aboard *U-124* had not improved his situation. Mohr's vote of confidence marked a breakthrough.

Henke did not disappoint on the next patrol. Together with *U-201* the boat departed Lorient on 16 September and proceeded due west, where on 20 September they encountered Convoy OG 74 on its southbound arc toward Gibraltar. Just before midnight, Mohr slipped into the rear of the convoy to attack. Henke's first night surface firings demonstrated his sharpshooting skills: three shots, three claimed hits, two merchantmen sunk.

Five days later BdU directed Mohr against Convoy HG 73, spotted by an Italian submarine and Luftwaffe reconnaissance en route to England. In a running battle over the next two nights, Mohr perilously steered past unwitting convoy escorts to sink four more steamers, all of which were torpedoed under Henke's direction. Exhausted by their exertions and narrow escapes, Mohr and his crew returned to port on 1 October after one of the shortest but most successful cruises of the war.

The patrol proved both rewarding and educational for Henke. For his marksmanship and overall performance, he received the Iron Cross, First Class, two days after returning to Lorient. Mohr's daring—or rashness—became Henke's own standard for U-Boat operations. His five torpedo misses against British escorts taught him something of the speed and maneuverability of warships in action. One trait he did not acquire from Mohr, however, was the tendency to exaggerate, as many German and American submarine skippers did, the size of their victims: The six vessels estimated at 44,000 tons by Mohr in reality amounted to less than 12,000 tons. Henke's own claims would correspond much more closely to actual tonnage sunk.[16]

Above all, Mohr's endorsement of his performance elevated Henke to command level. Sometime in October, as *U-124* underwent a complete overhaul, Henke received orders to report on 1 November to the Twenty-fourth U-Boat Flotilla in Danzig for commanders' school. It may be assumed that Henke did not detour for visits to girlfriends on this trip.

He would spend the next ten months in preparation for a combat command. During November 1941 he received extensive training in the use of the periscope and the submerged firing of torpedoes under various simulated combat conditions. The course also dealt with the many skills and command practices that had to be mastered: dives and crash dives under different weather and sea conditions, the duties of bridge-watches under various conditions and times of day, the latest developments in weaponry and equipment, and the maintenance of morale and peak performance by the crew.[17] Henke then spent a month studying the characteristics of current and new models of torpedoes at Gotenhafen (Gdynia).

On 12 January 1942, he reported to the commercial shipyards of the Deutsche Werft firm, in the Hamburg suburb of Finkenwerder. There he first saw the half-finished, cigar-shaped metal framework that was to become his submarine. The standard practice of *Baubelehrung* (literally "new construction acquaintance") enabled a U-Boat commander and his crew to familiarize themselves with the actual construction of the vessel prior to commissioning. This allowed a commander to discuss the submarine's capabilities and limitations with the designers and technical specialists.

It also provided the opportunity for a captain to become acquainted with his officers. The first watch officer, *Oberleutnant* Berthold Hashagen, was a Bremerhaven native only a few months younger than Henke; a reserve officer, he had earlier commanded a patrol boat flotilla. *Oberleutnant* Ernst Sauerberg, the II.W.O., passed through Mürwik with the December 1939 term of cadets and had just completed his preliminary submarine training. Finally, Georg Mahnken of Crew 37-B, promoted to the rank of *Oberleutnant (Ingenieur)* in April 1942, would serve as chief engineer for most of the history of *U–515*.[18]

The crew gradually assembled as the date of commissioning approached. Finally, on the frozen morning of 21 February 1942, submarine *U–515* entered the service of the German Navy. Each crewman received, courtesy of the shipyard, a photo album to record his memories. The crew also accepted gifts from the shipyard workers—probably an electric coffee machine and mixing bowl, as *U–512* had received a few months earlier. Werner Henke had received the greatest gift of all: a second chance.

The next several months followed the familiar pattern of training and shakedown cruises for all new U-Boats, delayed only by the packed ice in the Elbe River that kept *U–515* tied up until late March. She then traveled through the Kaiser Wilhelm Canal to Kiel for her acceptance trials with the U.A.K. (U-Bootsabnahmekommando, U-Boat Acceptance Command). These involved practice dives and simulations in the pressure dock to test the pressure hull, tests of the torpedo tubes, engines, radio equipment, and general seaworthiness of the craft. Then came silent running trials off the island of Bornholm to test the volume of noise emitted by the submerged U-Boat and its engines. More tests followed of the torpedo-firing mechanisms.

During these trials, Henke's submarine tied an underwater speed record for Type IXC boats set by *U–155* during her own trials several months earlier. To assess the underwater performance of the electrical engines, each boat's maximum submerged speed was timed over a stretch of one nautical mile. *U–515* achieved a top speed of 7.46 knots— still below the record for the Type VIIC, but an excellent performance for the larger, more sluggish class of submarine. This extra speed, a testament to both the quality of the engines and the engine-room personnel, would spell the difference between life and death in combat.[19]

In early May the *Fünf-fünfzehn* reported for tactical exercises to the Agru-Front (full name Technisches Ausbildungsgruppe für Frontunterseeboote, Operational Training Command), but commonly known to submariners as the "Fifth Column" for the rigorous tests they inflicted upon U-Boat trainees. The training officers on board would stage problems in the middle of exercises to introduce crews to the unexpected situations they would confront in combat. Damage to vital parts of the submarine would be simulated in the middle of crash dives or during submerged runs, with the trainees expected to master the situation before the vessel sank. Necessary as such tests were, they proved extremely nerve-wracking to the crews for the two weeks they lasted.

The submarine had just begun a new series of torpedo-firing exercises when the clutches on her diesel engines suffered damage, and *U–515* put into Stettin for repairs. Over a month was required to completely repair the defects before the submarine returned to the Baltic to complete her training. These involved daily torpedo-firing practices and emphasized simulated attacks on convoys as part of a "wolf pack," including night and underwater attacks. Here Henke combined his own experiences aboard *U–124* with the latest "Lessons Learned" distributed by the U-Boat Command, and updated technological improvements. At last, the submarine and her crew graduated from training. On 23 July

1942, *U–515* arrived in Kiel for a final overhaul and the crew departed for a last home leave; when they next embarked, it would be for real.[20]

Before turning to that day, however, it is appropriate to examine the crewmen of *U–515* and the submarine herself. From the moment of commissioning, Werner Henke's life and fate became inextricably bound with both.

NOTES

1. See Jak P. Mallmann Showell, *U-Boat Command and the Battle of the Atlantic* (Lewiston, NY: Vanwell Publishing, 1989), 37–46; and Günter Hessler, *The U-Boat War in the Atlantic 1939–1945*, vol. 1 (London: Her Majesty's Stationery Office, 1989), 50–57. These are the two best operational summaries of the U-Boat war from the German perspective.

2. Hessler, *U-Boat War*, vol. 1, 57–58, 64–65.

3. The basic information on these individuals is taken from the history of *U–124* by E. B. Gasaway, *Grey Wolf, Grey Sea* (New York: Ballantine Books, 1970.) Additional biographical data on Schulz and Mohr appear in Franz Kurowski, *Die Träger des Ritterkreuzes des Eisernen Krenzes der U-Bootwaffe 1939–1945* (Bad Nauheim: Podzun, 1987), 47, 66.

4. Karl-Friedrich Merten, letter to author, 31 May 1987, and interview with author, Waldshut, 12 September 1989; Jordan Vause, *U-Boat Ace. The Story of Wolfgang Lüth* (Annapolis, MD: Naval Institute Press, 1990), 97–98, 123–26; and Harald Busch, *So War der U-Boot-Krieg* (Bielefeld: Deutscher Heimat-Verlag, 1952), 340–58, for the most complete (but still expurgated) version of Lüth's views on "problems of leadership."

5. See *U–124* KTB, 16 December 1940–22 January 1941, on T1022/2973/PG 30114/4, and description in Gasaway, *Grey Wolf*, 88–94.

6. John Costello and Terry Hughes, *The Battle of the Atlantic* (New York: Dial Press/James Wade, 1977), 122.

7. Hessler, *U-Boat War*, vol. 1, 62–64, 67–69.

8. On general developments during this period, see Jürgen Rohwer and Gerd Hümmelchen, *Chronology of the War at Sea 1939–1945*, vol. 1, trans. by Derek Masters (New York: Arco Publishing, 1972–74), 75–82; U-Boat numbers are taken from V. E. Tarrant, *The U-Boat Offensive 1914–1945* (Annapolis, MD: Naval Institute Press, 1989), 96; Dönitz's decision is recorded in his *Memoirs: Ten Years and Twenty Days* (Annapolis, MD: Naval Institute Press, 1990), 152.

9. *U–124* KTB, 23 February–1 May 1941, on T1022/2973/PG 30114/5; Gasaway, *Grey Wolf*, 97–139 (Gasaway errs in his statement on 139n that Henke then departed *U–124*). Both sources credit Schulz with one more ship than is acknowledged in Jürgen Rohwer, *Axis Submarine Successes 1939–1945* (Annapolis, MD: Naval Institute Press, 1983), 45–50; I have followed the latter. For *U–124*'s meeting with *Scharnhorst*, *Gneisenau*, and *Scheer*, see Gerhard Bidlingmaier, *Einsatz der schweren Kriegsmarineeinheiten im ozeanischen Zufuhrkrieg* (Neckargemünd: Scharnhorst, 1963), 174–79, 193.

10. Public acknowledgment of the losses of Schepke and Kretschmer was

withheld until 25 April; that of Prien until 23 May. See Dan van der Vat, *The Atlantic Campaign: World War II's Great Struggle at Sea* (New York: Harper & Row, 1988), 166–71.

11. Interview with Albrecht Henke, Lüneburg, 18 September 1987.

12. See the first two volumes of F. H. Hinsley et al., *British Intelligence in the Second World War* (New York: Cambridge University Press, 1979–81), esp. vol. 1, 336–39, and vol. 2, 167–71; and Patrick Beesly, *Very Special Intelligence: The Story of the Admiralty's Operational Intelligence Centre 1939–1945* (Garden City, NY: Doubleday & Company, 1978), 73–75, 92ff. David Kahn's *Seizing the Enigma: The Race to Break the German U-Boat Codes, 1939–1943* (Boston: Houghton Mifflin, 1991), 1–14, 161–69, details the capture of *U–110*'s cipher.

13. See *U–124* KTB, 10 July–25 August 1941 (T1022/2973/PG 30114); KTB *BdU*, 30 July–25 August 1941 (T1022/4063/PG 30293–95); Gasaway, *Grey Wolf*, 140–49.

14. See Gasaway, *Grey Wolf*, 140 (the identification of Hans Köster as the new II.W.O. is incorrect). Heinz Eck later gained notoriety as the only U-Boat commander known to have ordered the execution of shipwrecked survivors. See John Cameron, ed., *The "Peleus" Trial*, vol. 1 of *War Crimes Trials*, ed. by Sir David Maxwell Fyfe (London: William Hodge and Co., Ltd., 1948).

15. KTB *BdU*, 30 July 1941, on T1022/4063/PG 30293.

16. *U–124* KTB, 16 September–1 October 1941 (T1022/2973/PG 30114); Gasaway, *Grey Wolf*, 150–66; and the vivid account in Busch, *U-Boot-Krieg*, 111–39. Actual tonnage sunk is taken from Rohwer, *Successes*, 66–67; the date of Henke's Iron Cross award is taken from his personnel record. A discussion of Henke's claimed and actual tonnage appears in appendix 1.

17. Henke's personnel record; letter, Karl-Friedrich Merten to author, 25 July 1991 (Merten served as commander of the 24th U-Boat Flotilla later in the war); and Eberhard Rössler, "Die deutsche U-Bootausbildung und ihre Vorbereitung 1925–1945," *Marine-Rundschau*, 68, no. 8 (August 1971): 453–66.

18. Henke's personnel file; data on Hashagen and Sauerberg taken from Walter Lohmann and Hans H. Hildebrand, *Die Deutsche Kriegsmarine 1939–1945*, vol. 2 (Bad Nauheim: Podzun, 1964), "Personalien 2," 91, 183; data on Mahnken from the U-Boot-Archiv, Cuxhaven.

19. Fritz Köhl and Axel Niestle, *Vom Original zum Modell: Uboottyp IXC. Eine Bild- und Plandokumentation* (Koblenz: Bernard & Graefe Verlag, 1990), 7; interview with Carl Möller, Lübbenau, 12 May 1992.

20. On *U–515*'s training period: *Kriegstagebuch* (hereafter KTB) *U–515*, 21 February–23 July 1942, on T1022/3067/PG 30553; British naval intelligence report, "Summary of Information on German U-Boots" (N.I.D. 08710/43), 29 November 1943, esp. 19–21, in Op-16-Z subject files, RG 38, NA); Rössler, "U-Bootausbildung"; and, from the Op-16-Z interrogation files in the same collection, "Final Report—Report on the Interrogation of Survivors from *U–515*, Sunk 9 April 1944, and *U–68*, Sunk 10 April 1944," 17 June 1944 (hereafter cited as "Final Interrogation Report").

6

The Boat

Werner Henke and *U–515*'s crew doubtless took great pride in their new vessel at the time of her commissioning in February 1942. Newly painted, filled with the smell of freshly lubricated machinery, the submarine and its maze of gauges, valves, and pipes seemed the embodiment of modern technology. But though these appearances mirrored the boat's newness, they merely disguised the age of her design.

Fünf-fünfzehn belonged to the Type IXC category of German submarines, the parent models for which had been conceived in late 1935 to carry out long-range missions and, later, to serve as flotilla commanders' boats in directing U-Boat groups at sea. These boats reflected the Naval High Command's prewar concept of the use of submarines for strategic purposes rather than commerce warfare. Where Dönitz preferred the smaller and more maneuverable Type VII boats as the primary weapon in an all-out war on merchant shipping, the Seekriegsleitung (Naval Operations Staff) intended the Type IX boats to perform mine-laying, reconnaissance, and even escort missions for blockade-runners.

The specifications for the IXC class represented by *U–515* remained essentially those laid out for the Type IX nearly five-and-one-half years earlier. The basic characteristics were:

Length: 246 ft.

Beam: 22 ft.

Draft: 14 ft.

Top Speed: 18.3 knots surfaced, 7.3 knots submerged

Maximum surface range: 11,000 nautical miles

Approved diving depth: 540 ft.

Armament: six torpedo tubes, twenty-two torpedoes; one 10.5cm deck gun (fore), one 3.7cm gun (aft), one 20mm flak gun (conning tower)

The 20mm antiaircraft gun and larger, more powerful engines constituted the most significant changes from the September 1936 Type IX, increasing the displacement tonnage from 740 to 1,120. (Throughout the war, Allied intelligence continued to refer to this class as 740-tonners.)

The true origins of Henke's submarine, however, reached back even further, for all Type IX boats merely represented updated models of First World War technology. In armament, speed, torpedo tubes, and range *U–515* enjoyed few or no advantages over *U–81* in 1915. Most important, both generations of submarine could only submerge for limited periods, during which they could barely move: They were not true submarines, but submersibles intended primarily for surface movement and action. With the suddenness of the U-Boat construction program of 1935–36, and the disinterest of the Naval High Command in a major role for submarines, there was neither enough time nor interest to redesign the technical capabilities of the submarine.

Ironically, one such breakthrough had been drafted as early as October 1933 by a German engineer. Professor Hellmuth Walter approached the navy with a radical design for a submarine propelled by highly concentrated hydrogen peroxide that would permit high speeds and extended periods underwater. The navy provided some support for Walter's research, but remained skeptical. The coming of war dictated increased production of existing models, especially as the staggering practical problems in developing Walter's design (including production costs and the huge amounts of fuel required) became more apparent. Dönitz, however, pushed for the development of this and similar projects in January 1942 to the Naval High Command. The reply to Dönitz's appeal, dated two days after *U–515*'s commissioning, accorded priority to immediate submarine needs and the uninterrupted production of existing types.[1]

Thus, *U–515*'s production typified the never-solved dilemma of German weapons production: New technologies were necessary to offset the material superiority of the Allies, but battlefield needs dictated the maximum production of existing weapon types. *U–515* represented a proven but obsolescent design, the wartime need for which precluded the development of more modern types necessary for German success. Unaware of this paradox, her captain and crew eagerly familiarized themselves with the vessel that would be their home for more than two years.

U–515's history, as with many other Type IX boats, began in the workshops and slips of the Deutsche Werft shipyard located in the southwestern Hamburg district of Finkenwerder. As part of a contract order placed in October 1939, her keel was laid on 2 December 1941, just before the collapse of the German offensive in Russia and Japan's attack on Pearl Harbor. As "Hull Number 311" she was completed in eighty days. Later in the war, U-Boats would be produced in greater numbers by building sections in different plants for final assembly at the shipyard, but at this time they were built as single units. The pressure-hull sections were built and assembled first, then the conning tower was added; fitting out the interior and adding the outer hull followed, though some overlap occurred in all phases. The final product required over 440,000 man-hours of construction work on the ship and its engines, at a total cost to the German government of perhaps two million Reichsmarks, equal to about half a million U.S. dollars at the time.[2]

The submarine, like her crew, drew its components from all of the Reich. The powerful diesel engines that drove *U–515* on the surface originated with the Maschinenfabrik Augsburg-Nürnberg (MAN), based in Augsburg; the electrical motors necessary for underwater propulsion, as well as the torpedo-attack computer in the conning tower, were built by the Siemens-Schukert firm located in Berlin's "Siemensstadt" district. The Junkers aircraft firm in Dessau provided the air compressors necessary for "blowing" air into and water out of the ballast tanks between the inner and outer hulls to allow the submarine to return to the surface. From Jena, the Zeiss concern supplied its expertise in precision optics with the periscopes and binoculars. The storage batteries that furnished the current for her electrical motors and onboard electrical systems were produced in the Akkumulatoren Fabrik's plants in Hannover, Posen, and Hagen. East Prussia's pine forests contributed the wood planks on the boat's deck and bridge.[3]

The Type IXC U-Boat invites comparison with its more famous and more numerous cousin, the Type VIIC. The latter was smaller (760-tons displacement vs. the IXC's 1,120) and, with a fuel capacity of 113 tons, limited to a cruising range of about 6,500 nautical miles. The smaller submarine bore the brunt of the North Atlantic convoy battles during World War II, averaging four to six weeks on each patrol. By contrast, with a fuel capacity of 208 tons and a cruising range of 11,000 miles, the IXC's natural operational areas included the Caribbean, the South Atlantic, and the west coast of Africa. The larger size meant slightly less cramped conditions than aboard the VIIC, but the crew could expect to be on patrol for a much longer period—an average of more than 100 days. The IXC's maximum surface speed of 18.3 knots marked an advantage of 1.3 knots over the VIIC, an edge necessary for the greater distances traversed and in escaping pursuing escort vessels. The IXC was also better armed for commerce warfare, carrying eighteen to twenty-two torpedoes (versus twelve to fourteen), two stern torpedo tubes (versus one) and heavier deck armament (the VIIC carried only one forward 88mm piece).

Yet the IXC—as reflected in her nickname, the *Seekuh* (Sea Cow)—was far less suited for combat than the VIIC. Her greater bulk and broader deck inhibited her ability to crash dive, requiring about thirty-five seconds against the VIIC's standard of thirty seconds. In those additional five seconds, an approaching B–24 Liberator bomber could close more than a third of a mile before releasing its bombs. The IXC's larger conning tower contributed to this sluggishness, and surrendered the advantage of the VIIC's lower silhouette. Dönitz pointed out other handicaps of the model when be protested their use in the approaches to Gibraltar in December 1941: "These boats are easier to locate than the Type VIIs, more complicated and therefore more vulnerable to depth charges and are more difficult to control when submerged." Nevertheless, the IXC boats accounted for roughly thirty-seven percent of all merchant sinkings during the war, despite the fact they never amounted to more than 12 percent of the U-Boat fleet.[4]

The greater vulnerability of the IXC was graphically demonstrated in April 1943, when Dönitz, pressed to maintain maximum strength in the North Atlantic, committed a number of the larger boats to the convoy battles. In less than a month, the effort had to be abandoned. Although the Type IXs constituted less than one-fourth the attacking forces, their losses amounted to twice those of the Type VIIs.[5]

In comparing the appearance of the two classes, the IXC's greater length (252 versus 220 ft.) and broader beam (22 versus 20 ft.) became obvious if the two vessels lay side by side, but other characteristics more clearly distinguished them. The main ballast tanks that hung outside either side of the Type VII's pressure hull (aptly dubbed "saddle tanks") produced obvious bulges below the deck level; the Type IX's double hull and broad deck casing completely enclosed these tanks. The unbroken line of rectangular flooding vents along the sides of Type IXs also contrasted with the irregular pattern of the VIIs.[6]

The IXC may also be compared with the *Gato* class of U.S. Navy fleet submarine, which saw extensive action in the Pacific. The two classes shared the same cruising range, but the *Gato* was much larger in terms of size (312 ft. long, with a surface displacement of 2,025 tons) and crew (80 in wartime, roughly 20 more than the IXC). The U.S. submarine not only carried two more torpedoes, she enjoyed the use of ten torpedo tubes (six bow and four stern); her top surface speed of just over 20 knots also rendered her faster than her German counterpart. American crew accommodations, even with the larger number of men, would have been envied by any German submariner: a bunk for each crewman, four toilets, several shower stalls and lavatories, a messroom, and a washing machine.[7]

Conditions aboard a Type IXC were much less comfortable but featured some unique touches that merit detailed description. (See Figure 6.1.) The U-Boat's bow contained the first main compartment, the forward torpedo room (*Bugtorpedoraum*), the most crowded and cramped area on board at the start of every patrol. A space that measured roughly seventy-five square feet served as the boat's weapons center, crews' quarters (known as the "Lords," German naval jargon for sailors), mess area, and general storage hold. The section closest to the bow held the breeches and firing mechanisms of four torpedo tubes, with only twenty-one inches separating the port (left side, looking forward) and starboard (right side) pairs of tubes. Each tube contained one *Aal* (eel, or torpedo), with four more in reserve beneath the compartment floor plates; others were stored above in external containers between the pressure hull and the deck casing. A chain hoist and trolley behind the torpedo breeches (generally stored to the side until needed) allowed for the loading of the reserve torpedoes. Further behind the tubes were ten suspended berths for crewmen, five on either side, that could be folded against the wall to permit more overhead storage for torpedoes. Four berths on each side were arranged in bunk fashion, with the lower berths—reserved for the one petty officer stationed there, the torpedo mechanic, and the senior ratings—enjoying a full twenty-two inches of headroom from the pillow to the spring-cushioned bottom of the top bunk. Those sleeping above had only seventeen inches of headroom to the top of the compartment. At least two men shared each berth throughout the duration of the patrol.

Along the walls in the forward compartment, each crewman had his own small wooden locker in which, theoretically, he could store his clothing, mess kit, and personal possessions; in fact, the storage of

Figure 6.1
Type IXC U-Boat, March 1944

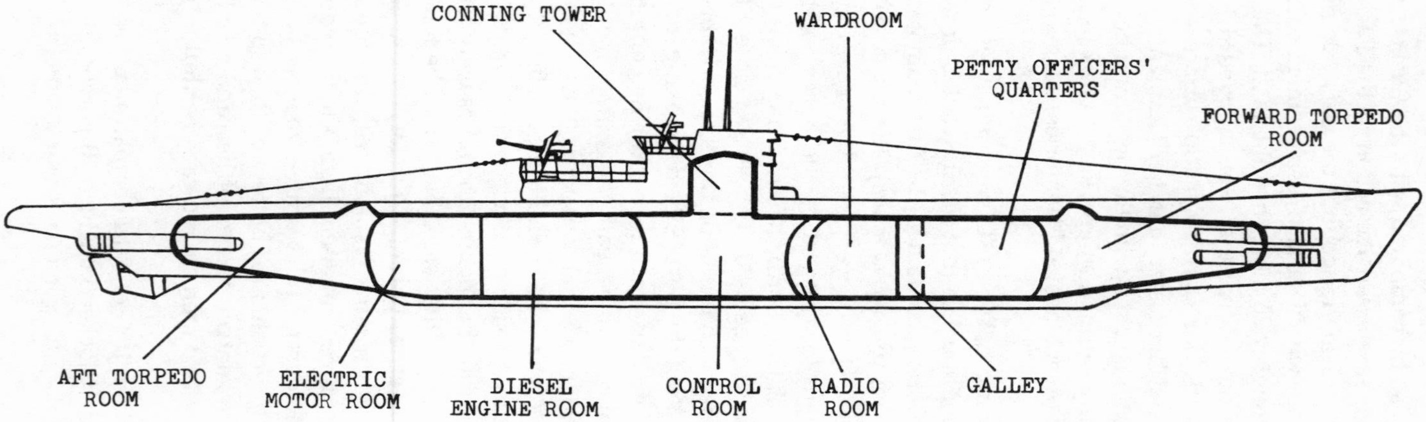

FORWARD TORPEDO ROOM

PETTY OFFICERS' QUARTERS

GALLEY

WARDROOM

RADIO ROOM

CONTROL ROOM

CONNING TOWER

DIESEL ENGINE ROOM

AFT TORPEDO ROOM

ELECTRIC MOTOR ROOM

provisions held first priority, and every locker substituted as a kitchen cabinet in storing canned foods. Sausages and other meats hung from convenient pipes overhead. Food also filled the bathroom on the starboard side at the back of the compartment, but this was such a tiny facility (a sitting man's knees would be grazing the wall) that it proved small loss. The food scattered throughout the compartment was not merely stored, but regularly inventoried (for the cook) and weighed (for the chief engineer, who required exact data for trimming adjustments). Only with the expenditure of torpedoes and foodstuffs did the crewmen here gain some breathing space.[8]

The torpedoes aboard *U–515* varied in number and type as the war progressed. For her first patrol in August 1942, she carried twenty-three eels divided between types G7a and G7e, the two standard models used early in the war. The former, powered by an internal combustion engine, could be trusted in combat but left a telltale wake, effectively limiting its use to night attacks. The electric G7e left no wake and carried a larger warhead, but suffered from less reliability, less range, and the need for constant maintenance and battery charging. Six torpedoes could be stored in containers between the pressure and outer hulls, but these required a lengthy time on the surface to be removed and stored below decks.

By 1944, Allied air power had gained such strength that U-Boats could no longer count on the time needed to complete such transfers. On his last two patrols, Henke carried only fifteen and seventeen torpedoes, several of which represented sophisticated new models. Torpedoes armed with a reliable magnetic detonator significantly improved striking power. The FAT (for *Federapparat Torpedo*, spring-operated torpedo) required a U-Boat only to parallel a convoy's course for it to be fired at an angle into the columns of merchant ships, where it ran a back-and-forth course until striking a target. Still another model, the T–5 Zaunkönig (Wren), represented an acoustic torpedo designed to home in on the propeller noises of escort vessels.[9]

From the forward torpedo compartment, a circular hatchway through the bulkhead led to the petty officers' and chiefs' quarters. (This differed from the arrangement aboard a VIIC, where petty officers were berthed just aft of the control room.) Six berths along either wall provided the senior noncommissioned personnel with individual beds; the top berths could be folded up to allow lower bunks to function as seats for meals on a folding table. The wooden storage lockers were larger, but they also held food items early in the voyage. Two wash basins provided some amenities, but only with salt water and the strong antiseptic lotion, *Colibri eau de cologne.*

The linoleum-tiled interval between the chiefs' quarters and the wardroom contained the ship's galley. This location marked another difference from the VIIC, where the galley separated the petty officers' area from the diesel engine room. In a sense, the cook could justifiably claim that his domain extended over the entire vessel, in view of the storage space required for the large quantities of food. On a typical twelve-week voyage, a Type IXC boat carried nearly fourteen tons of foodstuffs with her when she left port (see Table 6.1), occasionally supplemented by freshly caught fish.

Daily menus on board were not improvised, but followed a carefully planned schedule to maintain proper diet and calorie needs. Breakfast

Table 6.1
Foods Carried Aboard a Type IXC U-Boat for a 12-Week Voyage

494 lbs. fresh and cooked meats	1,728 lbs. milk
238 lbs. sausages	441 lbs. fruit juices
4,808 lbs. preserved/tinned meats	154 lbs. coffee
334 lbs. preserved fish	205 lbs. other drinks
3,858 lbs. potatoes	441 lbs. sugar
397 lbs. dried potatoes	132 lbs. salt
3,428 lbs. other vegetables	108 lbs. chocolates
1,226 lbs. bread dough	
2,058 lbs. preserved breads	
463 lbs. rice and noodles	
595 lbs. fresh eggs	
917 lbs. fresh lemons	
2,365 lbs. other fruits	
551 lbs. butter and margarine	
611 lbs. soup ingredients	
408 lbs. marmalade and honey	
309 lbs. fresh and preserved cheese	

Source: Jobst Schaefer, "Die Ernährung des U-Bootsfahrers im Kriege" (Doctoral dissertation, Christian-Albrechts-Universität zu Kiel, 1943), 156c-d.

usually consisted of coffee, buttermilk soup, biscuits, hardbread with butter or honey, and eggs; the main midday meal featured soup, potatoes, cooked meat and vegetables, and fruit; dinner included sausages or canned fish, cheese, bread, and coffee, tea, or chocolate. That such food preparations were required for three separate watches every day testifies to the workload carried by the *Smutje* (cook).[10]

All of this vast quantity eventually funneled through the diminutive galley, with a floor space only 59 inches long and 27.5 inches wide. On the starboard side of the passageway, the cook operated an electric range with three hotplates and two small ovens, which could be heated to three different levels. The remaining space somehow held a small refrigerator, a 40-liter (10.6 gallons) self-heating soup kettle, additional provision lockers, and a small enamel sink with hot and cold fresh water (distilled from sea water) and hot salt water. A locker in the adjacent wardroom held the kitchen utensils.

The wardroom represented the most attractive and comfortable compartment on board, with four berths for officers along the walls. Surrounding these were numerous storage lockers that contained the officers' possessions, additional provisions, and confidential papers and manuals. A small glass cabinet mounted on the starboard side of the passageway held a mix of chinaware, glass, and silver that originated in part as standard navy issue, and in part as items "liberated" from French restaurants and hotels.

Postwar American investigators were surprised by the extensive oak paneling used in the walls and lockers of U-Boat living quarters, an inefficient material that absorbed too much light and posed increased risks of fire and vermin or insect infestation. Where U.S. submarines combined greater crew comforts with the more pragmatic use of aluminum and reflective paint, the U-Boats tried to balance their more Spartan conditions with sleeping quarters more comfortable to the eye and the touch.[11]

The passageway aft from the wardroom led past two small starboard compartments. The first, the sound room, housed the monitor for the hydrophone equipment. Wires linked the monitor to an arc of underwater detection receivers along the underside of the U-Boat's bow designated the GHG (for *Gruppen-Horch-Gerät*, group listening apparatus). Under favorable conditions, these receivers could detect single ships at a distance of twelve miles and convoys more than sixty miles away. If the sound source lay directly ahead of or behind the submarine, however, the receivers proved less accurate.

In the adjacent radio room, a *Funker* (radioman) was always on duty to receive and transmit messages to Dönitz's headquarters regarding movement and operational orders, though a IXC on extended patrol required less radio direction than VIICs being formed into patrol lines and wolf packs. Next to the long- and short-wave transmitters and receivers sat the *Schlüssel M* (Enigma) machine for the encryption and decryption of operational messages. The radio room also contained the boat's phonograph player and supply of records, which aboard *U–515* always included a mix of jazz, Cole Porter, and Chopin. Ironically, listening to swing music in Germany could be punished with time in a concentration camp, but aboard a U-Boat the same music boosted a crew's morale.[12]

Directly across from the radio room lay the captain's stateroom, with only a cloth curtain to provide some privacy. In addition to a single berth and storage lockers, the *Kommandant* enjoyed the convenience of an overhead lamp and a desk that could be converted into a salt-water washstand.

Two strides and a step through a circular pressure hatch brought the commander into the *Zentrale* (the central control room) that constituted the boat's nerve center. The relative spaciousness of the compartment contrasted with the mass of handwheels, valves, and instruments that covered the walls: Most were color-coded or distinguished by shape or physical characteristics to permit easy identification in dim or no light. These included the controls for the rudder, bow, and stern hydroplanes; depth gauges for the submarine and its periscopes; gyro and magnetic compasses; trim indicators; engine order telegraphs; and valves to regulate air movement in the ballast tanks. At the room's center stood the periscope well that housed the attack periscope. A network of voice tubes, telephones, and a loudspeaker microphone allowed the captain to communicate with any part of the vessel. The navigation or "sky" periscope could be operated here to fix the boat's position. Five men regularly manned the *Zentrale* while cruising on the surface, ten while at submerged battle stations.

A ladder next to the periscope well connected the control room with the conning tower, the battle center for underwater attacks. Here the captain sat astride a bicycle-type saddle as he peered through the eyepiece of the attack periscope, adjusting its movements with foot pedals. Through the periscope lens Henke fixed upon his target, calculating the vessel's bearing, distance, course, speed, and the necessary angle of torpedo fire from the U-Boat's own course. A watch officer fed this information into the wall-mounted *Torpedovorhaltrechner* (torpedo attack calculator), which would determine the appropriate launching time and position. The information was then transmitted to the firing control panel in the conning tower and to receivers in the torpedo room to indicate the exact moment of firing. One or two other crewmen squeezed into the tower's confined space would assist the captain in working other controls or relaying orders by voice tubes.[13]

Following the successes of her first two patrols, *U–515* acquired the nickname of the "Hammer Boat." The exterior of her conning tower carried the emblem of a sledgehammer for the next couple of war cruises, but this was likely removed when Henke had the entire conning tower painted a whitish gray in late 1943 to reduce surface visibility.[14]

Aft of the *Zentrale* lay the power plant of the submarine, the diesel engine room. Each of the 2 nine-cylinder MAN engines supplied 2,170 horsepower (with superchargers, even more for brief periods) and weighed 27 metric tons. Their size occupied most of the size of the compartment, divided only by a walkway that measured 28 inches across. The engines powered the boat on the surface and could also be used to charge the electrical batteries stored beneath the deck. Four machinists stood their watches (expanding to six at battle stations) in this space or at the control stands at the front ends of the engines: confinement posed less of a problem than the heat generated by the engines and the carbon dioxide fumes that eluded the exhaust valves. In operation the diesels absorbed prodigious amounts of air, necessitating a rapid shutdown when the boat dived lest the crew be suffocated.

Under water the submarine relied upon its electric motors, located in the compartment just aft of the diesels. Two dynamotors rated at 493 horsepower provided the record submerged speed of 7.46 knots, though to conserve batteries the usual speed was limited to 4 knots. On the surface the motors functioned as diesel-driven generators for recharging the batteries.

Each electric motor was mounted on the drive shaft powered by the diesel engine immediately forward, with a connecting clutch in between. Another clutch behind the motor linked it with the propellor shaft. The use of these clutches determined the configuration of diesel and electric power necessary for traveling above or below the surface, charging the batteries, or a combination of surface travel and charging. During a crash-dive, the men stationed here rapidly disengaged the forward clutches and maintained the aft clutches' engagement to the propellor shafts for underwater power.

Two or three machinists worked in the electric motor room, manning the controls in the forward section of the compartment or working the motors on either side of a narrow walkway. The rear section on the starboard side of the compartment also held a 2,440-lb. air compressor which, driven by a separate electric motor, furnished the compressed air required to blow water out of the ballast tanks, to prime the diesel engines, and to fire torpedoes.

The final manned compartment of the boat, the aft torpedo room, presented a reversed image of its counterpart in the bow. Four folding berths and tiers of oaken lockers lined each wall close to the hatchway, while two torpedo tubes jutted out from the far wall. Though slightly smaller than the forward torpedo room (55- versus 75-sq. ft.), this compartment was significantly larger than the aft torpedo room on a Type VIIC, where only one stern tube was available. Several features, however, distinguished this compartment on a IXC. The submarine's main head (also known as "tube 7"), located just inside the hatchway on the starboard side, was larger and more comfortable than its forward counterpart—a full thirty inches separated the seat from the facing wall! And, in addition to the chain hoists for loading torpedoes, the interval between the berths and the tubes held the auxiliary steering wheel (for manual use in case of a breakdown in the control room) and a small lathe attached to the starboard wall.

The manned compartments covered only a portion of the submarine. Below and around the crewmen were tanks and cells used for diving and trimming, and for storing drinking water and waste water. The fuel tanks outside the diesel engine held approximately 200 tons of fuel oil. Beneath the decks fore and aft of the *Zentrale* lay two massive electrical batteries, with a combined weight of over 75 tons: Necessary for the submerged operation of the electrical motors, the 62 cells of each battery required continual warmth and constant recharging (usually requiring several hours of surface running time every day). A distiller near the galley provided up to 63.5 gallons of fresh water per day, divided between drinking and cooking purposes and electrical battery use. Artillery shells for the deck and flak guns were stored beneath the central control room. All of these systems demanded vigilant maintenance, for the malfunction or mishandling of any of these components jeopardized the submarine's operation and, therefore, the lives of every man aboard. There was no margin for error aboard a U-Boat.[15]

As will be seen, the deck armament underwent considerable revision in a losing battle to keep pace with Allied air power. In addition, *U–515* usually carried two light machine guns that were mounted on the bridge during the dangerous passages through the Bay of Biscay, where radar-equipped Allied aircraft waited to pounce on careless submarines.[16]

This was the world of *U-515* and her crew. With time, new weaponry and instruments would be added and new skills acquired in a desperate race against superior Allied technology. After May 1943 the Naval High Command, now directly under Dönitz, no longer denied the obsolescence of both the VIIC and the IXC in the Battle of the Atlantic. New generations of true submarines finally began to appear in German shipyards, including the Walter prototypes and other models that might redress the disadvantage under which German submariners had fought. The Type IX was to be replaced by the Type XXI, an "electro-boat" that employed a Walter hull design with high-powered electrical motors for extended underwater operations. In July 1943 the Deutsche Werft company that had produced *U-515* received its first contract for the production of Type XXIs; after September no more Type IXs were built.[17]

But it would take some time before these models could hope to appear in any numbers to make a difference. To attempt to buy that time, with an outdated warship against heavy odds, became the unrecognized yet ultimate purpose for *U-515* and the men who manned her.

NOTES

1. For technical information, see Eberhard Rössler, *The U-Boat. The Evolution and Technical History of German Submarines* (Annapolis, MD: Naval Institute Press, 1981), 103–5, 170–74, 336; and Fritz Köhl and Axel Niestle, *Vom Original zum Modell: Uboottyp IXC. Eine Bild- und Plandokumentation* (Koblenz: Bernard & Graefe Verlag, 1990), 5–8; on the planned use of Type IX, see Michael Salewski, *Die deutsche Seekriegsleitung 1935–1945, Bd. 1: 1935–1941* (Frankfurt/M.: Bernard & Graefe Verlag, 1970), 24–28; the continuity of design is pointed out by Jak P. Mallman Showell, *U-Boats Under the Swastika*, 2nd ed. (Annapolis, MD: Naval Institute Press, 1987), 70–76.

2. See Rössler, *U-Boat*, 130–41, and Erich Gröner, *Die deutschen Kriegsschiffe 1815–1945*, cont. and ed. by Dieter Jung and Martin Maass, *U-Boote, Hilfskreuzer, Minenschiffe, Netzleger und Sperrbrecher*, Bd. 3 (Koblenz: Bernard & Graefe Verlag, 1985), 105–8.

3. Most of the information is taken from the U.S. Strategic Bombing Survey (USSBS) report, "Introductory Notes on Submarines, The Submarine Industry and Operations," 20 February 1945, USSBS (Europe) Report no. 92a6, Records of the U.S. Strategic Bombing Survey, RG 243, NA. The wood-decking reference appears in the Report of the Portsmouth Naval Shipyard, "Surrendered German Submarine Report Type IXC," March–July 1946, item 2G-9C-S14, in the custody

of the Museum of Science and Industry, Chicago, IL (hereafter cited as "Portsmouth Report").

4. For technical data see Rössler, *U-Boat*, 335–36, and Gröner, *Kriegsschiffe*, Bd. 3, 71–72, 105–6; for a good comparison of the two types, see Martin Middlebrook, *Convoy* (New York: William Morrow and Company, 1976), 68–69; Dönitz's comment appears in his *Memoirs: Ten Years and Twenty Days* (Annapolis, MD: Naval Institute Press, 1990), 197–98; and the summary averages are taken from Köhl and Niestle, *Original*, 14.

5. See KTB BdU, 1 and 5 May 1943 (T1022/4064/PG 30323). The comparative strengths of the two classes in the Atlantic in April 1943 involved 166 VIIs and 50 IXs, with respective losses of 4 (2 in convoy actions) and 8 (5 in convoy actions).

6. In addition to the sources of technical data noted above, useful references to photographs and illustrations are provided in Köhl and Niestle, *Original zum Modell*.

7. See John D. Alden, *The Fleet Submarine in the U.S. Navy: A Design and Construction History* (Annapolis, MD: Naval Institute Press, 1979), 100a–103; and Paul R. Schratz, *Submarine Commander* (Lexington, KY: University of Kentucky Press, 1988), pp. 23–24.

8. The above is based on the "Portsmouth Report," 9C-S33 and 9C-S75, and on personal observations on board *U-505* at the Chicago Museum of Science and Industry. An extra berth was apparently added in the forward compartment after the exhibit was installed in 1954. Excellent photographs of the interior of a Type IXC are reproduced in Köhl and Niestle, *Original*.

9. See Eberhard Rössler, *Die Torpedos der deutschen U-Boote* (Herford: Koehler, 1984). The numbers and types of Henke's torpedoes are noted in the *Schussmeldungen* (torpedo-firing reports) for his first two patrols, held by the Bibliothek für Zeitgeschichte (BfZ), Stuttgart; "U-515 Final Interrogation Report," RG 38, NA; and occasional references in the submarine's war diary.

10. Jobst Schaefer, "Die Ernährung des U-Bootsfahrers im Kriege," Diss., Christian-Albrecht-Universität Kiel, 1943, 158–58b, details the daily menu for a Type IXC boat on a six-week patrol.

11. "Portsmouth Report," 9C-S33 and 9C-S34.

12. Hydrophone gear is described in Rössler, *Die Sonaranlagen der deutschen U-Boote* (Herford: Koehler, 1991), esp. 39ff; operation of the Enigma cipher machine is described in David Kahn, *Seizing the Engima. The Race to Break the German U-Boat Codes, 1939–1943* (Boston: Houghton Mifflin, 1991), 32–48; the selection of music is confirmed by group interviews in Steinhude, 25 May 1991, and letter of Carl Möller to author, 8 February 1990; punishments for "swing music" listeners are described in Detlev Peukert, *Die Edelweisspiraten. Protestbewegungen jugendlicher Arbeiter im Dritten Reich* (Köln: Bund, 1983), 153–59, 228–29.

13. "Portsmouth Report," 9C-S24; the operation of the *Torpedovorhaltrechner* is detailed in Rössler, *Torpedos*, 86–90.

14. Georg Högel, *Embleme, Wappen, Malings deutscher U-Boote 1939–1945* (Herford: Koehler, 1987), 144–46; Henke's paint scheme is discussed in chapters 14 and 15.

15. "Portsmouth Report," *passim*; "U–515 Final Interrogation Report," RG 38, NA; Robert C. Stern, *Type VII U-Boats* (Annapolis, MD: Naval Institute Press, 1991), 56–58, on engine arrangements; and personal observations and measurements on board *U–505*, Chicago Museum of Science and Industry.

16. On the use of light machine guns, see Hans Hahn, letter to author, 16 June 1992.

17. Rössler, *U-Boat*, 212ff.

7

The Crew of *U–515*

At the time of his capture, Henke described his men as "the best U-Boat crew anywhere, anytime," qualities for which he took full credit.[1] The crewmen of *U–515* certainly shared some unique characteristics and accomplishments, but in most ways they were representative of the entire German submarine service that fought the Atlantic campaign from 1942 through 1945.

Just as Henke marked a changing of the guard from such commanders as Prien, Schepke, and Kretschmer, so too his crew constituted a new generation. The crews that had begun the war aboard Germany's handful of submarines were already gone. Many were killed or captured (half of the twenty-eight boats lost in the war's first year went down with all hands), the rest promoted and dispersed throughout the rapidly expanding submarine fleet. British statistics for the ages of captured U-Boat personnel during the 1939–41 period document the transition from the prewar regulars to the much younger wartime recruits (see Table 7.1).

The men assembled for the commissioning ceremony on *U–515*'s deck that frigid morning of 21 February 1942 reflected the new character of their service, a mix of raw recruits leavened with veterans from other boats. The latter, now promoted to petty officers, included some from the prewar navy: Paul Wilde, a veteran of *U–27* who had enlisted in 1927; Carl Möller, who joined the Kriegsmarine in October 1938 and now had four patrols of experience aboard two other submarines; and Hans Stabwasser, another 1938 enlistee who had seen action aboard battleship *Scharnhorst*. At least three other *U–124* veterans accompanied

Table 7.1
U-Boat Prisoners of War in British Custody, 1939–41

		Age Categories (%)		
Period	No.	18-20	21-25	26-30+
Sep. - Dec. 1939	129	7%	73%	20%
Jan. - Dec. 1940	243	25%	56%	19%
Jan. - Dec. 1941	486	32%	50%	18%

Source: Op-16-Z, "Age Study of the Crews of German U-Boats from the Outbreak of the War in 1939 to the End of 1942," 22 February 1943, Special Activities Branch (Op-16-Z) subject file, Office of Naval Intelligence, RG 38, NA. Data applies only to petty officers and enlisted men.

Henke in the transfer to *U–515*, indicating some of the discretion afforded a commander in selecting his crew.[2]

The remainder consisted of young sailors serving on their first command. Nearly all had volunteered for U-Boat duty. Some were like machinist Günter Eckert, who preferred service aboard a motor torpedo boat but found himself assigned to submarine duty because his physical condition matched the high standards for U-Boat personnel. *U–515*'s recruits passed through three months of basic training with one of the *Schiffstammabteilungen* (naval training detachments) scattered along the coasts of Germany and Holland. This applied to all navy recruits and served primarily to accustom them to military life. Recruits then attended specialized training courses in radio, engineering, torpedoes, or artillery as these became available, passing the intervening time in general personnel depots.[3]

U-Boat recruits underwent a rigorous physical examination before beginning training with the U-Lehr-Division (Submarine Training Division) at either Pillau (now Baltijsk) or Gotenhafen (Gdynia). Those slated for specialized training, such as engine-room personnel and torpedomen, were organized into companies of 90 to 100 men, the rest divided into regular seamen classes of roughly 250 recruits each. All lived and trained aboard former passenger vessels converted to depot ships. In Pillau, for example, 3,000 trainees shared the quarters of the liner *Robert Ley*, formerly employed as a cruise ship for the "Strength through Joy" (*Kraft durch Freude*) program of the Nazi labor front. For three months (a period shortened later in the war) recruits endured a demanding schedule of classroom instruction and vigorous physical drills that tested their physical, intellectual, and spiritual capabilities. The drills included underwater escape exercises in submerged tanks while using a special breathing apparatus, timed races up and down ladders while carrying full pack and equipment, and complete changes of uniform within five minutes.

The graduates of this regimen represented a select group, men who could withstand physical stress and psychological pressure while performing complex technical tasks. Far from the automatons sometimes portrayed in Allied propaganda, German crewmen were skilled professionals who combined initiative with discipline. The lives of all depended upon each, whether in clearing the bridge as rapidly as possible, correctly loading a torpedo or effecting engine repairs while being depth-charged.

Yet, paradoxically, recruits acquired little actual experience on board submarines. With German shipyards straining to produce operational U-Boats, only the obsolete, diminutive Type II boats (known as "canoes") and the occasional Type VIIC retired from active duty could be spared for training. At Pillau in 1941, only the top five trainees from each company were permitted to train on these. For the rest, minesweepers usually sufficed. Most recruits left Pillau without ever boarding a U-Boat, except for brief evening visits to berthed submarines in port.[4]

Graduation from the Submarine Training Division meant immediate transfer to front U-Boats for some, but for most it signified assignment to submarines in the final stages of construction, to familiarize them with the workings of their new vessels at an early stage. Those detailed to the brand-new *U–515* arrived in Hamburg where they passed through a final screening by their new commander. Later transferees would also have to meet Henke's approval before they were accepted, though it is doubtful he followed the example of his friend Kaptlt. Peter 'Ali' Cremer (*U–333*) in favoring soccer players (for their teamwork) and musicians (for their entertainment value) among recruits.[5] The crewmen of February 1942, in any case, took their place beside the core of veterans at *Fünf-fünfzehn*'s commissioning. The weeks that followed blended captain, recruits, and veterans into a capable and confident team through the sea trials and combat training described in a previous chapter.

In addition to officers, the standard complement of a Type IXC boat numbered forty-four crewmen. In fact, *U–515* followed the practice of other submarines on extended patrols and carried more than this to allow for losses, increased gun crews, and easier duty shifts. On her final mission *U–515* carried six officers and fifty-four crewmen. The crew list drawn up after the fourth patrol (the first for which data is available) identifies seven officers and officer cadets, sixteen petty officers and thirty-four enlisted men.[6]

The fifty crewmen on this patrol were equally divided between "seamen" (including torpedo mechanics and radio operators) who carried out the vessel's combat functions, and "technical" personnel responsible for the vessel's seagoing capabilities. The latter effectively fell under the command of the chief engineer (*Leitender Ingenieur*, abbreviated L.I.), a post occupied for most of *U–515*'s history by Oblt.(I) Georg Mahnken. The fact that two of the three chief petty officers and seven of the remaining thirteen petty officers belonged to the *Techniker* reflected their greater skills and experience. An informal "caste system" further distinguished the diesel engine staff, normally under the chief diesel mechanic (*Diesel Obermaschinist*) and a diesel mate (*Dieselmaat*), from the more technically trained electricians, headed by a chief electro mechanic (*Elektro Obermaschinist*) with a mate (*Maschinenobermaat*). These petty officers and the enlisted men under them (designated *Maschinenobergefreiter* or *Maschinengefreiter*, the equivalent of the U.S. Navy's fireman 2d and 3d Class, respectively) stood their six-hour watches in the engine rooms, and generally lived apart from the rest of the crew.

Caste distinctions also applied among the "seamen" ranks, with the four radio operators (*Funker*) and the torpedomen (*Mechaniker*) enjoying the highest distinction. The petty officers in these classifications, as with their counterparts in the engine room, earned higher rates of supplementary pay than that received by all other noncommissioned and enlisted personnel. Most of the latter held the rank of *Matrosenobergefreiter* or *Mechanikerobergefreiter* (the equivalent of seaman 1st class) and mounted two four-hour watches per day on the bridge or in the torpedo rooms. The cook (*Smut* or *Smutje*) merited special consideration for his full-time cooking responsibilities. The *Matrose* (apprentice seaman) occupied the lowest rung, but the technical requirements of a U-Boat kept such inexperienced seamen to a minimum: Only one can be found on the roster for the fourth patrol.

In the cramped control room, the senior petty officer (and usually the oldest member) of the crew, the *Obersteuermann*, was responsible for navigation and provisions, usually assisted by a control room mate (*Zentralmaat*). At action stations, two men manned the hydroplane wheels while the rudder controls were operated by the "battle helmsman"—on *U–515*, a task performed by *Matrosenobergefreiter* Herbert Bölke, a former truck driver for a small delivery service outside Magdeburg.[7]

On the conning tower bridge above the *Zentrale* could be seen one of

U–515's distinguishing features, the use of extra lookouts. For most of the war, U-Boats lacked radar equipment. To search the sea for ships and the sky for aircraft, standard U-Boat practice called for four lookouts. Henke, by contrast, usually employed six and sometimes seven men for observation, allowing each to focus upon a smaller area of the horizon.

The crewmen's clean-shaven faces betrayed another trait not common to German submariners. To conserve the limited quantity of water on board, most U-Boat crews did not bother shaving while on patrol. Henke, however, required his men to shave regularly. As most of their time was spent in the tropics, he explained to his men, the growth of facial hair increased the risk of lice and other disease-bearing pests. Some crewmen felt that their captain simply did not like beards.[8]

But if these men were submariners by choice, they remained warriors only of necessity. What had they been before the war? Did they constitute a cross-section of German society, or were they more representative of specific groups and classes? And was *U–515*'s crew typical or unique among U-Boat sailors in general?

Personnel data for 61 noncommissioned crewmen of *U–515* provides some revealing answers to these questions.[9] In a few general areas, the crew does reflect the society for which it fought. The crewmen's urban backgrounds parallel that of greater Germany: As 24 percent of all Germans lived in cities of 250,000 or more, so too did 26 percent of the submariners. In its predominance of Protestants over Roman Catholics (71% vs. 26%), the crew more closely matches the religious preferences of pre-Anschluss Germany (62% vs. 33%) before the addition of Austria's heavily Catholic population. Above all, the crew could claim its members from all corners of the Reich, ranging from the Hanseatic ports of the north, industrial cities of the Ruhr and Saxony, the streets of Berlin, Pomerania's farmlands, East Prussia's marshes, and the densely wooded hills of the Hunsrück south of Koblenz.

Yet this distribution was not equal in terms of population. Of the fifty-five crewmen whose hometowns could be placed in specific German states (the hometowns for six were too small to be readily identified), only seven came from southern Germany (Bavaria, Baden, Württemberg, and Austria), a region that held more than a quarter of Germany's inhabitants. The rest originated in northern or central Germany, with heavy representation from the populous and industrialized areas of the Ruhr and Saxony. An interesting contrast is provided by the presence of four men from the Sudetenland (population 2.9 million) against only two from Austria (7 million).

This pattern of regional distribution was not unique to *U–515*. A sample of 558 other U-Boat sailors (the captured survivors of 33 submarines sunk by U.S. forces during the 1942–44 period) reveals the same bias toward northern and central Germany, with the heaviest concentrations still from the Ruhr and Saxony-Thuringia; Austria is again the least-represented state. Henke's crew stands out, however, in its inclusion of 3 Berliners (against only 11 for the larger sample) and 4 Sudetenlanders (only 5 could be identified among the sample). We do not know if the broad patterns of representation reflect specific recruitment policies of the Kriegsmarine or the level of geographic interest in U-Boat service, but the data for Berlin and the Sudetenland suggest Henke's independent judgment in selecting his crew members.[10]

The ages of *U–515*'s crewmen largely conform to the pattern of the larger sample. The average age of Henke's 61 crewmen was 21.9 years. The three youngest sailors went to sea as 18-year-olds, one-half the age of the senior petty officer. Over 44 percent of her crew fell into the 21 to 23 age bracket (37% in the sample), while 12 men (all petty officers) were 24 or older. One difference can be seen in the number of 22-year-olds: Where Henke's crew included 12 (20%), the sample counted only 61 (12%), the significance of which will be discussed below. (By contrast, the U.S. Navy in 1945 included proportionately more 18- and 19-year-old sailors.) In any case, the data clearly disputes the contention of writer Lothar-Günther Buchheim and others that large numbers of teenagers served among the crews, virtually rendering the U-Boat war a "children's crusade."[11]

The most striking characteristic, however, occurs in the area of prewar civilian occupations. Virtually all of *U–515*'s crew received only the requisite eight years of primary education before entering trade schools, and were working as apprentices when war broke out. The vocational fields involved are not at all representative of all German society, but reflect a narrow range of specialized skills, as surprising as they are logical in manning a submarine.

Of students, clerks, unskilled factory workers, miners, and farmers—that is, the majority of the German labor force—only a single representative of each category found a place on board. Three others were salesmen. The crew included only two professional sailors, with a third experienced in ship engine construction—not surprising when one considers the merchant marine's small size before war. Two electricians and a radio technician fulfilled obvious shipboard functions. There were also a relatively large number of bakers (7) and butchers (3), which suggests that a variety of recipes and dishes were available on board.

The remainder of the crew, nearly 60 percent of the total, may be generally characterized as skilled labor and craftsmen. Specialized workers included 5 professional mechanics or machinists, 4 plumbers or tinsmiths, 4 lathe operators, 3 smiths, 2 metal cutters, a carpenter, and a bootmaker. The largest single category consisted of 16 men identified as *Schlosser*, often translated as "locksmith" but more generally applied to any metalworker who had not yet received advanced or specialized training in his field. Granted the ages of these men, it is apparent they had just begun their careers as apprentices when war broke out.

Nor is this predominance unique to *U-515*'s crew. A review of the civilian occupations of our larger sample reveals the same patterns (see Table 7.2).

The large number of metalworkers and machinists commands attention, particularly in relation to the overall German labor force. Even before the war, the German Navy demonstrated a preference for recruiting metalworkers for the technical skills and training they brought into the service. It will be noted that only a few of the sample had advanced to specialized positions in metalworking, leaving the burden of wartime service to young workers at the beginning of their careers. With the manpower demands of other parts of the Wehrmacht, the new generation of metalworkers contributed far more than their share to the most hazardous military service of the Reich.

The advantages accruing to Dönitz in recruiting metalworkers are obvious. Men already trained in the use of metal tools, pipes, and fittings could effect repairs and improvise needs at sea, reducing the need for layovers in port. Training in the mechanical aspects of submarines could be trimmed and other areas accelerated to produce more crews. Most important, the crews would be more homogenous, with the opportunity to "talk shop" and exchange knowledge and experiences: the cement, perhaps, that held the U-Boat crews together through hours of tedium and moments of terror, in spite of physical deprivation and horrific casualties.[12]

For all these characteristics common to German submarine crews, Henke's boat differed from the majority in one key area: the experience and continuity of service of her crewmen. Standard U-Boat personnel policy, as determined by Admiral Hans-Georg von Friedeburg, required a regular turnover of crew members to distribute experienced submariners throughout a constantly expanding U-Boat fleet. Typically, a crewman served two or three patrols on one boat, then attended specialized training classes that qualified him for advancement before he returned

Table 7.2
Main Civilian Occupations of 558 U-Boat Sailors[1]

Occupation	Pct. of Work Force	No. in Sample	Pct. of Sample
Agriculture	28.5%	19	3.4%
Commerce/Banking	11.7%	27	4.8%
Administration and Services[2]	6.8%	16	2.9%
Industry: Basic Materials[3]	5.6%	20	3.6%
Industry: Construction[4]	3.6%	29	5.2%
Industry: Metalworking[5]	9.5%	310	55.6%
Other Industries[6]	9.1%	70	12.5%
Transportation[7]	5.4%	35	6.3%
All others[8]	19.8%	32	5.7%

[1]Data follows the employment categories and job classifications defined by the German Statistisches Reichsamt in their survey of the German labor force as of 31 May 1939, a total of 39,414,600 individuals. Sources: Bernhard R. Kroener, Rolf-Dieter Müller, and Hans Umbreit, *Organisation und Mobilisierung des Deutschen Machtbereichs*, Bd. 5/1 of *Das Deutsche Reich und der Zweite Weltkrieg*, comp. Militärgeschichtliches Forschungsamt (Stuttgart: Deutsche Verlags-Anstalt, 1988), tables on 810A; *Statistisches Jahrbuch für das Deutsche Reich, 1939–40* (Berlin: Statistisches Reichsamt, 1940); and United States Strategic Bombing Survey, "The Effects of Strategic Bombing on the German War Economy" (October 1945), 210.

[2]Includes 1 dentist, 1 druggist, 4 barbers, and 10 university students.

[3]Includes 11 miners and 9 factory workers (not further identified).

[4]Includes 8 masons, 10 laborers, 3 contractors/consultants, and 8 painters/paperhangers.

[5]Includes 113 mechanics and locksmiths (including *Schlosser*), 19 specialist mechanics (e.g., auto mechanics), 37 machinists, 37 electricians, 26 lathe-operators, 19 machine toolmakers, 21 blacksmiths and metalsmiths, 11 plumbers, 9 shipyard workers, 6 iron- and metalworkers, and 12 others (stonecutters, riveters, molders, steel technicians).

[6]Includes 23 carpenters and other woodworkers, 23 backers, 9 butchers, 6 cooks, 3 confectioners, 2 brewers, 2 weavers, 1 textile designer, and 1 shoemaker.

[7]For the U-Boat sample, includes 5 Reichsbahn (state railway) employees, 3 truck drivers, 1 radio operator, 1 streetcar conductor, and 25 merchant marine sailors.

[8]Includes 6 draftsmen, 3 artisans, 3 career navy men, 2 waiters, 2 typesetters, and 6 miscellaneous occupations. Ten men in the sample did not indicate employment.

to front-line duty with another submarine. This practice also minimized the loss of too many experienced personnel when a U-Boat was sunk.

Henke, however, preferred to keep his crew intact to maintain maximum combat proficiency. He could not have gotten away with this earlier in the war, against the imperative of submarine expansion. But his tardiness on the scene probably worked to his advantage, as the tremendous losses suffered in the spring of 1943 evidently convinced von Friedeburg of the benefits of keeping a proven commander and crew together. Such concessions might account for the higher percentage of twenty-two-year-olds among the crew, men who normally would have been training and qualifying for promotion ashore. Henke did not always have his way: Before her fourth patrol in August 1943, *U–515* took on twelve new men. But even here, five of the twelve had previous experience aboard Type IX boats.

As a result, *U–515* fought her campaign with a veteran and thoroughly familiar crew. At the time of her loss, 19 of the 54 crewmen had served on all 6 of her patrols; 15 others had served on 3 to 5 patrols. Altogether, roughly 100 petty officers and enlisted men served aboard the submarine at some time during her wartime career.[13]

But if these represented some of the collective characteristics of *U–515*'s crew, the question remains: who were they as individuals?

Maschinistenmaat (Fireman, 1st class) Carl Möller, a petty officer responsible for the operation of the electric motors when the boat was submerged, was a Hamburg native who learned his trade in constructing ships' engines for the Hamburg-Amerika Line. In 1938, he opted to fulfill his military service by joining the navy. Like his father, he volunteered for the U-Boat arm. Dönitz's prewar corps constituted a true elite, where more than one tooth cavity could disqualify a recruit; of the 150 volunteers in Möller's group, only 50 passed the physical tests, of whom only 20 survived the written examinations. Ironically, the Kriegsmarine Personnel Department fell below these standards, for they committed a bureaucratic error in spelling Möller's Christian name as "Karl," and no effort by the submariner over several years succeeded in correcting it.

When war broke out, Möller served for several patrols aboard the very successful *U–25* (Korv.kapt. Viktor Schütze) in the North Sea, the North Atlantic, and the approaches to Gibraltar. An illness that sent him to the hospital saved him from the fate of his crewmates in August 1940, when his boat struck a mine and went down with all hands. Later he sailed under Dönitz's son-in-law, Günter Hessler, aboard *U–107* off Freetown, Liberia, in what became the most successful U-Boat patrol of the war (14 ships totalling nearly 87,000 tons sunk). Possessing the best command of English on board, Möller carried out many of the interrogations of survivors of sunken merchantmen during his five patrols with Henke.[14]

Another petty officer in the engine room, *Maschinistenmaat* Edmund Simon, was a Berliner who left his mechanic's apprenticeship in an electric lamp factory to join the navy in January 1941. In April he volunteered for submarine duty, drawing an assignment to *U-160* (Oblt. Georg Lassen). Simon served aboard the Type IXC boat from the final stages of construction through fifteen months of patrols off the east coast of the United States, in the Caribbean, and off the South African coast. After attending noncommissioned officers' school in Kiel, Simon joined *U-515* for her last two patrols.[15]

Bruno Deussen, a former accountant and statistician from Düsseldorf and the largest crewman aboard (6 feet, 180 lbs.), served as senior torpedoman on board. For him, the perils of front-line duty aboard *U-221* (Oblt. Hans Trojer) and two *U-515* cruises paled beside the grim toll already exacted on his family by the war, with one brother killed on Crete, another brother dead in Russia, and his father and two sisters victims of Allied bombs in Düsseldorf. Yet his pleasant and easygoing nature remained unscarred, prompting even U.S. Navy interrogators to describe him as "a wonderful guy."[16]

U-515's crew featured another unusual characteristic in the presence of two brothers. Hermann and Helmut Kaspers, from the industrial town of Mörs in the Rhineland, served together with Henke for two years. Hermann, the elder by three years, came over with other veterans of *U-124* as a petty officer among the sailor contingent. Helmut, an apprentice *Schlosser* before the war, found his place in the U-Boat's engine room staff.

The backgrounds and experiences of enlisted crewmen varied considerably. *Matrosenobergefreiter* (Seaman, 1st class) Hans Hahn was a happy-go-lucky Sudeten German from a village nestled among the hills along the former Czechoslovakian border; a baker by trade, he became the self-appointed photographer of *Fünf-fünfzehn* and her crew from the date of commissioning through the day of her sinking.[17] Before boarding *U-515* for her last patrol, radioman Alex Schneider's three-year naval career included nineteen months as a typist in a naval headquarters in Paris (doubtless a source of many inquiries and anecdotes for his comrades), a stint aboard a minesweeper off the Danish coast, and several training courses in radio and radar schools.[18] Rolf Taubert, who at eighteen left his electrician's apprenticeship in Leipzig for action with Dönitz's corps, served for over two years aboard *U–257* (Oblt. Heinz Rahe) and *U–515* with the unusual distinction of never having fired a torpedo at an enemy.[19] Some additional crewmen will be met in the next chapter.

One key question concerns the attitudes of crewmen toward Hitler and National Socialism. With the exception of the officers and the two men who successively served as *Obersteuermann*, no one aboard *U–515* was old enough to have voted in the last free election in Germany in 1932, or even to remember a time before Hitler assumed power. Nearly all had participated in the Hitler Youth, in which membership had become compulsory from the age of ten in December 1936.[20] All had joined the navy by 1941 and thereafter lived a sequestered existence, broken only by home furloughs. Dönitz, extremely loyal to Hitler, established the tone of an ideological commitment to the struggle after he became commander in chief of the navy in January 1943.[21] Some commanders, particularly U-Boat ace Wolfgang Lüth, incorporated discussions of National Socialism in lectures to his crew.[22] Although Henke never followed this example, the men of *U–515* went to war with firm notions of what they were fighting for.

These beliefs can be seen in the interrogations of eight crewmen on questions of morale. Working from prepared questionnaires, U.S. Army interrogators queried their captives on attitudes toward the regime, public opinion, and the war. The answers they received were strikingly consistent. Germans stood united in support of Hitler; the air raids were bad but would not bring about a psychological collapse; German soldiers remained the best, and only the U.S. weapons and equipment approximated Germany's in quality; despite the high risks in submarine duty, morale aboard U-Boats had not deteriorated; Germany would yet win the war, or at least a favorable compromise peace. The crewmen's favorable assessment of Hitler consistently rested upon one foundation: "He did away with unemployment. . . . He gave everyone work. . . . He relieved unemployment. . . . Order and employment was restored. . . . He has helped the working man."

Though not specifically asked about Hitler's policies against Jews, one crewman offered the following comments:

> The injustices toward minorities would have ceased eventually, prisoner thinks, just as injustices against Indians and Negroes will eventually stop in this country. Furthermore, there are many deserving Jews and former

Communists who have not been molested by regime, as long as they
played ball with it. . . . Prisoner still has hopes that the U.S. will make
common cause with Germany. . . . The two peoples would, for instance,
get together about the Jewish question and solve it in no time—the German
way preferably, but giving the Jews a better break, nevertheless, as a
concession to the U.S.[23]

The perceptiveness of the crewman's remarks about the United States
underscores his ignorance of National Socialism's true nature in his own
society. Such attitudes and illusions were probably common throughout
the U-Boat service, but ideological precepts did not furnished the submarine sailor with the reason for his endurance. "We only knew what
we were told: our duty. We got the feeling that someday we would die
together. . . . But we had given our oath. That's a bad soldier, who forgets
he put up his three fingers" (the traditional form used in the German
military for swearing an oath).[24]

There were, of course, grievances among *U–515*'s crew. The delays
in promotions that resulted from Henke's keeping the crew together
naturally rankled. Moreover, in spite of his own record, Henke proved
a harsh disciplinarian on his vessel, as *Maschinenobergefreiter* Günter Eckert could attest. Once Henke received a drenching when he opened the
conning tower hatch before the boat had completely surfaced; Eckert
was blamed by the chief engineer for improper readings of depth gauge
and buoyancy, and received a week's punishment of washing the crew's
laundry in off-duty hours. A similar incident occurred on the last patrol,
when another crewman drew a like punishment.[25]

Balanced against these stood the bonds forged by similar vocational
backgrounds, common generational experiences and attitudes, and,
above all, by shared combat experiences. With a skilled and successful
commander, reinforced by Henke's own policy of keeping his crew together for as long as possible, *U–515* represented an exceptional blend
of talent and experience. Unrecognized at the time, Henke's "greed"
paid dividends for all concerned. The transfer of veteran crewmen to
other boats with less-experienced commanders would have simply
added their names to those who were lost at sea; in turn, *U–515* might
well have been lost with all hands on an earlier patrol without the calm
expertise of the older men. The final testament to this U-Boat crew lies
not in their tallies of sunken shipping, but in the fact that most survived
the war. Of their 40,000 comrades, 28,000 never returned.

NOTES

1. "Final Interrogation Report," RG 38, NA.

2. Data from *U–515* crew list, U-Boot-Archiv. Surprisingly, a new and unproven U-Boat commander could request—and receive—highly qualified personnel from the submarine he had just left as a watch officer, without the prior knowledge of the latter's captain. Such an incident occurred to Korv. kapt. Karl-Friedrich Merten of *U–68*, a leading U-Boat ace, who did not realize why he had lost his best crewmen until after the war (Merten's letter to author, 15 March 1990).

3. File "German Naval Training Establishments," 15 May 1943, Op-16-Z subject files, RG 38, NA; Jak P. Mallmann Showell, *U-Boats Under the Swastika* (Annapolis, MD: Naval Institute Press, 1987), 109; interview with Günter Eckert, Steinhude, 25 May 1991.

4. "ONI Interrogation Report of Survivors of *U–128*, sunk 5–17–43," Op-16-Z interrogation files, RG 38, NA; interview with Eduard Vogt, Rockville, MD, 27 January 1990.

5. Peter Cremer, *U-Boat Commander*, trans. by Lawrence Wilson (Annapolis, MD: Naval Institute Press, 1984), 67.

6. *U–515* crew lists, U-Boot-Archiv.

7. Mallman Showell, *U-Boats*, 115. Extensive data on pay and allowances for U-Boat crewmen is found in Op-16-Z, "Memorandum no. 103 for Op-16-W: Pay in the German Navy," 30 January 1943, Op-16-Z subject files, RG 38, NA; Herbert Bölke interrogation, 8 May 1944, G–2 Division (MIS-Y Branch), RG 165, NA.

8. Henke's recommendation on lookouts in his messages to BdU of 11 June 1943 and 24 January 1944, SRGN nos. 19678 and 30856, RG 457, NA; letter to author from Hans Hahn, 16 June 1992; and interview with Carl Möller, Steinhude, 25 May 1991.

9. Data taken from the crew list of September 1943 (as noted above), supplemented by POW personnel records for eleven additional crewmen captured after *U–515*'s loss (located among the preliminary interrogation reports, Op-16-Z, RG 38, NA). Statistical data for Germany as a whole is taken from the annual publication by the German Statistisches Reichsamt, *Statistisches Jahrbuch für das Deutsche Reich 1939–40* (Berlin, 1940).

10. For more detailed analysis, see Timothy P. Mulligan, "German U-Boat Crews in World War II: Sociology of an Elite," *Journal of Military History*, 56, no. 2 (April 1992), 261–81.

11. See, for example, Lothar-Günther Buchheim, *Zu Tode Gesiegt: Der Untergang der U-Boote* (Munich: C. Bertelsmann Verlag, 1989), 56.

12. See Mulligan, "Sociology."

13. Data taken from *U–515* crew lists, U-Boot-Archiv, combined with *U–515* POW personnel data in Op-16-Z files, RG 38, NA.

14. Correspondence of Carl Möller with author, 11 November 1987; and interviews in Hamburg, 30 August 1989 and 26 May 1991; on Hessler's patrol, see Dönitz, *Memoirs. Ten Years and Twenty Days* (Annapolis, MD: Naval Institute Press, 1990), 176.

15. U.S. Army interrogation of Edmund Simon, 11 May 1944, G–2 Division records, RG 165, NA.

16. *U–515* crew list, U-Boot-Archiv; preliminary interrogations of *U–515* crew, Op-16-Z, RG 38, NA.

17. *U–515* crew list, ca. August 1943, U-Boot-Archiv, Cuxhaven; interviews with Hans Hahn and Hermann Kaspers, Steinhude, 25 May 1991.

18. U.S. Army interrogations of Alexander Schneider, 19–21 May 1944, G–2 Division, RG 165, NA.

19. U.S. Navy preliminary interrogations of Rolf Taubert, 3–6 May 1944, Op-16-Z, RG 38, NA.

20. H. W. Koch, *The Hitler Youth: Origins and Development 1922–1945* (New York: Stein and Day, 1975), 113.

21. For varying views of Dönitz, see Peter Padfield, *Dönitz: The Last Führer* (New York: Harper & Row, 1984); Michael Salewski, *Die deutsche Seekriegsleitung 1935–1945, Bd. 2: 1942–1945* (Munich: Bernard & Graefe Verlag, 1975), esp. 225–29, 432–38; and Charles S. Thomas, *The German Navy in the Nazi Era* (Annapolis, MD: Naval Institute Press, 1990), 228ff.

22. See Jordan Vause, *U-Boat Ace. The Story of Wolfgang Lüth* (Annapolis, MD: Naval Institute Press, 1990), esp. 147ff.

23. U.S. Army interrogations of Edmund Simon, Herbert Bölke, Ernst Heimann, Erich Busse, Georg Rettenbeck, Wilhelm Heinemann, and Josef Fellinger, G–2 Division, RG 165, NA.

24. Statement of *U–505* sailor Hans Göbeler quoted in Studs Terkel, *"The Good War." An Oral History of World War Two* (New York: Pantheon Books, 1984), 403.

25. Interview with Günter Eckert, Steinhude, 25 May 1991; preliminary interrogation of Werner Bloch, Op-16-Z, RG 38, NA.

8

First Patrol

At Kiel, the early morning of 12 August 1942 hinted at the approach of autumn—cool and cloudy, with the possibility of rain. Long before first light, the submarine pens on the east side of the harbor had been bustling with activity as crews and workers finished the last preparations for long voyages. On the quay, Kaptlt. Werner Henke stood beside the commanders of *U–514* and *U–516*, Kaptlt. Hans-Jürgen Auffermann and Korv.kapt. Gerhard Wiebe, respectively, to receive the farewell greetings and wishes for success by the commander of the Fifth U-Boat Flotilla. Each then returned to his boat for final checks before departure. At 0700, the three Type IX boats cast off their lines and slipped into the channel. Several escort vessels joined them to form a small convoy in the Kieler Förde, the inlet that led to the Baltic Sea.

Left behind was a "certificate" from Henke and his crew, an acknowledgment of gratitude in doggerel verse so common in the German Navy:

> Flanked by escorts, we're leaving in style,
> After our last night home for quite awhile.
> How long 'twill be, we cannot say
> For our voyage takes us far away.
>
> Our stay in Kiel has drawn to a close
> Our fittings complete, we've plugged all the holes.
> So, crammed full of food, and with filled tanks,
> To our gracious hosts, Five-one-five says thanks.

The steadily broadening inlet took the submarines past the modest memorial to the First World War U-Boat dead at Möltenort, then past the mammoth Navy Memorial at the inlet's mouth, Laboe. The nearly 300-foot tower remained in sight long after the boats entered the Baltic, gradually disappearing on the southern horizon. *U–515* had left German waters, never to return.[1]

Periodically changing escorts, the outbound submarines proceeded through the Kattegat and into the Skagerrak, the waterways linking the Baltic with the North Sea, arriving at Kristiansand on the southern tip of Norway in the early evening of 13 August. After topping off their fuel and water tanks, the three U-Boats departed with new escorts at 0500 on 15 August, cruising along the Norwegian coast to a point north of latitude sixty degrees north. There the three boats split up to begin their individual break-outs into the Atlantic through the Faroes-Iceland passage, and toward their ultimate operational area, the Caribbean.

Henke's break-out posed few problems. British minefields were well known and Allied air power was spread too thinly to seriously interfere. Only one harmless air attack occurred during the passage, which Henke accomplished almost entirely on the surface. Employing his merchant sailor's knowledge of Atlantic currents and winds, Henke steered a more southerly course across the central Atlantic to save fuel. Steaming virtually unchallenged, the voyage offered little change from training routines of practice crash dives and gun drills. Only a fruitless pursuit of a lone steamer 500 miles west of Ireland interrupted the trans-Atlantic cruise.

This quiet contrasted sharply against the backdrop of the Battle of the Atlantic. The day of Henke's departure saw eighty-nine U-Boats in action on the seas: Type VIICs in "wolf packs" deployed along North Atlantic convoy routes, Type VIID and XB minelayers operating in the Caribbean and the Gulf of Mexico, and Type IXs scattered from the Gulf of the St. Lawrence, the Caribbean, the Brazilian coast, and off West Africa, with Type XIV "milk cow" supply tankers ferrying fuel and food to all. Henke did not realize that he had returned to action as the Battle of the Atlantic approached its climax. While Dönitz marshalled his strength for the decisive struggle in the North Atlantic, Henke and the rest of the Type IXs sank tonnage and tied down escorts in far-off waters.

These were no longer easy diversionary operations, as Allied defenses in the Caribbean improved dramatically over the summer of 1942. *Fünf-fünfzehn* and the boats that had sortied from Kiel with her were all directed to the Caribbean periphery of Trinidad-Tobago, a shipping traffic intersection for tankers en route from Venezuela to Britain or Gibraltar and freighters carrying bauxite to American factories. The area had grown increasingly dangerous for the U-Boats, with two submarines lost less than two weeks before Henke's arrival.[2]

After nearly a month's journey, Henke eased into the warm waters west of the islands of Trinidad and Tobago on 10 September. Henke narrowly missed his first kill the next morning, a 7000-ton freighter approaching Port of Spain on Trinidad's west coast: The ship proved too far away and picked up an escort before Henke could close. "With a heavy heart, I had to let her go," the disappointed commander confided to his war diary.

He did not have to wait long. The next morning at 0928 ship's time (roughly 3:30 A.M. Trinidad time),[3] a lookout spotted a large shadow three to four miles distant to the southeast. Binoculars trained on the shape revealed a large tanker, unescorted and not zigzagging, steaming northwest. A target at last!

Seven months of training now culminated in thirty minutes of preparations for attack. In the *Zentrale*, Chief Engineer Mahnken transmitted Henke's sharp commands for course and speed alterations as *U-515* maneuvered for a favorable firing position; the forward torpedo room readied for imminent action; bridge lookouts sharpened their search for escorts and aircraft. With the dark western horizon at her back, the submarine worked her way to within 1,000 meters of her target's port beam. On the bridge, Oblt. Berthold Hashagen peered through the UZO (*Überwasserzieloptik*, also known as the *U-Boot-Ziel-Optik*), the special aiming sight for night surface firings, as Henke reckoned the appropriate distance, course, and speed of the target for the torpedoes. Henke opted for a double-shot from bow tubes I and IV. At a range of 800 meters, Henke gave Hashagen permission to fire.

The Panamanian tanker *Stanvac Melbourne* (10,013 gross tons), proceeding from Belem, Brazil, to Aruba via Trinidad, carried nothing more than 21,500 barrels of sea water in ballast on this trip. Her lookouts had seen nothing on this calm, moonless night when first one, then a second torpedo ripped into her port side. Staggered, the tanker listed severely to port—there was no point to manning the 5-inch gun on the aft section. Distress signals were immediately sent, but without answer. As nothing could be done to save the ship, the captain ordered her abandoned. All but one of her forty-nine-man crew embarked on three lifeboats. A crewman who had run below to retrieve his money was never seen again.

Henke watched the lifeboats pull away, but noted the tanker refused to sink. With salvage tugs and port facilities so close, he could not take any chances. Through the conning tower he shouted new orders to Mahnken to close on the tanker and swing the U-Boat about to bring the stern tubes to bear: that would leave bow tubes II and III free for any contingency. Just in case, however, he ordered all tubes reloaded immediately after firing.

U–515 backed toward her stricken target to a range of 500 meters, then fired a "finishing shot" (*Fangschuss*) from tube V, but nothing happened: The torpedo apparently passed under her hull. A torpedo from the second stern tube, adjusted to a shallower depth, finished the tanker with a hit in the engine room. Following procedure, the U-Boat steered among the lifeboats to inquire after her first victim's name, size, home port, and the health of the survivors.[4]

Even as the brief interrogation ended, a bridge lookout sang out: "Shadow bearing 140 degrees!" Binoculars swung around to the southeast—another tanker! The men in *Stanvac Melbourne*'s lifeboats watched their attacker turn eastward before they too spotted the burning lights of another vessel.

The Dutch tanker *Woensdrecht* (4,668 tons) was completing a journey from Ango-Ango in the Belgian Congo (now in Angola) to Trinidad, en route ultimately to Curaçao. Like *Stanvac Melbourne*, the only cargo she carried was water in ballast; and like her fellow victim, she had ceased zigzagging with nightfall and now steered a northwest course at twelve knots. In addition to her thirty-seven crewman, *Woensdrecht* carried thirty-four survivors of the British merchantman *Cressington Court*, sunk on 19 August by U–510 (Kapt.z.S. Karl Neitzel) off Brazil's northeastern coast. The glare seen off the starboard bow that marked *Stanvac Melbourne*'s torpedoing prompted no action by the Dutch captain. Thirty minutes later the lookouts just had time to see the telltale wake rushing toward the starboard bow before the torpedo struck at the waterline.

Woensdrecht immediately stopped her engines and most of her crew and passengers abandoned ship. The captain and a handful of others, including the Royal Navy gunners manning her solitary deck gun, remained on board and discovered the damage was not fatal—a hit in the forepeak and foretank. Suddenly a shout went up as the U-Boat was spotted on the starboard bow. The gun crew promptly opened fire, and believed two of their seven shots came close before the submarine dived out of sight. In fact, several of their rounds landed perilously close to *Stanvac Melbourne*'s lifeboats.

Aboard U–515, a disgusted commander slammed shut the conning tower hatch as his vessel submerged. Only one, nonfatal hit with two shots, then forced under by a tanker's deck gun! Advised that tube I was reloaded, Henke fixed the starboard beam of the target in his periscope sights and fired again at a range of 1,000 meters. The detonation that followed ninety seconds later doubtless brought satisfaction to all aboard, but only for a moment—the tanker still remained afloat. Henke barked out more orders to Mahnken to close to 500 meters and rotate the boat to bring the reloaded stern tube V to bear. After thirty minutes of maneuvering, Henke was in position to fire again. This time, the audible *clank* of the torpedo striking the tanker's hull announced to the crew that their efforts had resulted only in a dud.

Henke refused to quit. He moved in closer, to 400 meters, and turned the U-Boat again to fire from tube III. The third *Fangschuss* lived up to its name, exploding in the engine room and breaking off the stern section. With dawn approaching, however, Henke did not come to the surface. *Woensdrecht's* monitored distress signals provided the name and tonnage of his second victim, and the likelihood of responding Allied warships and aircraft entering the area did not induce him to linger. He moved off to the protecting deeper water to the east even as a destroyer (USS *Barney*) arrived to pick up survivors. He did not know that the bow and forward compartments of *Woensdrecht* remained afloat to be towed into Trinidad. In the absence of a regular cargo of highly inflammable oil, all of her crew and passengers survived uninjured.[5]

U–515's first action was over. The crew, exhausted by two and a half hours of exertions in operating engines and manhandling torpedoes in tropical heat, had no energy left to celebrate her success. Henke and Hashagen found little cause for joy in the expenditure of 9 torpedoes— nearly 40 percent of their total—to sink 2 tankers, but such was the inevitable price of combat experience in torpedo attacks. Still, the first victory pennants could be sewn for eventual display upon returning home. What none aboard could know was that *U–515* had just joined a select minority of German submarines: the 321 (out of nearly 1,200 commissioned) that survived long enough at sea to attack an Allied vessel.[6]

In view of the heat and the daytime presence of Allied air patrols, Henke determined to lay low by day and hunt by night. When he surfaced just before sunset, he was rewarded almost immediately by a sighting of smoke on the southwest horizon—a freighter making for Trinidad. After a hurried conference with *Obersteuermann* Wilde to triangulate a course of interception, Henke ordered Mahnken to come to the new course with *"AK (Äusserster Kraft) voraus!"*—"All ahead full!"

Two hours and twenty minutes later, *Fünf-fünfzehn* had narrowed the twelve miles separating her from her target to 1,000 meters. Night had fallen, but the freighter's silhouette could easily be seen against a clear sky and calm sea. The first torpedo missed; Henke adjusted for a slower target speed, closed to 800 meters and fired again at the freighter's starboard beam.

The British steamer SS *Ocean Vanguard* (7,174 tons) had sailed independently from Capetown, South Africa, on 19 August with fifty-one crewmen. Captain Wilfred Brett hoped to continue an uneventful trip to Trinidad before proceeding on to New York. At 8:45 P.M. (Trinidad time), Brett's second officer saw the torpedo track mere seconds before it struck on the starboard side between the engine and boiler rooms. Hot steam from the boilers blocked the passage of the engine room crewmen as Brett ordered all hands to prepare to abandon ship. The radioman began dispatching the signal "SSS"—"attacked by submarine." Henke read the signal, however, and as the ship remained afloat, he fired another torpedo into her. *Ocean Vanguard* foundered swiftly, taking eleven men with her. The survivors, after a brief interrogation shouted from the submarine's bridge, began the fifty-mile journey to Trinidad.[7]

Henke decided to move off to the east and transfer the four torpedoes stored between the deck and the hull into the boat proper. This entailed removing deck plates, setting up a winch, and easing each twenty-three-foot eel and its nearly two-ton weight through a narrow hatch at a difficult angle. This laborious process required several hours of work, during which the U-Boat would be extremely vulnerable to attack. Illuminated only by the starlight above them, the straining crewmen had been at their task for two hours when another shadow appeared on the southwest horizon. A different commander would have opted to ignore it and finish reloading—but not Henke.

Without hesitation, he ordered his men below and set off in pursuit. An hour later he claimed his fourth kill, SS *Nimba*, a 1,854-ton Panamanian freighter bound for Trinidad with 3,000 tons of bauxite. A single torpedo knifed into her starboard side and sent her to the bottom in less than 30 seconds, with the loss of 19 of her 31 crewmen and passengers. After obtaining a garbled account of his victim's identity from survivors, Henke returned to the interrupted task of transferring torpedoes below deck. The broiling sun was well up in the east before the crew completed the job, and just in time: A patrolling aircraft could be seen even as Henke ordered a return to the depths.[8]

By now Henke had noticed that U.S. air power generally did not operate from one hour before sunset to one hour after sunrise. With the additional precaution of six lookouts instead of the usual four during daylight hours, Henke felt he could take more chances. When he surfaced again that evening, he resolved to locate the primary traffic lane used by shipping to approach Trinidad. *U–515* sped along the surface all night and into the next morning, when another steamer was spotted to the southwest.

The *Kommandant* and crew experienced another first, a daylight underwater attack, with results that underscored their improved marksmanship: a stern tube shot from 1,000 meters struck the British freighter *Harborough* (5,415 tons) amidships on the port side. The stricken vessel began to settle slowly by the stern, as Capt. F. N. Hibbert and all but two of his forty-nine crewmen took to lifeboats.

To conserve torpedoes, Henke came up to finish his prey with artillery. As reported by the British captain, a minor yet revealing incident occurred, one not deemed important enough by Henke even to record. When *U–515* surfaced, *Harborough*'s lifeboats lay between Henke and his target. According to Hibbert, the submarine

> fired a shell over the ship, a second shell was fired and fell short, and the third one I estimated would have struck the ship, only instead of firing a third shell the submarine fired a pom-pom [the 20mm gun mounted on the conning tower] into the water near the lifeboat—*I think this was to warn us to get out of his line of fire,* so we rowed further away from the ship." (emphasis added)

Hibbert continued that the U-Boat sailed round to the opposite (starboard) side to finish the bombardment, then made off to the northeast.[9]

The morning encounter on 14 September cost Henke time and the chance to fasten onto the shipping lane, as the danger of escorts forced him again to submerge by day. Yet this sinking testified both to his skills as a torpedo marksman, and to his humanitarian conduct, as far as possible, of an inhumane form of warfare. No greater contrast is evident to Hitler's view of the same subject, expressed in a conference with Dönitz and Raeder exactly two weeks later: "The Führer calls attention to the fact that it is very much to our disadvantage if a large percentage of the crews of sunken ships is able to go to sea again on new ships."[10]

Henke's failing in this area was confirmed the next day, when he encountered and sank *Sörholt* (4,801 tons), a Norwegian vessel bound for New York via Trinidad with a cargo of leather, hides, and wool.

Determined to obtain specifics on shipping matters, Henke located and brought on board *Sörholt*'s captain, Jorgen Alfred Jacobsen, who described Henke as "tall, fair, clean-shaven, with night glasses on a strap around his neck," and mentions a subordinate who spoke English well (very likely Carl Möller, whose command of English was the best on board); both Germans wore khaki shirts and shorts.

After inquiries as to *Sörholt*'s particulars, the subordinate apologized for sinking her: "You know you are carrying a cargo to a nation with whom we are at war. I'm sorry we had to do this . . . we are doing our duty." Jacobsen replied, "So are we." After providing the merchant skipper with two tins of biscuits and three packages of cigarettes, the subordinate escorted Jacobsen back to his raft: "There have been many ships sunk here lately. I assume you will soon be picked up by a destroyer . . . you won't be long on the raft." In fact, after *U–515* moved off to the southeast, Jacobsen and his thirty-one crewmen waited thirty-seven hours for rescue.[11]

As he departed the scene, Henke finally radioed headquarters to report his latest sinking and the status of his available fuel and torpedoes. The expenditure of three to sink *Sörholt* left him only six, necessitating a rendezvous and resupply from another boat if Dönitz expected him to remain for any time. In any case, Henke had determined to abandon the Trinidad area to pursue the main shipping lane to the south. That meant surface steaming by day to cover distance.

On the morning of 16 September, lookouts spotted another solitary steamer to the northwest: not only another target, but evidence they might have found the traffic lane. Henke pursued for ninety minutes before being forced under by an air attack, the first to cause damage (albeit minor) aboard *U–515*. Any questions among the crew as to their commander's persistence were quickly answered. Though held under for nearly three hours by circling aircraft, Henke found his original target after an eighty-minute surface search. An eight-hour chase ended with Henke catching his unsuspecting prey just after midnight about 100 miles north of Georgetown, British Guyana (now Guyana). Henke and Hashagen had grown quite proficient: Although the moon had set and the target was zigzagging, a single torpedo scored a hit in the aft section of the merchantman's starboard side.

The victim was SS *Mae* (5,607 tons), a United States freighter of the Alcoa Steamship Company, en route to Georgetown from Trinidad to pick up a load of bauxite. The naval armed guard rushed to man the deck gun but reconsidered when a searchlight from *U–515* trained on them. The submarine crept close enough for German crewmen to steady the rope ladders as the armed guard climbed down. Only one crewman, a Filipino sleeping near the point of impact, was lost. As the last sailors made off, Henke's 10.5cm deck gun opened fire on the hulk and finished her.[12]

As a reward to the crew, and with water temperatures rising to fifty degrees centigrade, Henke decided some rest was due. He moved off to the northeast and submerged for the rest of the day, except to air out the boat in the afternoon. That evening he surfaced and transferred the last torpedoes below decks.

After two days of fruitless patrolling northeast of Guyana, Henke caught the British steamer SS *Reedpool* (4,838 tons) en route to Trinidad in the early hours of 20 September. One week earlier *Reedpool* had recovered sixteen survivors of the freighter *Medon*, adrift for thirty-five days after being sunk by the Italian submarine *Giuliani*. Now a torpedo hit amidships broke *Reedpool*'s back and put former rescuers and rescued into the lifeboats. As they rowed away Henke's second shot cut the freighter in half.

Determined to acquire some intelligence as to shipping traffic patterns, Henke went in among the survivors and identified *Reedpool*'s captain, William J. Downs, and brought him aboard *U–515* to take back to Germany as a prisoner. Under interrogation, Downs told Henke what the latter expected: The shipping lanes previously used had already been changed because of the U-Boat threat.

The interrogation was broken off when Henke received an urgent summons to the bridge. There lay the inert form of nineteen-year-old *Matrosegefreiter* Matthias Biazza. While trying to clear a jam in the light machine gun kept on the bridge, a round still in the barrel went off, killing him instantly. *Fünf-fünfzehn* had suffered her first casualty. Henke ordered him taken below, and had Mahnken steer a course due west.[13]

But misfortune's visit aboard *U–515* continued. Henke radioed BdU another status report, including news of Biazza's death, but the main transmitter gave out with the message's completion. A subdued crew ate their meal and carried out their duties as their former comrade was prepared for burial at sea. That evening, Henke presided over a brief service as Biazza's shipmates placed his body over the side. The rest of the night, and the next two, passed without any sightings as Henke began working his way back toward Trinidad.

Finally, on the night of 22–23 September, Henke bagged two ships within five hours. The small Norwegian steamer *Lindvangen* (2,412 tons), trying to slip along the coast with 2,800 tons of bauxite, disintegrated when a torpedo hit caused the boilers to explode. Only 8 of her 23 crewmen survived.[14]

Four hours later the American freighter *Antinous* (6,034 tons) was taking more bauxite to Georgetown from Trinidad when she crossed *U–515's* sights. Henke and Hashagen fired their last torpedo and achieved a hit on the port bow, about 40 feet forward of the bridge. *Antinous* stopped, but did not sink; her naval armed guard opened fire from the aft 5-inch gun and scored two near misses before the U-Boat dived. At a distance of 3,500 meters Henke resurfaced, but opted not to finish his prey with artillery fire, with air support likely any moment in the growing daylight. With her rudder and propeller protruding from the water, *Antinous* appeared doomed, so Henke moved off to deep water and submerged.[15]

The next day, as Henke moved south toward the Venezuelan coast, he radioed his latest successes to BdU with his secondary transmitter. As he had expended all torpedoes and was low on fuel, he also requested permission to return home. But had anyone heard their messages?

Morning on 26 September brought two items of news. First, *U–512* (Kaptlt. Wolfgang Schultze) reported to BdU that she had completed the sinking of *Antinous* shortly after Henke had departed—*U–515's* radioman picked up the message and spread the news. More important was Dönitz's direct signal to Henke: "*U–515* well done. Return to base without resupply." As Henke noted in his war diary: "Heading home. Great rejoicing on board."

"Home" was the familiar port of Lorient, over 3,000 miles to the east. The voyage took 18 days, marked by a gale that forced the submarine under for much of one day and by several crash dives to avoid Allied aircraft in the Bay of Biscay. At 1500 hours on 14 October, with 10 victory pennants flapping from the sky periscope, *U–515* tied up in Lorient as the band of the 10th U-Boat Flotilla provided a musical greeting.[16]

For Henke and his crew, the patrol had been a major success. In 64 days they journeyed more than 10,266 nautical miles, sank ten vessels (including *Antinous*) totalling 52,807 tons, took one merchant captain prisoner, and secured important intelligence regarding Allied shipping in the region. *U–515's* sinkings represented more than a third of all those accomplished in the Trinidad area during September (29 ships, 143,249 tons) by a total of eight U-Boats. Only Hitler might have been disappointed that crew and passenger losses totalled only 63 men, less than 14 percent of the total number on board.[17] Dönitz could point to this patrol as a validation of his strategy of *Tonnagekrieg*, the maximum sinking of shipping regardless of location and cargo and at minimum loss in U-Boats.

Yet from the perspective of the Battle of the Atlantic, it remained a minor victory. Most Allied convoys were still eluding the submarines. The mathematical yardstick by which the U-Boat Command measured success—the average of estimated Allied merchant tonnage sunk per day per U-Boat at sea—had recorded its highest scores in October 1940 with an average of 920 tons. In September 1942, though Henke himself averaged 825 tons, the overall totals dropped from 220 tons the previous month to only 153 tons. On 28 September Dönitz reported to the Naval High Command, "There is ample evidence to suggest the enemy has gained the upper hand."[18]

NOTE

1. *U–515* KTB provides little on her departure, but more is available in the KTB's of *U–514* (T1022/3067/PG 30552) and *U–516* (T1022/3068/PG 30554). The German original of the Kiel "certificate" is located in the U-Boot-Archiv, Cuxhaven.

2. See Günter Hessler, *The U-Boat War in the Atlantic 1939–1945* (London: Her Majesty's Stationery Office, 1989), pt. 2, 39–41; for Allied improvements in the Caribbean during this period, see Samuel E. Morison, *The Battle of the Atlantic 1939–1943*, vol. 1 of *History of United States Naval Operations in World War II* (Boston: Little, Brown and Company, 1975), 257–65, 346–50.

3. *U–515*'s chronometer, as with all German submarines, remained set on German time throughout her voyages. By contrast, the reports filed by the U.S. Navy on Henke's victims followed Greenwich mean time, two hours earlier than German time; British reports filed with the British Admiralty generally provide both Greenwich and local (Trinidad) time.

4. This action is based on Henke's KTB and on the report, "Summary of Statements by Survivors of the SS *Stanvac Melbourne*," 28 September 1942, in the Chief of Naval Operations (CNO) Intelligence records, World War II Command Files, Operational Archives, Washington Navy Yard, Washington, DC (hereafter cited as OpArchives).

5. *U–515* KTB and "Summary of Statements by Survivors of the MV *Woensdrecht*," OpArchives; additional details of torpedo attacks are provided in the *Schussmeldungen* (torpedo-firing reports) available in the Bibliothek für Zeitgeschichte, Stuttgart.

6. Jak P. Mallmann Showell, *U-Boats Under the Swastika*, 2d ed. (Annapolis, MD: Naval Institute Press, 1987), 16–18. Even allowing for training boats, milk cows, and obsolete models, at least 550 operational U-Boats sank nothing during the war (Mallmann Showell, *U-Boat Command and the Battle of the Atlantic* [Lewiston, NY: Vanwell, 1989], 27n).

7. *U–515* KTB, and the Shipping Casualties Section/Trade Division "Report of an Interview with the Master, Capt. W. L. Brett, SS *Ocean Vanguard*," 2 December 1942, file ADM 199/2142, Admiralty Records, Public Record Office, Kew Gardens (hereafter cited PRO).

8. *U–515* KTB and "Summary of Statements by Survivors SS *Nimba*," 29 September 1942, OpArchives. Henke misidentified his victim as SS *Senta*.

9. *U–515* KTB and Shipping Casualties Section/Trade Division, "Report of an Interview with the Master, Captain F. N. Hibbert, SS *Harborough*," 8 December 1942, file ADM 199/2142, PRO.

10. "Report of the Conference with the Führer in the Reich Chancellery on Monday, September 28, 1942, from 1630 to 1830," in *Führer Conferences on Naval Affairs 1939–1945* (Annapolis, MD: Naval Institute Press, 1990), 294–97.

11. *U–515* KTB; "Summary of Statements by Survivors of MV *Sörholt*, Norwegian Cargo Vessel," 29 September 1942; and accompanying survivor interview of Jacobsen at Headquarters, Third Naval District, New York, 24 October 1942, both in OpArchives.

12. *U–515* KTB; "Summary of Statements by Survivors of the SS *Mae*, American Freighter," 5 October 1942, OpArchives; "Report of Survivors of SS *Mae*," 21 September 1942, among Shipwrecked Survivors Reports, Records of the Bureau of Medicine and Surgery, RG 52, NA; and additional data in Arthur R. Moore, *A Careless Word . . . A Needless Sinking* (Kings Point, NY: American Merchant Marine Museum, 1983), 177–78. The "summary of statements" confirms that *Mae*'s crew deliberately misled the Germans in identifying their vessel as the British freighter *Mary*, but mistakenly believed they had been attacked by two U-Boats.

13. *U–515* KTB; Shipping Casualties Section/Trade Division, "Report of an Interview with the Chief Officer, Mr. F. R. Lawson, SS *Reedpool*," 15 January 1943, file ADM 199/2142, PRO.

14. *U–515* KTB; CNO, "Summary of Statements of Survivors of SS *Lindvangen*," 24 October 1942; and Caribbean Sea Frontier war diary, 25 September 1942, both in OpArchives.

15. *U–515* KTB; CNO, "Summary of Statements by Survivors of SS *Antinous*," 10 October 1942, OpArchives.

16. All data taken from *U–515* KTB.

17. Merchant crew casualty data is provided in appendix 2. Prompted by Hitler's queries, German naval intelligence in December 1942 calculated that merchant crew losses on vessels sunk by U-Boats amounted to 33 percent, a very accurate estimate against the actual rate of 30 percent among British merchant crews (cf. the German Foreign Ministry and *Abwehr* reports of 14 and 18 December 1942, T1022/2097/PG 33350, and the statistical table in Terry Hughes and John Costello, *The Battle of the Atlantic* [New York: Dial Press/James Wade, 1977], 329).

18. Hessler, *U-Boat War*, Part 2, 57–58; V. E. Tarrant, *The U-Boat Offensive 1914–1945* (Annapolis, MD: Naval Institute Press, 1989), 108, 116; and Mallmann Showell, *U-Boat Command*, 99, 110. Copies of the monthly calculations prepared by BdU's Operations Department are located in files PG 30953 and PG 30956 (T1022/3403).

9

The Highest Recognition

The successful completion of their first patrol brought little respite to the crew of *U–515*. The flotilla commander coupled his congratulations to Henke with a warning to be ready to sail within three weeks. Half the crew received no leave at all during the layover. The radiomen and officers took crash courses on the newly installed radar-detector equipment, the FuMB (Funkmessbeobachter) 1 Metox, named after the Paris firm that produced them. Popularly known to U-Boat crews as the "Biscay Cross" (*Biskayakreuz*) from the mounting of the antenna on a wooden cross structure, the Metox provided warning of approaching radar-equipped British aircraft at a range of 30 kilometers (18.6 miles).[1]

In mid-October, Henke met with Dönitz and the Chief of U-Boat Operations, Admiral Eberhard Godt, at BdU headquarters on the Avenue Marechal in Paris. Already indebted to Dönitz for a second chance, Henke probably shared the affection and esteem of nearly all U-Boat commanders for their charismatic commander. No record of their conversation survives, but Dönitz and Godt likely appraised Henke of the nature and significance of his future missions.

"Your success is gratifying," declared Dönitz, using the familiar "Du" as he did with all of his submarine captains, "particularly as this will be the type of mission you will have for the foreseeable future. The situation has much improved since your days aboard *U–124*: At last there are enough boats to do real damage. For the past three months, thirty new boats per month have become ready for operational duties. Most, of course, will fight the decisive convoy battles to come in the North Atlantic.

"You and the other Type IXC commanders will carry the fight to distant waters. Your first patrol acquainted you with the Trinidad-To-bago area; your previous missions with Schulz and Mohr familiarized you with conditions off Freetown and West Africa. The Gulf of the St. Lawrence in Canada and now Brazil offer additional opportunities. You will not encounter the increasingly difficult convoy defenses we now confront in the North Atlantic, but the need for success on your part becomes all the more necessary.

"We are doing everything we can to ensure that the fighting efficiency of our boats keeps pace with the enemy's defensive devices. With the FuMB search receiver, you will have some warning that you have been located by enemy radar in time to react. We are increasing your flak armament. The new magnetic pistol torpedoes, which are about to become operational, should have the same effect as doubling the number of torpedoes you carry—each should suffice to kill one ship.

"The enemy's shipping constitutes one single entity. Tonnage must be sunk wherever it is found and most easily destroyed. In so doing we also force the Allies to spread their defenses ever thinner. These are your tasks."

Godt interjected a mild qualifier: "Of course, strategic developments may arise that force us to reconcentrate, so you must be prepared for any situation."

In a sterner tone, Dönitz continued: "You will recall my order of 17 September regarding the non-rescue of survivors, which you received on the passage home. The basis for that order was the attempted rescue of survivors—most of them Italian POWs—from the passenger liner *Laconia*, sunk by *Kapitänleutnant* Hartenstein. Against my better judgment, I supported the action. As a result, we nearly lost Hartenstein (*U–156*) when the Tommies, despite a deck crowded with survivors and lifeboats in tow, despite messages sent in the clear and a prominently displayed Red Cross flag, bombed the boat. We will no longer risk our lives to save enemy survivors when the enemy is willing to risk his own people to try to sink us. We must be harsh in this war."[2]

In contrast to this admonition, the crew of *U–515* made sure to obtain a small Christmas tree before departure, in expectation of a long patrol. To keep it fresh, the tree was stored in the cargo area between the pressure hull and the main deck. There it rested beside eight spare torpedoes for most of the coming patrol. U-Boat sailors had little time to reflect on the incongruity of such arrangements.[3]

Henke and his crew left Lorient on 7 November. They were likely intended for a return to the Trinidad area when, only two days out, an urgent message from BdU informed him of the major Allied landings in the Vichy French colonies of Morocco and Algeria.[4] Godt's caution had proved correct: To combat Operation TORCH, he directed Henke and fourteen other submarines to concentrate off the Moroccan coast at top speed. Later that day Henke received another signal designating *U–515* as one of eight boats of group *Schlagtot* to operate against the invasion fleet off Casablanca and Fedala. Yet another message from Dönitz to all boats offered the following encouragement: "We must relentlessly carry out the Führer's will with our tested brutal means of attack. The sinking of transports will have great significance for the American attack and the French defense."[5]

Behind this rhetoric, however, lay another disagreement in the long-running debate between the U-Boat Command and the Naval High Command. The latter, caught completely off guard by the invasion, ordered four more U-Boats into the Mediterranean and the deployment of an additional twenty in the area west of Gibraltar and off the Moroccan coast. Dönitz's orders anticipated such a reconcentration, but he strongly criticized this diversion from the tonnage war in the North Atlantic, especially when it would likely prove costly. The Seekriegsleitung compromised with BdU on 21 November, reducing the number of boats west of Gibraltar to twelve, but Dönitz still objected to this dispersion of his forces.[6]

Henke, for example, never got anywhere near Casablanca. On the afternoon of 11 November, roughly 150 miles south of Cape St. Vincent, *U–515* experienced a close call when an Allied bomber attacked and temporarily knocked out her fire control apparatus. That evening, the bridge lookouts sighted what appeared to be a task force of two *Birmingham*-class cruisers and three destroyers ahead of them steaming east, toward Gibraltar. Henke did not hesitate for a second. He shouted the order for a turn to port and plotted an intercept course to the southeast. Though badly outnumbered and unsure of his fire control, he would nevertheless go after them by himself. Thus Henke entered his first battle with Allied warships.

The odds were not quite as one-sided as they appeared, but they were impressive enough. Henke had spotted a Royal Navy force comprising four ships: the old and partially disarmed cruiser *Vindictive*, the destroyer depot ship *Hecla*, and two screening destroyers, the twenty-three-year-old *Venemous* and the two-year-old *Marne*. *Venemous*, like the rest of her class, had been modified to include the latest antisubmarine weaponry. Both destroyers were equipped with Asdic (sonar) and radar. In the twilight, HMS *Hecla* was easy to mistake as a cruiser, with a displacement of 10,850 tons and eight 4.5-inch guns; completed in January 1941, she also carried radar.[7]

For the next five hours *Fünf-fünfzehn* steamed at full speed to try to reach an attack position ahead of the task force. On several occasions Henke had to veer off when the Metox alerted him to radar-scanning by the screening destroyers. Ironically, this would provide him the opening he needed.

At 10:15 P.M. (Greenwich mean time, as that kept aboard British ships; 11:15 P.M. on board *U–515*), destroyer *Venemous* made radar contact with an object 4,000 yards off her port beam. She turned to investigate, but lost contact at 2,200 yards. For more than 20 minutes *Venemous* vainly searched the area before giving up and heading back to the formation. Her signaled intentions, however, were picked up only by *Vindictive*, and then only tardily: The formation had proceeded as if *Venemous* had kept her place. Into this gap *U–515* gratefully sailed, aided even more by the formation's zigzag course that turned toward the U-Boat at the right moment.

Vindictive, just ahead of *Hecla*, spotted a bow wake one mile off her port beam at 11:11 P.M. but assumed it was the screening destroyer. It was actually Henke, crossing astern the formation to then pivot and place himself in the best firing position. Distrustful of his fire control system's capacity for setting depths on his torpedoes, Henke set all of them for a depth of only two meters, much shallower than normal for large ships. Four minutes later *U–515* fired a full spread of four torpedoes at the closest "cruiser." A deafening explosion amidships on his target stopped her dead in the water.

Henke and First Officer Hashagen were disappointed with what they believed to be only one hit in four shots. In fact, two torpedoes had struck *Hecla* simultaneously. The other two just missed *Vindictive*, which had just begun her next turn in the zigzag: The torpedoes passed by on either side of the cruiser, which made good her escape to the east at high speed.

Venemous now rejoined *Marne* in an attempt to protect the stricken *Hecla*, but neither radar nor star shell revealed a target. Having moved off to reload torpedoes, Henke returned an hour later to apply the *coup de grace*. Over the next forty minutes he fired four individual shots, three of which struck *Hecla*; the last blew off the stern of the *Marne*. On the last run the U-Boat was spotted and hotly pursued by *Venemous*. The destroyer's guns scored near misses as Henke received the alarming news of a malfunction in the steering gear. Suddenly, the switchboard in the control room caught on fire. With the destroyer only 200 yards away and steadily gaining on him, Henke ordered a crash dive.

Observers on *Venemous* saw the U-Boat's periscope slip beneath the waves not ten yards off the destroyer's port side. Depth-charges followed *U–515* into the depths, the 250-lb. explosive charge of each shaking the boat about and causing additional damage and minor leaks. The "Wabos" (for *Wasserbomben*, the German term for depth-charges) continued to explode about the U-Boat even at a depth of 160 meters (525 ft.). Fortunately for Henke, one depth-charge detonated with such force as to damage one of *Venemous'* dynamos, resulting in a temporary loss of power. Mahnken then employed the record-setting underwater speed of his motors to move off. When the destroyer subsequently conducted a fruitless sonar search, she presumed she had probably sunk the U-Boat and returned to the damaged *Marne*.

For an inexperienced U-Boat crew, the British assessment would likely have been accurate. But the veterans of *U–515* mastered the problems, plugged the leaks, and began reloading their torpedo tubes. With Allied help doubtless on the way, Henke wanted to be sure that the cruiser was sunk.

He did not realize that he had already accomplished that in his last run. *Hecla* turned over and sank stern first at 1:16 A.M. even as Henke was crash diving to escape *Venemous*. When he came up to periscope depth two hours later, Henke mistook the crippled *Marne* for his earlier target, and resolved to finish her once and for all. But after surfacing and cautiously approaching his prey, Henke was spotted and driven down again by shellfire from both ships and more depth-charges from *Venemous*.

At 5:13 A.M., *U–515* surfaced once again and began a curving approach designed to provide the bow tubes a broadside shot on *Marne's* port beam. After nearly 40 minutes, he fired one shot at a range of 2,000 meters, followed by a second a minute later. Even as the torpedoes sped away, *U–515* came under fire from the vigilant *Venemous*, which had picked up the U-Boat's approach on radar and made straight for her in an attempt to ram. As a shell from a 4.7-inch gun scored a near miss and 20mm fire from the destroyer's Oerlikons struck the bridge, Henke once again crash dived. As depth-charges exploded about them yet again, the sound of another explosion convinced Henke that one of his torpedoes had found its mark.

Henke could only have heard an end-of-run detonation, for his torpedoes struck nothing. *Venemous* launched more depth-charges, but Henke played his final card and released *Bold*, the sonar decoy (also known as the *Pillenwerfer*) that generated a mass of underwater bubbles to simulate the sonar echo of a submarine. The ploy worked—the British sonar operators lost contact. Dawn broke on a silent battlefield and exhausted antagonists.

The ordeal was not yet over for Henke and his crew. Allied aircraft arrived with daylight, and over the course of the next day fresh escort vessels relieved *Venemous*. The escorts combed the area, often chasing phantoms but sometimes coming close enough to rattle the ship's crockery. While they remained, Henke could neither surface nor slip away. *U–515* remained submerged for twelve hours, during which hundreds of depth-charges detonated in their vicinity. Everyone knew that neither the oxygen nor the electric motors would last indefinitely.

What happened next aptly illustrated Henke's character. Carl Möller, at his battle station in the *Zentrale*, recalled

> Henke stood, ramrod-stiff, by the navigation table. The Chief Engineer was bent double with stomach pains. As the next series of Wabos burst near us, all eyes turned to the captain, looking for some words of inspiration or comfort. Conscious of this, Henke announced: "What are you looking at me for? What can I do about it?" That broke the spell.

Finally, at 6:19 P.M. on 12 November, the boat surfaced to a clear horizon. Henke radioed to BdU his claim of one cruiser sunk and a destroyer damaged.

Thus ended a confused but classic battle between submarine and surface warships. The "fog of war" not only clouded Henke's vision, but left the British convinced they had fought two U-Boats, one of which was "probably sunk" and the other "probably severely damaged." With slightly more luck, *U–515* might have sunk three ships—a little less, and the boat might never have seen another day. As it was, an important vessel had been lost to the Allies, together with 13 officers and 266 men of her crew; 548 survivors were rescued. In addition, a destroyer was put out of commission for some time. Dönitz's own assessment of Henke's performance bears repeating: "The attack on the cruiser unit, carried out with exemplary determination, deliberation, and tenacity against the strongest defense, brought about a well-earned success. Because of its special boldness and courage, this attack merits the highest recognition."[8]

Dönitz's praise applies equally to *U–515*'s crew. For nearly twelve hours they remained continuously at battle stations, coaxing the utmost power from the diesel engines or manhandling torpedoes into firing position in record time. They absorbed the psychological strain of crash dives and depth-charges without complaint, repaired the physical damage to their vessel, and went on about their jobs. There can be little wonder why Henke wanted to keep his crew together for the rest of the war.

The overwhelming Allied material superiority in the area, however, allowed them no time to celebrate their success. Omnipresent air patrols compelled *U–515* and the other U-Boats operating west of Gibraltar to spend most of the daylight hours under water. Notwithstanding the tactical success of Henke and other individual commanders in specific attacks, the strong Allied defenses prevented any serious interference with the consolidation of the invading forces' position in Morocco and Algeria.

Henke's subsequent experiences typified this frustration of the submarine effort. On 16 November he attacked another cruiser formation but managed only two long-range shots (both misses) before being shelled and driven under, there to be heavily depth-charged. Twelve hours later, the U-Boat surfaced; twelve minutes later, an approaching plane forced another crash dive. The next night, Henke gave chase to a convoy but a radar-equipped escorting cruiser surprised him and forced him down again as the convoy escaped.

U–515 was luckier than some. Three boats—*U–98* (Oblt. Kurt Eichmann), *U–411* (Kaplt. Johann Spindlegger) and *U–173* (Oblt. Hans-Adolf Schweichel)—were all lost by 19 November in the area west of Gibraltar, and five others badly damaged. *U–155* reported it was forced to stay submerged twenty hours per day because of Allied air and sea patrols. On 21 November, Dönitz designated the remaining sixteen submarines as Group *Westwall* and ordered them westward out of the range of Gibraltar-based aircraft. When they failed to find any convoys, he shifted them farther west, to sweep the area north and west of the Azores for Mediterranean-bound convoys from the United States. This allowed Dönitz to uphold the Naval High Command's strategy of countering Operation TORCH, but at the same time returned a significant number of U-Boats to the general campaign against Allied merchant tonnage.[9]

Ironically, the futile campaign against TORCH marked the last time Dönitz's forces enjoyed a major advantage against their adversaries. Since the introduction of the fourth rotor on the Schlüssel M (Enigma) encryption machine at the end of 1941, U-Boat communications had been secure from Allied eavesdropping. While the German Navy's B-Dienst continued to crack Allied convoy codes, British and American cryptanalysts could not break into the signal traffic exchanged between Dönitz and his commanders at sea. But the recovery of some key documents from the sinking *U–559* in the eastern Mediterranean in October 1942 gave British intelligence the opening it needed. On December 13, the four-rotor U-Boat key, known as "Triton" to the Germans and termed "Shark" by the British, was broken. A current reading of communications would not be achieved until January, but cryptanalysts in the meantime solved the intercepted (but not yet decrypted) messages for an eight-day period in November. One of those messages was Henke's action report from the engagement with *Hecla*.[10]

Oblivious to these fateful developments, *U–515* at last enjoyed some relative quiet in moving westward to the Azores. The most significant event involved a typical experience for U-Boats with the Metox radar detector. The "Biscay Cross" had more than proved its worth during the patrol with timely warnings of approaching aircraft and warships. Yet the only way to dismount the fragile wooden frame during the crash dive was to hurriedly throw the entire mounting down the hatchway, with the bridge watch following close behind. The force of the descending boots often broke the frame and the antennae, although this could usually be repaired with little difficulty.

On 20 November, however, a crash dive by *U–515* resulted in severe damage to the cables that connected the mounting with the receiver in the radio room. This required Henke to rendezvous with the supply tanker ("milk cow") *U–461* (Korv.kapt. Wolf-Harro Stiebler) to pick up replacement equipment, after which he speeded west to take up his alloted position in *Westwall*.

No greater contrast with the early days of the patrol could be imagined than the period that followed on station north and west of the Azores. The war seemingly vanished, and the boat and its crew had the ocean to themselves. After the rendezvous with the supply tanker, *U–515* spent the next ten days alone on the sea, except for a brief meeting with the *Westwall* boat to its south, *U–155* (Kaptlt. Adolf-Cornelius Piening). Henke's was the fourth in a line of ten boats, stretched over 260 miles from north to south, that continually moved further west as Dönitz groped for a convoy. The deployment this far from Gibraltar meant that convoys from Britain to the Mediterranean had an open door in the rear, but Dönitz reasoned that if he could catch one convoy from the United States headed in the same direction, the operation would be a success.[11]

In fact, Dönitz's move of *Westwall* caught Allied intelligence flat-footed. Unable to read BdU's messages to determine U-Boat dispositions and movements, British and American naval intelligence utilized all available evidence—sightings, espionage, decryption of lower-grade cyphers, and especially radio direction-finding of U-Boat transmissions at sea—but inevitably had to make deductions and informed guesses as the basis for planning. Unwilling to believe that Dönitz would leave open the avenue from Britain to Gibraltar, the British Admiralty placed the *Westwall* boats at varying distances west and northwest of Gibraltar. Dönitz would never realize that—perhaps for the last time in the war—he had a wolf pack invisible to Allied intelligence.[12]

Sunday, 6 December 1942, passed in the manner of the previous ten days for *U–515*. The cloudy sky and horizon remained empty until, at 1838 ship's time two plumes of smoke appeared in the distance. Henke and his lookouts trained their binoculars on the spot and made out a 7000-ton freighter and a 4-masted passenger liner, steaming on a south-easterly course at a speed of about 17 knots. If they were headed toward Gibraltar, as their course indicated, they had a good head start with the advantage of speed.

The larger ship was the obvious target, though Henke and his first officer debated its exact size. The captain wasted no time, however, in deliberation over his next course of action. He ordered a pursuit course to be plotted for the larger ship and shouted the order to the engine room: "*AK voraus!*"—All ahead full!

To overtake its prey required *U–515* to maintain maximum speed for more than five hours—a risky business, since the strain pushed the engines to their limit. That they held up testified to the resourcefulness of the engine-room personnel, in terms of both the condition and maintenance of the engines and their handling of the machines that evening. At one point the exhaust manifold began to leak, necessitating a quick repair before the accompanying fumes overpowered the crewmen in the compartment. Even Henke began to doubt his ability to catch up to his quarry, for at 2142 hours he radioed his sighting of both steamers to BdU, a signal he knew would be picked up by other boats in the area. (In fact, the two ships had separated long before then, and *U–155* had already sighted and set off in pursuit of the smaller freighter.)

But by 2359, after a "forced march" of roughly 100 nautical miles,

Henke had overtaken his quarry. The navigator noted their position on the German Navy grid chart as quadrant CD 2927. Maneuvering through the ship's wash into attack position on her starboard side, Henke began his run on the massive target.[13]

NOTES

1. On lack of crew leave, see preliminary interrogations of Hermann Brandt, 6 May 1944, *U–515* interrogations, Op-16-Z, RG 38, NA; on the Metox, see Robert C. Stern, *Type VII U-Boats* (Annapolis, MD: Naval Institute Press, 1991), 122–24.

2. Where possible, Dönitz's remarks are taken from his *Memoirs. Ten Years and Twenty Days* (Annapolis, MD: Naval Institute Press, 1990), for example, 228, 238–40, 256–63, 266–71; for a very readable account of the *Laconia* incident, see Leonce Peillard, *The Laconia Affair*, trans. by Oliver Coburn (New York: G. P. Putnam's Sons, 1963).

3. Letter of Hans Hahn to author, 1 November 1991.

4. This is based on the comments of Günter Hessler, *The U-Boat War in the Atlantic 1939–1945*, II (London: Her Majesty's Stationery Office, 1989), 57–59, regarding the relative U-Boat dispositions and success in the various operational areas.

5. *U–515* KTB; KTB BdU, 9 November 1942 (T1022/3980/PG 30313a).

6. See KTB BdU, 18–21 November 1942, and especially the overall assessment of 18 November (appended to the KTB for 1–15 November), T1022/3980/PG 30313-b, and Michael Salewski, *Die deutsche Seekriegsleitung 1935–45, Bd.II: 1942–1945* (Munich: Bernard & Graefe Verlag, 1975), 173–84.

7. Data compiled from the following sources: Anti-Submarine Warfare Division, Naval Staff, "Analysis of Attacks by a U-boat on HMS *Hecla* at 2315, 11th November 1942," 25 January 1943, file ADM 199/1274 (7969), PRO (hereafter cited as "*Hecla* Analysis"); Charles Hocking, ed., *Dictionary of Disasters at Sea During the Age of Steam* (London: Lloyd's Register of Shipping, 1969), 309; and *British Vessels Lost at Sea 1939–45*, reprint of two official publications in 1947 regarding losses of Royal Navy and British merchant ships (Cambridge: Patrick Stephens, 1977), Pt. 1, 22.

8. Sources for the action are *U–515* KTB, 11–12 November 1942 and patrol assessment; *U–515 Schussmeldungen*, Bibliothek für Zeitgeschichte; and ASW Division, "*Hecla* Analysis," ADM 199/1274 (7969), PRO. Carl Möller's story is taken from his letter to the author, 20 November 1987; and from an interview with the author in Hamburg, 30 August 1989. Data on the loss of personnel aboard *Hecla* taken from Hocking, ed., *Dictionary*, 309. Both Dönitz (*Memoirs*, 281–82) and Hessler (*U-Boat War*, vol. 2, 64–65) quote extensively from Henke's war diary as a tribute to his performance.

9. *U–515* KTB; KTB BdU, 18–25 November 1942 (including assessment of situation on 18 November but appended to the KTB for 1–15 November 1942), T1022/3980/PG 30313a–b. A good map of *Westwall*'s changing positions is reproduced in Hessler, *U-Boat War*, vol. 2, 66.

10. See F. H. Hinsely et al., *British Intelligence in the Second World War*, vol. 2 (5 vols. in 6 parts; New York: Cambridge University Press, 1981), 547–56, 747–52; and David Kahn, *Seizing the Enigma. The Race to Break the German U-Boat Codes, 1939–1943* (Boston: Houghton Mifflin, 1991), 220–27. Henke's message of 12 November 1942 is located among the SRGN (German U-Boat) signal intercept series, SRGN no. 6441, Records of the National Security Agency/Central Security Service, RG 457, NA.

11. *U–515* KTB, 13–25 November; KTB BdU, 18 November–1 December 1942, T1022/3980/PG 30313b–30314a; and Stern, *Type VII*, 122–23, regarding Metox damage.

12. The above is based on the commander in chief, U.S. Fleet (COMINCH) daily situation maps, 25 November–6 December 1942, in COMINCH files, OpArchives. These situation maps indicate the presumed locations and anticipated movements of German U-Boats for each day of this period. The equivalent Admiralty maps are not yet available for public use. On Allied processing of intelligence data and deduction in U-Boat dispositions, see Patrick Beesly, *Very Special Intelligence. The Story of the Admiralty's Operational Intelligence Centre 1939–1945* (Garden City, NY: Doubleday & Company, 1978), 116–20; and Donald McLachlan, *Room 39. Naval Intelligence in Action 1939–1945* (London: Weidenfeld and Nicolson, 1968), 104ff.

13. *U–515* KTB, which acknowledges the contribution of the engine-room staff; *U–515*'s *Schussmeldung* of 7 December 1942, 0000 hrs. (Bibliothek für Zeitgeschichte), illustrates Henke's attack approach; the text of the radio message is contained in SRGN No. 6942, RG 457, NA; and the debate with Hashagen (who correctly believed the ship to be larger than Henke's assessment) is noted in Carl Möller's letter to the author, 20 November 1987.

10

Ceramic

The passenger liner *Ceramic* had weathered many storms of man and nature in her long life. She came from the same shipyards in Belfast that had produced the *Titanic* only a year before her, and entered service for the White Star line in 1913 on the passenger routes to Australia. During World War I she remained on this route, ferrying Australian troops to European battlefields. In 1934, when the White Star and Cunard lines merged, *Ceramic* was sold to the Blue Funnel & Shaw Savill Line, but continued to grace the cruise routes from Britain to Australia. The outbreak of war in 1939 found her in the operational area of the German pocket battleship *Admiral Graf Spee*, but she managed to elude capture.

With a length of 655 feet and a beam of 69 feet, she was roughly four-fifths the size of the Cunard liner *Lusitania*, but her shallower draft and single smokestack made her appear smaller. Displacing 18,713 tons, she possessed a top speed of 15 knots. After being requisitioned by the Ministry of Transport in February 1940, *Ceramic* completed an internal refit in autumn 1942 that converted her lower passenger quarters and facilities into troop quarters. She also carried one four-inch gun and a smaller twelve-pound gun, though as with all merchant vessels this armament served little purpose beyond legitimizing the ships as military targets.[1]

On the morning of 23 November 1942, *Ceramic* pulled away from her familiar dock at Liverpool to join with other ships assembling in the Irish Sea to form Convoy ON 149. Under Capt. Herbert Elford, *Ceramic* would accompany the convoy on its route to Halifax and New York until the mid-Atlantic was reached, when the liner and six other vessels would depart and proceed unescorted to southern destinations. *Ceramic's* scheduled stops included St. Helena in the South Atlantic, Capetown and Durban, South Africa, and ultimately Sydney, Australia.

Ceramic carried a varied assortment of crew and passengers on this voyage. There was the normal complement of 264 crewmen, with an additional 14 DEMS (for Defensively Equipped Merchant Ships, the British equivalent of naval armed guards) gunners to man the two artillery pieces, for a total crew of 278. The number of passengers classified as "military" amounted to 226, consisting of 43 British Army officers, mostly representing the artillery, engineers, and medical services; 11 Royal Navy officers; 9 Merchant Navy officers; 30 nurses, most of whom belonged to the order of Queen Alexandra's Imperial Military Nursing Service; a 50-man unit of Royal Engineers; and a mix of 83 military and naval other ranks, including some merchant seamen designated for reassignment. Finally *Ceramic* carried 152 civilian passengers, comprising 90 men (including 11 homeward-bound inhabitants of the Belgian Congo), 50 women, and 12 children. Most of the women and children were dependents of officers traveling on board. The bulk of the space below decks, however, held the ship's principal cargo on this trip, some 12,362 tons of general and government stores, including aircraft spare parts.[2]

Had *Ceramic* carried no passengers at all, her cargo capacity alone marked her as a valuable target. The supplies she carried on this trip equaled the amount carried by two or three average-sized merchant ships. The same space could also accommodate four thousand soldiers: In less than two months, *Ceramic* alone could ferry an entire division from the United States to Britain. On the return run of this voyage, the liner probably would have departed Sydney with reinforcements for the Royal Air Force's Bomber Command and a full load of beef and butter for the troops assembling in England.

The story has also been advanced that an unscheduled stop was planned for Takoradi, on the Gold Coast of West Africa. According to this theory, *Ceramic*'s passengers included some airfield specialists whose expertise was so urgently required as to determine the ship's ultimate course. No available evidence supports this version except for the importance of its source: Capt. (later Commodore) Rodger Winn, the Admiralty officer responsible for plotting the positions of German U-Boats in the Atlantic. Winn would play a critical role in the drama about to unfold.[3]

ON 149 departed the Irish Sea on the afternoon of 26 November with a total of fifty merchant ships—five American, thirty-one British, and fourteen of other Allied nations—escorted by only two destroyers and five corvettes. The convoy rounded the tip of northern Ireland and began the long trek across the North Atlantic at an average speed of eight knots. Three days out, one of the screening escorts reported a sonar contact; though it could not be confirmed as a submarine, the convoy altered its course. On 1 December, the convoy received a message from the Commander in Chief, Western Approaches, Admiral Sir Max Horton, ordering another change in course and specifying that the southbound ships of the convoy "were not to be detached until further notice." Later that day, the U.S. Navy issued an "urgent U-Boat warning" to the convoy commodore that a submarine radio transmission within 100 miles of their position had been identified.[4]

Effective control of the convoy's movements lay in Capt. Rodger Winn's Tracking Room at the Admiralty, where the positions and movements of German U-boats were daily calculated and plotted on the basis of the latest intelligence. Next door stood the Trade Division's section for the movements of Allied shipping, so that the latest developments in U-Boat dispositions could be immediately translated into evasive convoy routing around the danger. The British, like the Americans, had picked up the radio transmission of *U–603* (Oberlt. Hans-Joachim Bertelsmann) on 30 November. Had ULTRA decryption been available, they would have read that the U-Boat had spotted four ships of the convoy in the early afternoon, and had maintained contact by hydrophone monitoring of the convoy's propeller noises.

Dönitz, mistakenly identifying the convoy as ON 151, disposed six submarines across its anticipated route, but it was too late. The course alteration took ON 149 away from the threat, and on 1 December the German commander cancelled the operation. Unaware of this order, and unwilling to take risks, Horton ordered another course change on 3 December. In reality, ON 149 had already left its moment of danger behind.[5]

On 4 December, the Admiralty signaled its approval for the detachment of the convoy's southbound ships. Specific routing instructions were provided for each of the seven ships scheduled to depart, three bound for West African ports and four—including *Ceramic*—for South Africa. According to Winn, this approval came reluctantly and only after pressure had been applied by the Ministry of Shipping, as all of the detached vessels would be exposed to long voyages without escort. Much of this passage ran the length of the "air gap," beyond the range of air cover from either North America or Britain. Winn preferred to

leave *Ceramic* in convoy all the way to New York, then move her south
with coastal convoys to the Caribbean and Recife, Brazil, with only a
short trip remaining across the South Atlantic. Though this probably
represents faulty memory and hindsight, Winn's acceptance of ultimate
responsibility underscores the role of intelligence in what was about to
happen.[6]

For Dönitz's *Westwall* boats, it will be recalled, had been misplaced
by Winn and his American colleagues. Instead of lying in the western
approaches of Gibraltar, this group of submarines now formed a picket
line more than a thousand miles away, west and north of the Azores.
To intercept convoys from U.S. ports bound for Gibraltar, Dönitz deployed the boats between thirty-nine degrees and forty-two degrees
north latitude, astride the great circle routes between Gibraltar and all
American ports from Norfolk to Boston. As of 6 December, Allied intelligence placed only one U-Boat slightly northeast of this position, with
a second one transiting the area on its way home. In reality, ten U-Boats
lay there in ambush.

But Dönitz, too, had guessed wrong. Not until late in December did
the B-dienst's radio intercepts reveal that the expected convoys had been
routed further south. *Westwall*'s boats awaited a battle that would not
come. They would not, however, be completely disappointed.[7]

On the evening of 5 December, ON 149 detached its southbound ships
at latitude forty-five degrees North, longitude forty-six degrees West.
All steered a southeasterly course—straight into *Westwall*.

Ceramic followed her planned route for the next twenty-four hours,
accompanied for much of the time by the Dutch freighter *Serooskerk*. The
passenger liner possessed one advantage over all the other independents, her speed; and as dusk fell on the evening of 6 December, she
pulled away from her companion at fifteen knots. One of her passengers,
twenty-year-old Eric Munday, a sapper in the Royal Engineers, recalled
no particular sense of danger as *Ceramic* maintained only a four-hour
submarine watch per day. The trip had been very pleasant to this point,
with enough opportunities to enjoy cigarettes, drinks, and girls. Zigzagging through moderate seas but with light rain and poor visibility,
Ceramic had by 8:00 P.M. (Azores time, as kept on board the liner) reached
a point roughly 600 miles northwest of the Azores. None aboard realized
that they were in the sights of a U-Boat ace.[8]

U–515 now stood 1,200 meters off on *Ceramic*'s starboard beam. Following procedure, First Watch Officer Hashagen worked out the details
of the torpedo attack under Henke's supervision. Mechanically, the com-

mands from the bridge and the confirmations from the bow torpedo room echoed through the submarine in the same manner as a practice run.

"Tubes I and IV, prepare for a surface firing!"

"Flooding tubes I and IV, opening outer caps . . . Tubes I and IV ready!"

"Double shot with deflection calculator!"

"Switched angle of spread for double!"

"Depth five meters . . . Torpedo speed 40 . . . Target's speed 15.5 knots . . . Target's bows on right, bearing 80 degrees . . . Range 1200 meters . . . Target's length, 200!"

"All Set!'

"Follow!" With this command, the attack computer in the aft section of the conning tower determined the deflection angles and firing times. A silent countdown followed as the submarine's chronometer, four hours ahead of time kept aboard her target, turned to 0000 hours and the first seconds of 7 December 1942.

"Fächer—los! (Salvo—Fire!)"[9]

Thirty seconds later, a muffled, invisible explosion sounded across the water. Immediately after, those on the U-Boat's bridge heard the metallic thud of the second torpedo striking the hull—a dud. Henke believed he had hit the engine room of the liner, but he had actually struck the ship's forward section.

In *Ceramic*'s lounge, Eric Munday felt the explosion and the beginning of a list to starboard, but noted no lessening of speed and no interruption in the hum of the engines. "Action stations" was sounded, but nothing could be seen in the blackness about them. *Ceramic*'s radio operator immediately issued a distress call, picked up by *U–515*'s own *Funker* and relayed to the bridge.

At last aware of his target's identity, Henke could also see that *Ceramic*'s wound was not mortal. He swung the boat around to bring the stern tubes to bear, and at a range of 1,000 meters fired again at 0018 hours. Another hit, and *Ceramic* stopped immediately. The liner's lights suddenly illuminated the night as Captain Elford gave the order to abandon ship. On *U–515*'s bridge, Henke could see lifeboats swinging out and being lowered. To finish her off, he ordered the second stern tube to deliver the *coup de grâce*.

To Munday, the third torpedo hit seemed to come almost immediately after the second, but in fact twenty minutes had passed. Munday proceeded to his lifeboat on *Ceramic*'s port side. He later recalled, "There was a little panic, probably owing to our having women and children on board, but it was nothing serious, and quite understandable as it was so very dark that slight confusion was inevitable."

The list on the starboard side apparently prevented the use of some lifeboats there, as Munday discovered that his own lifeboat contained more than fifty occupants. After a "slight struggle," however, the lifeboat was successfully lowered and pushed away from the liner. Munday could see six or eight other lifeboats in the water as well as numerous life rafts.

Henke described the same sight in his war diary, together with the observation of uniformed military personnel in the lifeboats. He had no doubts now that *Ceramic* was a troopship bound for the Mediterranean theater. Conceivably she had been en route to a rendezvous with an Allied convoy, whose escorts might even now be steaming to the spot in response to *Ceramic*'s distress call. The overworked state of his diesel engines after the long chase did not favor Henke in any engagement with a destroyer. A full hour had passed since the first attack, and still *Ceramic* remained afloat. He would waste no more time.

At Henke's command, the boat pivoted again and fired another torpedo from tube II. This was *Ceramic*'s death blow, breaking the ship apart and leaving no trace on the surface within ten seconds of detonation. Suddenly another nearby explosion occurred—possibly the liner's boilers or ammunition stored aboard her—but Henke feared it might signify the arrival of an escort vessel, so he turned and made off to the northwest, to resume his position in the picket line. *U–515*'s radioman transmitted the report of the success to BdU, identifying *Ceramic* as a troop transport.[10]

This message joined a growing collection of reports at U-Boat Command headquarters in Paris of activities of *Westwall* boats during the night. When Henke had first radioed his sighting and pursuit of two vessels, BdU alerted all submarines in the area to look out for independent ships. During the night of 6–7 December, three other ships that had detached from ON 149 fell victim to *Westwall* boats. Reviewing the reports the next morning, Dönitz and Godt pondered the significance of this sudden activity in the area. Had a convoy somehow broken up and been dispersed? Or were these unescorted ships detached from a North Atlantic convoy to make a run for West African ports? If so, it might mean the Allies had abandoned, at least for the moment, the Great Britain–Sierra Leone convoy route. But what about Henke's claimed troopship? Such a vessel could only be headed for the Mediterranean—if she was a troopship. These were important questions, as they might indicate new patterns of Allied shipping in the aftermath of the North African operation.[11]

Therefore, at 0730 on 7 December, BdU radioed the following query to Henke: "REPORT AT ONCE WHETHER TROOP TRANSPORT WAS LOADED WITH TROOPS AND WHETHER THERE WAS ANY INDICATION OF ITS PORT OF DESTINATION."

The signal doubtless surprised Henke and probably confused him. Why would Headquarters doubt his earlier message? What did they want him to do about it now, especially as rescue ships and escorts might be in the area? On the other hand, perhaps the desired information possessed an intelligence value not obvious to a U-Boat captain. The only way to obtain the information, however, was to go back for it. After weighing the possible risks, Henke turned the submarine about and headed back to the site. At 1147 he sent the following message back to BdU: "CERAMIC FULL OF TROOPS. AM GOING TO THE SITE OF SINKING IN ORDER TO CAPTURE THE CAPTAIN."

If Henke selected the wording of the message to suggest a waste of time and effort, and bring about a countermanding order, he was disappointed. *U–515* retraced her path through darkening skies and ever-rougher seas, with a rising wind gauged at force 7 on the Beaufort scale (about 35 mph).[12]

Ceramic's survivors spent a listless but uneventful night in their lifeboats. The crowding in sapper Munday's boat did not permit much moving about, and "as there were mostly military personnel in the boat nobody knew very much about handling it." With daylight, however, came rain, winds, and a rising sea, all with rapidly increasing intensity. A northerly gale had caught them in its grip. Munday recalled,

> Huge waves were breaking over the boat, we bailed furiously, but it was impossible to free the boat of water before another wave crashed over, swamping it so that it capsized and we were all thrown in the water. After a struggle the boat was righted, but it was three-quarters full of water; two or three men climbed in and tried to bail it out, but again it was capsized by the huge waves.

Munday decided to swim off and chance things on his own. Soon he lost sight of his companions and other lifeboats. He held on briefly to a piece of wreckage for support, but the sea soon washed it away. Though the full battle dress he wore beneath his lifejacket provided some warmth, the soldier's ordeal nevertheless pushed his endurance to the limit. After four hours, with his strength failing, Munday wondered if the shape that suddenly appeared between the waves was a submarine or an illusion.[13]

Aboard *U–515*, the chronometer read 1600 hours—sixteen hours since the attack on *Ceramic*, and more than four hours since they had turned back. The track led the boat straight into the gale encountered by the liner's survivors. For those on the bridge, the scene they beheld matched any nightmare. The storm's violent fury engulfed them with rain and hailstones from above, high swells lifting them from below and plunging them back into deep furrows of grey water. The sea and sky conditions were far less unnerving, however, than the grisly field of wreckage tossed about in the storm. The corpses of *Ceramic*'s passengers and crew were all around them, mixed with the smashed fragments of lifeboats, aircraft parts, and other cargo.

Henke knew he could not expect to find a surviving senior officer, but would be lucky to recover any living member of *Ceramic*'s complement. One moving figure could be seen near the boat before he disappeared behind a wave. Henke gave the order to stop all engines as Hashagen and a crewman, secured by ropes to the bridge, lowered themselves to the deck and prepared to throw out a line. But when the next wave carried the man closer, he still could not reach—or lacked the strength to reach—the offered rope. Just as it seemed the sea would carry him away, a wave suddenly washed the man onto the deck of the U-Boat.

Eric Munday was close to death, his stomach swollen from the water he had swallowed. Two crewmen immediately took him below, where they forced the sea water out of his stomach and lungs and kept him from swallowing his tongue. Later he received dry clothes and warm condensed milk to drink, but his only conscious response was to say, "I won't talk."

The primary reason for his rescue, of course, had been to obtain intelligence. Interrogated shortly after his rescue, Munday (according to *U–515*'s war diary) told his captors that *Ceramic* carried 45 officers and about 1,000 men. He said he knew nothing of her cargo or destination. As the weather precluded further rescue attempts, and no further intelligence could be obtained, Henke could only conclude that *Ceramic* had been carrying troops to the Mediterranean. This remained the German view after the war.[14]

The gale that had doomed *Ceramic*'s survivors continued for several days, forcing *U–515* to remain submerged for much of the period to avoid the worst of its fury. The Portugese destroyer *Dao*, which departed the Azores' port of Horta on the morning of 9 December to look for survivors, suffered considerable damage in the storm and had to turn back. British light cruiser HMS *Enterprise*, which only arrived in the Azores on the evening of 8 December, left the next day to join the search. Riding into the gale, *Enterprise* reached the position of the sinking on 11 December but encountered typhoon-like conditions, with winds rising from force 7 to force 12 (over 75 mph) in a span of 15 minutes; she had to abandon the effort.

Nature's violence and the lack of rescue vessels wrote the epilogue to the tragedy of the *Ceramic*. With warships tied up in Operation TORCH and on convoy duty, none could be spared when distress calls came out of the middle of the Atlantic. The loss of life on the other independent ships caught in *Westwall's* net, though smaller in number than that aboard the liner, was no less total. Of the sixty-five persons aboard *Henry Stanley*, sunk by *U–103* during the night of 6–7 December, only the captain survived, removed from his lifeboat by the U-Boat before the storm arrived. There were no survivors among the sixty-seven crewmen and passengers aboard the *Peter Maersk*, though *U–185* (Kaptlt. August Maus) observed three lifeboats in the water after torpedoing the steamer on the morning of 7 December.[15]

As with every disaster, a combination of variables—what might be termed fate—shaped the course of *Ceramic's* final voyage. Had Allied intelligence broken the German Navy's Enigma cypher two weeks sooner . . . had Winn not guessed incorrectly about the deployment of *Westwall* . . . had the U-Boats shadowing Convoy ON 149 maintained contact for one more day, forcing cancellation of the detachment of southbound ships . . . had *U–515's* diesels not been so well maintained, or the leaking exhaust manifold not been quickly repaired . . . had the storm not struck . . . had rescue vessels been available in the Azores. Any of these variables might have averted *Ceramic's* sinking, or reduced the loss of life among her passengers and crew. But none occurred, and *Ceramic* took all save one of the 656 souls aboard her to a watery grave.

On the evening of 11 December, Dönitz ordered the withdrawal eastward of the *Westwall* boats. In nearly three weeks, the sinking of the four ships detached from ON 149 represented the group's only successes. The time spent on this distant station had moreover drained the submarines' fuel tanks, reducing the options for their future employment. A disappointed Dönitz ordered them to reconcentrate in the area west of Portugal, hopeful of catching some British traffic bound for Gibraltar.[16]

In fact, U–515 would not see another ship after *Ceramic*. For the remainder of the patrol, a number of diversions provided welcome relief from the tensions and terror that had characterized much of this mission. Eric Munday, dubbed by the crew "Johnny" (from "John Bull," the personification of England), received various duties to perform (for example, peeling potatoes) aboard the submarine as soon as he had recovered his strength—Henke himself had informed the Englishman that he had to "help out."

On 14 December, the U-Boat encountered a floating field of wooden cases, the debris from a recently sunk ship in the area. The watch recovered one of the cases and opened it, to discover the unexpected treat of fresh New Zealand butter. Quickly the crew collected fifty cases and stored them below deck. The large quantities of butter not only furnished numerous cream tortes for Christmas dinner aboard, but enough remained to provide donations to the officers' and noncommissioned officers' messes back at Lorient, as well as a pound for each man to take home on his next leave.

That Christmas on board U–515 was particularly memorable, the first celebrated aboard the submarine and the first at sea for many crewmen. The small Christmas tree that had been carefully stored between the pressure hull and the main deck was removed and set up in the forward torpedo room. Crewmen decorated the tree with silver filaments, colored ribbons, and figures fashioned from rope. On Christmas Eve a string of colored lights provided the finishing touch.

After sunset, Henke submerged the boat to allow the entire crew to participate in the festivities. Freshly shaven and in their good uniforms, the crewmen sat along an improvised table to receive treats of *stollen*, baked cookies, and butter creme tortes. At a given signal, the ship's lights were extinguished, and the Christmas tree illuminated—an effect that Eric Munday described as "very moving." The sailors then sang the traditional Christmas carols before enjoying a round of hot punch and chocolate. Munday himself received a Christmas present of a special portion of chocolate.[17]

One celebration, however, represented a very special occasion within the *U-Boat-Waffe*. On 19 December 1942 BdU signaled U–515 that her commander had been awarded the Knight's Cross of the Iron Cross. In the message Dönitz also congratulated Henke's "brave crew and their demonstrated willingness to fight." On just his second patrol, Werner Henke had earned a decoration bestowed upon only sixty-nine U-Boat officers before him. The radioman notified the rest of the crew before passing the message to the captain, so that a small surprise could be arranged. *Maschinistenmaat* Hans Stabwasser fashioned an oversized Iron Cross from some scrap metal in the engine room, and in an informal ceremony in the control room the crew presented the "decoration" and accompanying radio message to Henke.[18]

Though not a sentimentalist, Henke was touched by his crew's gesture. He gave the oversized award to his mother on his next visit home. It remains with the family today.

On 31 December, yet another special event occurred on board with the marriage by proxy of *Funkmaat* Schoppmann-Ketting. At 1100 hours, a special radio hook-up allowed the young radioman to exchange vows with his sweetheart in Germany as Henke and a local magistrate officiated the ceremony. That evening the crew celebrated the New Year quietly with a round of hot punch.

As Dönitz suspected, the reconcentration of *Westwall* boats west of Portugal failed to achieve any successes, and on 23 December he disbanded the group. *U-515* received permission to hunt independently in the area, but nothing turned up. Dwindling fuel reserves compelled Henke to order a return to base on 2 January 1943. The submariners needed little inspiration to apply themselves to their tasks on the voyage home. They remained blissfully ignorant of the Allied breakthrough on 13 December in decrypting German naval ciphers, and unaware that Dönitz's congratulatory message and Henke's return to base signal had been intercepted and read by the enemy.[19]

The story of the *Ceramic* was not yet over.

NOTES

1. Data taken from Charles Hocking, ed., *Dictionary of Disasters at Sea during the Age of Steam* (London: Lloyd's Register of Shipping, 1969), 129; from Frank C. Bowen, *The Flag of the Southern Cross 1939–1945* (London: Shaw Savill & Albion Co., n.d.), 33–34, 48–49; and the narrative by Gordon W. Haddon, "The Loss of the *Ceramic*," November 1989 (copy available in the U-Boot-Archiv, Cuxhaven). Haddon's manuscript is based upon available British sources.

2. In addition to Haddon's manuscript, the accounts of *Ceramic*'s voyage and loss are taken from "ON 149 Convoy Folder," U.S. Tenth Fleet Convoy and

Routing Files, OpArchives; the official report by the only survivor, "Shipping Casualties Section, Trade Division, SS *Ceramic*' Report of an Interview with Sapper Eric Munday, R. E.," 14 August 1945, file ADM 199/176 (7534), PRO; and Munday's subsequent account related to German author Hans Herlin, reproduced in Herlin, *Verdammter Atlantik. Schicksale deutscher U-Boot-Fahrer* (Munich: Wilhelm Heyne, 1982), 119–21. The version appearing in Daniel V. Gallery, *U–505* (New York: Paperback Library, 1967), 194–210, is largely fictional.

3. The story was apparently told by Winn to Donald McLachlan, then serving on the personal staff of the Director of Naval Intelligence. See McLachlan, *Room 39. Naval Intelligence in Action 1939–1945* (London: Weidenfeld and Nicolson, 1968), 118.

4. The texts of both messages are included in the "ON 149 Convoy Folder," OpArchives.

5. See the messages for 29 November–3 December 1942 in the "ON 149 Convoy Folder," OpArchives; and the BdU KTB, 29 November–1 December 1942 (T1022/3980/PG 30313b–30314a).

6. The account in McLachlan, *Room 39*, 118, contains too many discrepancies against official, declassified documents: There are no course indications for routing *Ceramic* to Takoradi, no references to "two destroyers" assigned as escort (there were only two destroyers for all of ON 149!), and the other southbound ships are not mentioned at all.

7. See the COMINCH situation map of U-Boat dispositions, 6 December 1942, in COMINCH files, OpArchives; and Hessler, *U-Boat War*, vol. 2, 66. The COMINCH map reflects the best available information to both British and American intelligence.

8. Munday's account in Herlin, *Atlantik*, 120.

9. The firing command sequence is provided in the German Navy technical manual (*Marine-Druckvorschrift*, or M.Dv.) Nr. 416/3, *Torpedo-Schiessvorschrift für U-Boote, Heft 3: Feuerleitung auf U-Booten* (Berlin, 1943), in the collection of German technical manuals, RG 242, NA. The data for the attack is taken from the *Schussmeldung*, BfZ, Stuttgart.

10. *U–515* KTB and Munday's August 1945 interview; I have offered my own conjecture of Henke's reasoning. The message to BdU is located in the SRGN collection of radio intercepts, SRGN nos. 6967 (original copy) and 6988 (corrected copy), RG 457, NA. It must be remembered that these intercepts were not decrypted until after mid-December, hence the information was not available to Allied intelligence.

11. This assessment relies upon the comments in the BdU war diary of 6 December 1942 (T1022/3980/PG 30314a); and the views of the commander of *U–103*, who sank one of the vessels (KTB *U–103*, 6–7 December 1942, T1022/3037/PG 30099).

12. Both messages are in the SRGN collection, SRGN nos. 6968 and 6996, RG 457, NA.

13. Munday, August 1945 interview (including quotation) and comments quoted in Herlin, *Atlantik*, 122–23.

14. *U–515* KTB and Herlin, *Atlantik*, 123–26, for general information; Munday's rescue and immediate treatment is described by Carl Möller in his letter to the

author, 20 November 1987; and interview with author, 30 August 1989; and Günter Hessler, *The U-Boat War in the Atlantic 1939–1945* (London: Her Majesty's Stationery Office, 1989), vol. 2, 66, for the continued belief in *Ceramic*'s Mediterranean course.

15. Rescue efforts are described in Munday, official interview, August 1945; and in Haddon, "Loss of Ceramic," 7–8; the number of lives lost on the other vessels is given in John M. Young, *Britain's Sea War: A Diary of Ship Losses 1939–1945* (Wellingborough: Patrick Stephens, 1989), 174; the sinkings of the latter are described in the war diaries of *U–103* (T1022/3036/PC 30099) and *U–185* (T1022/2885/PG 30172). I have been unable to determine the loss of life aboard the Dutch freighter *Serooskerk*, sunk by *U–155* at the same time, but the situation is almost certainly the same.

16. KTB BdU, 11 December 1942 (T1022/3980/PG 30314a).

17. Munday's diary, quoted in Herlin, *Atlantik*, 127–28; Hans Hahn, letter to author, 1 November 1991; Carl Möller, interview with author, 30 August 1989.

18. On the overall significance of the award, see Franz Kurowski, *Die Träger des Ritterkreuzes des Eisernen Kreuzes der U-Bootwaffe 1939–1945* (Bad Nauheim: Podzun, 1987), 5, 24; and Gordon Williamson, *Aces of the Reich* (London: Arms and Armour, 1989), 197–201. The message is reproduced in the SRGN collection of intercepts as SRGN no. 7741, RG 457, NA; a description of the crew's response is provided in Karl Alman, "Kapitänleutnant Werner Henke," *Der Landser-Ritterkreuzträger Nr. 2*, Nr. 680 (1971), 57–58.

19. Hessler, *U-Boat War*, vol. 2, 66; *U–515* KTB; copies of the messages are located in the SRGN collection of intercepts, SRGN nos. 7741, 8444–45, and 8547, RG 457, NA.

1. An early recruit for the Kaiser's Navy: Werner Henke and his mother, ca. 1914. Courtesy of Albrecht Henke.

2. Werner Henke (fourth from left, standing) with transport pilots, Spanish Nationalist militia, civilians, and fellow crew members of the *Admiral Scheer* during the Spanish Civil War, probably in the autumn of 1936. Courtesy of Albrecht Henke.

3. *Oberleutnant* Werner Henke, ca. 1938. Courtesy of the U-Boot-Archiv, Cuxhaven.

4. Aboard the *Schleswig-Holstein*, Henke (left) directs one of the first shots of World War II at Polish fortifications outside Danzig, 1 September 1939. Intended for antiaircraft defense, the 88mm gun is already proving its versatility. Courtesy of Albrecht Henke.

5. A U-Boat ace and two in training: Henke (right) is the Second Watch Officer, Jochen Mohr (left) the First Officer, and Kaptlt. Georg Schulz the commander on the bridge of *U-124*, sometime in 1941. Courtesy of the U-Boot-Archiv, Cuxhaven.

6. Henke displays the oversized Knight's Cross of the Iron Cross fashioned for him by his crew, December 1942. The liquid refreshment and hanging tinsel in the upper right indicate the Christmas celebration on board. Courtesy of the U-Boot-Archiv, Cuxhaven.

7. Henke reciprocates by congratulating his crew after the return to Lorient, January 1943. Courtesy of Albrecht Henke.

8. Henke on the bridge. Courtesy of the U-Boot-Archiv, Cuxhaven.

9. Henke receives the Oakleaves to the Knight's Cross of the Iron Cross from Adolf Hitler, July 1943. Courtesy of the U-Boot-Archiv, Cuxhaven.

10. *U-515* departs on her fifth patrol, November 1943. The expanded lower platform for increased antiaircraft armament allows half the crew to come up and wave farewell to the escorts. Courtesy of the Marineschule Mürwik.

11. 9 April 1944: Smoke pours from the wreckage of the lower platform shortly before the mortally wounded *U-515* takes her final plunge. U.S. Navy photo, courtesy of the National Archives.

12. Transferred aboard the U.S. escort carrier *Guadalcanal*, Henke begins his final journey. Courtesy of the U-Boot-Archiv, Cuxhaven.

11

War Criminal No. 1

Not until *U–515* tied up to the dock at Lorient could her crew appreciate how many people were awaiting her: the band of the Tenth Flotilla, a military honor guard, members of the Womens' Naval Auxiliary (the German equivalent to the WAVES), and a crowd of off-duty well-wishers. Flotilla commander Kaptlt. Günter Kuhnke and his adjutant separated themselves from the throng and boarded the submarine to greet Henke and present him with the regulation-size Knight's Cross of the Iron Cross.

Among those waiting to congratulate Henke as he stepped onto the pier was a radio broadcaster with a recording machine, who transcribed the captain's observations on the sinking of the *Ceramic*. The crew disembarked, half of whom would soon begin their homeward journey with extra portions of butter packed with their clothing. Lastly, armed guards escorted Eric Munday to the naval arsenal for an hour-long interrogation. Then he too was briefly interviewed by the radio broadcaster, before boarding a train to Wilhelmshaven and captivity for the rest of the war.[1]

In a separate ceremony, the crew of *Fünf-fünfzehn* formally celebrated her captain's award of the Knight's Iron Cross. In full dress uniform, the crew presented Henke with flowers as the captain, in his turn, passed among the ranks to congratulate each crew member.

Henke departed for Paris and a cordial debriefing by Dönitz. The *Grossadmiral*'s memoirs record his commendation from that day: "The perseverance and tenacity of purpose with which Henke persisted in his efforts to sink his opponent (the *Hecla*) deserve the highest praise." In his assessment of the patrol, Dönitz also acknowledged the "worthy hardness" demonstrated by Henke in extracting the utmost from his engine-room staff in the pursuit of the *Ceramic*.

Most important for Henke, Dönitz assured him that his personnel record had been wiped clean. As of 1 December 1942, Werner Henke returned to full career status as a naval officer, and with a promotion to the rank of *Kapitänleutnant* (lieutenant-commander) backdated to 1 April 1941 to match the promotion of his comrades in Crew 33.[2]

Thus, Werner Henke left Paris for his first home leave in nearly a year, aware that he had conquered his past and regained his future. He could not know that the first steps toward his destruction had been taken.

On 21 February 1943—the very day that Henke led *U–515* out on her next patrol—Radio Berlin delivered its daily shortwave radio broadcast to the Western Hemisphere. There was little positive to report in any land campaigns, as the remnants of the Sixth Army had surrendered at Stalingrad less than three weeks before and the Afrika Korps now held only Tunisia. Only at sea could German victories still be touted, and on this day the radio station chose to use the recordings of Henke and Munday. Disputing Allied claims of low casualties among troop transports during the North African operations, Radio Berlin claimed that "several thousand soldiers" had been lost on a single transport, citing the testimony of the U-Boat commander who sank the *Ceramic* and its sole survivor.

Henke's recorded comments actually offered little proof of the claim. He acknowledged that *Ceramic* represented his first "really big steamer— we had always wanted one of those"; he described the attack on the liner, consistent with the account in his war diary; and he confirmed that he observed aircraft parts among the wreckage. Most forceful was his description of the scene:

Whether this was purely a troop transport, I couldn't really say, but certainly there were many soldiers on board. When we returned to the site the next day, a gruesome sight awaited us. I could see many bodies in the water. The dead British soldiers and sailors had been battered by the floating wreckage. The lifeboats had completely disintegrated. . . . It was not a pretty picture. I tried to save some individuals, but in the heavy seas and strong winds no real rescue action was possible. I managed to get one survivor aboard, but even that nearly cost me my first officer and a crewman. I broke off the attempt to save any more, because ultimately my mission was not to rescue survivors but to wage war.

Munday's only comments in the broadcast concerned his impression that he was the only survivor, and the observation that the *Ceramic*'s captain had always cautioned passengers to keep their lifebelts nearby.[3]

As propaganda, the broadcast exaggerated the losses of military personnel and erroneously included the *Ceramic* with the North African invasion. Yet it certainly underscored the perils of overseas transport aboard unescorted liners, and at precisely the moment when Allied reliance on such measures was increasing. In August 1942, the British Admiralty and the U.S. Navy began to employ such fast luxury liners as the *Queen Mary* and the *Queen Elizabeth* as troopships on a regular basis, gambling that their superior speed would enable them to outrun any submarine. Without being slowed by escorts, each of these liners could carry up to 15,000 troops across the Atlantic in half the time of the fastest convoy.

The *Ceramic*, however, demonstrated the potential for disaster if the gamble failed. U-Boat sinkings of the smaller, escorted army transports *Dorchester* and *Henry R. Mallory* in the North Atlantic in January–February 1943, with a combined loss of nearly 1,000 lives, added further proof of the risks involved.[4]

The number of listeners to Radio Berlin's broadcast, beyond the monitoring authorities, probably constituted a very small audience. Yet the brief address produced a result out of all proportion to its content. To understand why, one must consider both the general and specific direction of propaganda in the United States and in the navy, respectively.

The degree to which American citizens listened to enemy broadcasts during World War II remains unknown. In the spring of 1943, however, the available evidence worried U.S. authorities. When these broadcasts released the names of American prisoners of war, for example, relatives received as many as fifty or sixty letters from amateur radio operators who had monitored the announcements. Every one of these individuals was breaking the law, but the military hesitated to take action lest the accompanying publicity provide Axis propagandists with proof of their success. To attempt to find everyone who listened, of course, proved impossible.[5]

Combatting these influences required ever stronger domestic propaganda. The American motion picture industry proved the most effective medium in this regard, guided by the directives of the Office of War Information (OWI). In early 1943 the film *Action in the North Atlantic* drew audiences to the theaters with a tribute to the American merchant marine; the movie included scenes of laughing U-Boat crews running down survivors of torpedoed ships. When the March 1943 screenplay by John Steinbeck, *Lifeboat*, included a sympathetic view of an ordinary U-Boat crewman as a victim of his system, Hollywood and OWI revised the portrayal to that of a powerful, murderous U-Boat captain who must eventually be executed by the other survivors.[6]

The *Ceramic* broadcast, heard by an unquantifiable American audience, refuted such depictions with a closer version of the truth. Munday's participation in the broadcast demonstrated that survivors could be spared and rescued. At the time, American propagandists could not know that only one proven case of a U-Boat killing the survivors of a torpedoed ship would occur, and that not until March 1944.[7]

To the need for effective counterpropaganda, the special interest of a new agency provided added weight. Within the navy's Office of Naval Intelligence (ONI), the establishment of the Special Warfare Branch (Op-16-W) in October 1942 reflected a small but significant victory for the proponents of psychological warfare. Under Commander Cecil H. Coggins, a naval surgeon with a flair for intelligence work, Op-16-W sought an operational role as a combat propaganda unit, in addition to coordinating propaganda activities with the Office of War Information. Coggins hoped to complement the work of the Admiralty's NID/17/Z, which utilized the most recent intelligence (short of ULTRA intelligence, to which neither the British nor the American propaganda units were privy) in broadcasts to German submarine crews to attempt to undermine their morale.[8]

After three months Coggins's organization remained small, but it had established a strong relationship with the Special Activities Branch (Op-16-Z), the ONI intelligence office responsible for interrogating prisoners of war and evaluating captured enemy equipment. The first fruits of this collaboration blossomed in January 1943 with the initial broadcasts of "Commander Robert Lee Norden," the omniscient, German-speaking intelligence officer who informed U-Boat crews of the fates of missing comrades, passed on the latest gossip of Nazi party scandals, criticized the promotion policies of the German Naval High Command, and otherwise displayed an astounding knowledge of German naval affairs. (Unlike the "black" propaganda broadcast by NID/17/Z, which posed as a German radio station, the Norden broadcasts did not pretend to be anything other than a U.S. Navy operation, or "white" propaganda.) "Norden" was in fact the liaison officer from Op-16-Z, Lt. Cdr. Ralph G. Albrecht, an international lawyer holding a wartime commission.[9]

Less than ten days before the *Ceramic* broadcast, a policy directive of the Office of War Information singled out the U-Boat service for propaganda attack, and established the specific themes for emphasis. These included the "unrestricted and inhuman character" of Germany's submarine campaign that would require a harsher peace settlement; U-Boat successes as the fabrications of "excited or corrupt submarine commanders"; and the German people's deception by the "ruthless and reckless leaders" of the U-Boat war, who were "indifferent to the consequences of their private war and corrupted by their own prominent position." Chief among the latter, of course, was Dönitz, "a fanatic pledged to vindicate himself" for his capture in World War I, whose reliance on his submarines to bring victory "is a case familiar to psychiatrists, known as frustration-compensation."[10]

The tenor of this directive for propaganda suggests that it was itself a product of the same views it espoused. The propaganda legacy of World War I, when the sinking of the *Lusitania* and other passenger ships by German U-Boats had first inflamed American public opinion, and the common images of submarine warfare depicted on the silver screen, doubtless influenced Op-16-W's staff. More immediate, however, was the seriousness of the U-Boat threat to the Allied conduct of the war, for without secure lifelines across the Atlantic there could be no invasion of the continent. The British and American Combined Chiefs of Staff underscored the importance of this threat on 19 January 1943 when they agreed that "the defeat of the U-Boat must remain a first charge on the resources of the United Nations."[11]

Thus, in February 1943 the Special Warfare Branch combined an eagerness to prove its worth with a sense of mission against the U-Boat menace. At precisely this moment, the transcript of Radio Berlin's broadcast on Henke and the *Ceramic* arrived. Any German propaganda would have been challenged, but the *Ceramic* broadcast represented the most dangerous form of propaganda—the truth. It placed Allied propagandists on the defensive, and demanded a strong response.

Retaliation was not long in coming. The Op-16-W official and future popular historian who claimed authorship of the reply, Ladislas Farago, subsequently wrote that listening to the "fanatical Nazi [and] big blonde bully" Henke and the "poor, brainwashed" Munday had so sickened him that he composed a blistering counterattack while his anger "was still fresh." In this he identified Henke as "War Criminal no. 1"—that is, the first to be named. Farago's postwar account of the Henke episode contains numerous errors,[12] but there is no reason to doubt his authorship of the response. What is most interesting to note is that, in contrast to the essential truth of Radio Berlin's version, the "Norden" reply that followed constituted an outright lie.

The broadcast, no. 23 in the Norden series, went out on 25 March 1943. As with all Norden talks, the broadcasts were presented over various frequencies, and repeated five times a week to reach the widest possible audience.[13] The broadcast hammered home its theme from the opening lines. "I accuse! I accuse Lt. Werner Henke of murder! Lieutenant Henke has murdered 264 helpless survivors of a sinking." Directly acknowledging Radio Berlin's account of the *Ceramic*'s sinking, Norden claimed that eighty-five other survivors of the passenger liner had been recovered by Allied forces.

> The 85 have a different story to tell than Lt. Henke. They reported that the storm during the sinking of the ship by no means assumed such proportions as to preclude rescue. . . . Lt. Henke had apparently forgotten that such things as articles of war existed. He combed the waters with his searchlights and wherever he found a boat with survivors, women or children . . . he had his guns trained upon them. Yes, he ordered the survivors slaughtered with machine guns. He drove his crew to supreme efforts in order to murder as many of the helpless people as possible.

That Henke had "forced" a survivor "to tell fairy tales over the German radio" would not save the U-Boat commander from the "day of judgment . . . on which he will have to answer for his crime, before himself, before the German people, and before humanity."[14]

A careful reading of the text might have raised some questions about its contents. Why, for example, did the U.S. Navy break the story about a war crime committed against British subjects, aboard a British vessel? If the story was true, why had Henke spared eighty-five survivors? And since the incident has occurred the previous December, why had the alleged survivors not told their story for more than three months?

Lost in the spectacular accusations was Norden's statement that Henke and other war criminals would be brought to trial before *German* courts after the war. No such policy existed, as no serious thought had yet been given to the postwar prosecution of war crimes. That any U-Boat captain should be labeled as "war criminal no. 1" indicates the Allies' ignorance in 1943 of the truth of Auschwitz and the Final Solution. Concrete planning for war crimes did not exist before autumn 1944, when the U.S. War Department first outlined the judicial proposals that culminated in the Nürnberg trials.

Even in the courtroom at Nürnberg, the relationship of unrestricted submarine warfare and war crimes proved thorny and equivocal. Though some Allied officials recommended his acquittal, Karl Dönitz would eventually be convicted and sentenced to ten years' imprisonment largely for his conduct of the U-Boat war, though the International Military Tribunal agreed to announce that the navy commander in chief had been convicted on other grounds.[15]

For Farago and his colleagues in 1943, however, war crimes constituted only a propaganda issue. Ironically, had Op-16-W held back for a few months, they might have produced a less caustic but more effective propaganda piece. In August 1943 Op-16-Z provided them with a fairly accurate sketch of Henke's career, based on information obtained from captured U-Boat crewmen. This included knowledge of Henke's earlier punishment for going AWOL and hearsay about the strict discipline he enforced on his submarine, contradictions that could have been exploited with adroit propaganda handling.[16]

Instead, Farago and his fellow propagandists moved on to other subjects, and Henke was left tarred with the brush of "war criminal"—the first to be publicly identified as such by the Allies. This notoriety certainly did not affect his performance as a submarine commander, as we shall soon see. But it produced a deep and permanent psychological scar, and the specter of a British trial—despite the contrary wording of the broadcast—began to haunt him.

The effect of the broadcast on the U-Boat service as a whole is impossible to gauge. No one knows how many submariners secretly listened to the Norden broadcasts, especially in early 1943. A copy of the broadcast appended to *U–515*'s war diary reveals that Henke's crew at least knew it for precisely what it was. Probably this particular address had little general impact, since it seemed so improbable and the crewmen of *U–515* could easily debunk the story in Lorient.

Op-16-W did not improve its veracity with a second "war criminal" broadcast in April 1943, one that named *Korvettenkapitän* Hans Erdmenger as criminally responsible for the heavy personnel losses inflicted aboard two obsolete Norwegian ironclads sunk off Narvik in April 1940. The ironclads, given the option to surrender, had chosen to offer a courageous but futile resistance. Why Erdmenger, who had not even been in command of the action, was chosen for this distinction remains unknown. Neither he nor Henke appeared in the initial list of potential war criminals compiled by the United Nations War Crimes Commission, adding further proof that Op-16-W could only grasp at straws in identifying Kriegsmarine war criminals.[17]

With the deterioration of the military situation, however, the broadcasts gained in popularity. German submariners tuned in for the same reasons that American amateur radio operators listened to Radio Berlin— as a source of information on the fates of missing comrades. At the same time, the navy's propaganda improved with a reliance upon more accurate intelligence data. When Norden spoke of the navy's "launching" of more admirals than U-Boats over a given period, or the relative lack of high-level decorations to enlisted personnel, the issues raised actually brought about changes in Kriegsmarine policy.

For these reasons, postwar assessments cite the Norden broadcasts as a prime example of a successful psychological warfare operation.[18] The claimed credit for the "surrender" of U-Boat survivors in the water, however, exaggerates the success achieved.[19] The far more significant contribution—that the intelligence knowledge openly displayed by Norden facilitated the interrogations of U-Boat POWs—has not been systematically studied. A more appropriate question to ask might be: What did Op-16-W and its British counterparts hope to accomplish *at the time*?

In the course of 1943, an idea took root in the minds of senior Allied officials, particularly in Britain, that 1918 might repeat itself. The defeats in Russia, North Africa, and the Atlantic left Germany in a comparable military position to the last year of World War I, and Italy's withdrawal from the Axis in September 1943 recalled Austria-Hungary's peace manifesto two months before the Armistice. The 1918 analogy was developed on a point-by-point basis by the British War Cabinet's Joint Intelligence Subcommittee on 9 September 1943, which concluded that "Germany is, if anything, in a worse position today than she was at the same period in 1918. . . . The end will come when we have *broken Germany's will* to continue the struggle. . . . If therefore the Allies press home attacks by land and sea, maintain and intensify the air offensive, and pursue a vigorous political and propaganda campaign, we may [defeat Germany] before the end of the year" (emphasis added).[20]

Another British intelligence assessment of October 1943 compounded this wishful thinking with national stereotypes: "The Germans are a hard but brittle people and snap suddenly. It remains to be seen how long fear will make them endure."[21] Sir Arthur Harris, the head of RAF Bomber Command, sought to give life to these attitudes with an all-out area bombing campaign, which he predicted in August would "push Germany over by bombing this year."[22]

Op-16-W shared the same mentality. The text of a briefing lecture prepared for naval intelligence officers in September 1943 indicates the objectives of the Norden broadcasts:

> Let me impress this upon you with all the power at my command: It is not the first hundred Norden broadcasts which may be of decisive importance. It's the last ten, the last five, even the last one, conceivably, which may bear a message which can break the spirit of that enemy we have chosen for our target! The cumulative effect of the dozens and dozens of "Norden talks" already broadcast, and of those still to be written, cannot fail to play a part in the achievement of that purpose for which we are working—the complete breakdown of morale in the German Armed Forces, and, specifically, of the German Naval forces.[23]

By its own standards, Op-16-W's campaign failed. The reading of the vulnerability of German morale was as flawed as all those already quoted. Allied operational commands possessed a clearer view of German attitudes. In March 1944 the British Admiralty, when asked by Churchill about the quality and character of U-Boat crewmen captured, found "no marked deterioration in the fighting spirit of either officers or men while still engaged in war," nor "any proven cases of refusals to carry out orders by commanding officers or by crews"—even though 50 to 75 percent of the prisoners believed the war to be lost.[24]

Perhaps this accounts for the major change in emphasis when Werner Henke next appeared in a propaganda broadcast. In June 1944, the British black propaganda radio station, Soldatensender Calais, commenting on the reported loss of Henke, offered nothing but compliments concerning the U-Boat captain. Nothing was said about the *Ceramic*; rather Henke received praise for not following an alleged (and untrue) directive for the killing of shipwrecked survivors. At the time, no one realized that broadcast would become an obituary.[25]

NOTES

1. See the descriptions in Karl Alman, "Kapitänleutnant Werner Henke," *Der Landser-Ritterkreuzträger Nr. 2*, Nr. 680 (1971), 59; and in Hans Herlin, *Verdammter Atlantik. Schicksale deutscher U-Boot-Fahrer* (Munich: Wilhelm Heyne, 1982), 129–30.

2. Dönitz's comments are taken from the *U–515* KTB (after the entry of 6 January 1943) and from his *Memoirs: Ten Years and Twenty Days* (Annapolis, MD: Naval Institute Press, 1990), 282; Henke's personnel record provides the rest.

3. "Transcript of Shortwave Broadcast, Station Berlin, February 21, 1943,

Time 1810–1825 hrs.," among the intercepted radio broadcasts, Records of the Foreign Broadcast Intercept Service, RG 262, NA.

4. See Samuel Eliot Morison, *The Battle of the Atlantic 1939–1943* (Boston: Little, Brown and Co., 1975), 329–36.

5. See Lt. Cdr. Ralph Albrecht to Cdr. John L. Riheldaffer, "Enemy Broadcasts of P/W Messages and their reception and Dissemination in this Country," 19 April 1943, in file "Radio Broadcasts," Op-16-Z subject files, RG 38, NA.

6. See Clayton R. Koppes and Gregory D. Black, *Hollywood Goes to War: How Politics, Profits, and Propaganda Shaped World War II Movies* (Los Angeles: University of California Press, 1987), 114–19, 309–16, 356n.

7. This involved the sinking of the Greek steamer *Peleus* by *U–852* in the South Atlantic, 13 March 1944, as a result of which the submarine's captain, Kaptlt. Heinz Eck, and three of his officers were tried, convicted, and executed. See John Cameron, ed., *The "Peleus" Trial* (London: William Hodge and Co., Ltd., 1948).

8. See the account of NID 17-Z's propaganda in Peter Cremer, *U-Boat Commander* (Annapolis, MD: Naval Institute Press, 1984), 122–29.

9. On the organization and activities of Op-16-W see "United States Naval Administration in World War II: Office of Naval Intelligence," 1341–81, in the World War II Organizational Histories, OpArchives; William E. Daugherty, "Commander Norden and the German Admirals," in William E. Daugherty and Morris Janowitz, eds., *A Psychological Warfare Casebook* (Baltimore: Johns Hopkins University Press, 1958), 494–97; and, with caution, the accounts by Op-16-W staff member Ladislas Farago in his *Burn After Reading: The Espionage History of World War II* (New York: Walker and Company, 1961), 276–82; and Farago, *The Tenth Fleet* (New York: Paperback Library, 1964), 141–46. The records of Op-16-W, including transcripts of the "Norden" broadcasts, staff directives, and office correspondence are now located with other ONI records in RG 38, NA.

10. Office of War Information, Overseas Operations Branch, "For Week Feb. 5–12, 1943, Submarine Annex," Op-16-W subject file "Central Directives," RG 38, NA.

11. C.C.S. 155, "Conduct of the War in 1943," 18 January 1943, published in U.S. Department of State, *Foreign Relations of the United States: The Conferences at Washington, 1941–42, and Casablanca, 1943* (Washington, DC: Government Printing Office, 1968), 760.

12. In *Burn* (281–82), for example, Farago misspells Henke's name ("Hanke"), does not mention Radio Berlin's broadcast but refers to "secret intelligence reports" as the source for information about the *Ceramic*, and states that Henke was sunk a week after his own counterbroadcast—an error of one year. *Tenth Fleet* (146–50) corrects these factual errors, but invents conversations for Henke and erroneously places him in a POW camp at Papago Park, AZ, at the time of his death. Neither publication notes that the "Norden" broadcast on the *Ceramic* is a complete fabrication.

13. Broadcast practices are described in "Naval Administration," 1380, in OpArchives.

14. The original script of the broadcast, including annotations as to tone and emphasis, is located in file "Norden Broadcasts" among the Op-16-W subject

files, RG 38, NA; the English translation can be found in the "Norden Broadcasts" of CNO/ONI, World War II Command Files, OpArchives. A monitored German version, dated 30 March 1943, is appended to the war diary of *U–515* in the custody of the Bundesarchiv-Abt. Militärarchiv, Freiburg/Br.

15. See Bradley F. Smith, *Reaching Judgment at Nuremberg* (New York: Basic Books, Inc., 1977), 27–29, 247–65.

16. Op-16-Z, "Memorandum no. 939 for Op-16-W: Werner Henke, Klt.," 19 August 1943, Op-16-Z subject file "Memoranda for Op-16-W, nos. 900–1303 (July-December 1943)," RG 38, NA. This collection of memoranda represents the basic intelligence data forwarded to Op-16-W for use in the Norden broadcasts.

17. The actual commander, *Kommodore* Fritz Bonte, was killed shortly thereafter; see R. K. Lochner, *Als Das Eis Brach: Der Krieg zur See um Norwegen 1940* (Munich: Wilhelm Heyne Verlag, 1983), 176–84; and Norden Broadcast no. 34, "J'accuse-no. 2—KK. Erdmenger," 21 April 1943, Op-16-W subject files, RG 38, NA. The U.N. War Crimes Commission initial list of German criminals, December 1944, is located among the Miscellaneous Library Materials, National Archives Collection of World War II War Crimes Records, RG 238, NA.

18. Daugherty, "Commander Norden," 496–97; Robert D. Wells, "Persuading the U-Boats," *USNIP*, 90, 12 (December 1964), 53–59.

19. See the letters of Carl Strohmeyer and Roland E. Krause in response to Wells' article, in *USNIP*, 91, 4 (April 1965), 105–6.

20. J.I.C. (43) 367 Final, "Probabilities of a German Collapse: Report by the Joint Intelligence Subcommittee," 9 September 1943, in ABC File 381 Germany (1–29–43), Sec. 1-A, Records of the Operations Division (OPD), War Department General and Special Staffs, RG 165, NA.

21. General Headquarters India Intelligence Summary, 28 October 1943, in file 385/306 of the Ordnance Committee Data Files, 1940–45, Records of the Office of the Chief of Ordnance, RG 156, NA.

22. See Max Hasting's excellent *Bomber Command* (London: Michael Joseph, 1979), 306.

23. Untitled briefing in file "Lectures," Op-16-W subject files, RG 38, NA. The briefing refers to the Norden broadcasts "within the past eight months," thus September 1943.

24. Donald McLachlan, *Room 39. Naval Intelligence in Action 1939–1945* (London: Weidenfeld and Nicolson, 1968), 175–76.

25. Broadcast of *Soldatensender Calais* of 3 June 1944, copy in Op-16-W subject file "Broadcasts," RG 38, NA.

12

Night of the Long Knives

The crew of *U–515* reassembled in Lorient in early February 1943. The faces remained the same, except for a change in watch officers. Lieutenant Hashagen departed for final training before receiving his own command, *U–846*, in May 1943. Lieutenant Sauerberg moved up to replace Hashagen as first watch officer, while newly arrived Lt. Heinrich Niemeyer assumed the duties of II.W.O.

In equipment, *U–515* received some of the new torpedoes now being issued to all submarines. This included the familiar G7e electrical torpedo armed with a new detonator designated Pi–2 (for *Pistole*, pistol). This detonator restored the torpedo's capacity to explode by the proximity of the magnetic field generated by a ship's steel hull. A single torpedo would break the back of a ship if set at the proper depth. Potentially far more destructive than the simple contact torpedo, this weapon could double a U-Boat's ship-killing capabilities.[1]

U–515 slipped out of the massive Keroman bunker in Lorient on the late afternoon of 21 February 1943, destined for one of the longest and most eventful operational cruises of the war. It began, however, with the assertion of Allied air dominance as patrolling aircraft twice forced the U-Boat to submerge during the first night's voyage.

In accordance with standard procedure, crewmen were not informed of their ultimate destination until long after departure. Yet none could fail to notice that from the morning of 27 February they steered a westerly course. Only the officers knew that before dawn a radio signal arrived from BdU with the laconic message: "PROCEED TO ORDERED AREA AT NAVAL QUADRANT CA 50." *U–515* was headed toward New York.

The move reflected a dilemma that had confronted U-Boat Command since September 1942, when Dönitz finally attained a steady operational strength in the Atlantic of roughly 100 submarines. Yet because of the expanded capabilities of radio direction-finding equipment to pinpoint U-Boat radio transmissions, most Allied convoys continued to evade their opponents over the next four months. Moreover Dönitz, who on 30 January 1943 succeeded Raeder as commander in chief of the Kriegsmarine, how had to consider strategic needs beyond the tonnage war. To relieve the tightening Allied pressure against Rommel in Tunisia, for example, action was demanded against Allied supply lines to the Mediterranean.

To meet these challenges, Dönitz decided on the desperate measure of employing Type IX submarines for the same missions as those for Type VII U-Boats. Some would be committed to convoy battles in the North Atlantic, for which they were ill-equipped. Six Type IXC boats would be sent to operate off American ports, there to track and attack Gibraltar-bound convoys once the latter were beyond the protection of land-based aircraft. Given the strong state of American defenses, the vulnerability of the Type IXCs, and the Allies' renewed ability to read German radio messages, the mission amounted to little less than suicide.[2]

On the evening of 4 March, while northwest of the Azores en route to her destination, *U–515* encountered her first Allied merchant ship. The 8,300-ton British freighter *California Star*, sailing independently from Panama to Liverpool with 7,000 tons of food and general cargo, suspected nothing until two torpedoes slammed into her starboard side. Two more torpedoes (both armed with the magnetic detonator) finished her, with the loss of fifty of the seventy-four men on board. Henke took his submarine among the lifeboats, looking to take the captain prisoner, but had to settle instead for the merchantman's second officer. The sinking provided valuable experience with the new Pi–2 detonators, especially in determining the most effective depth-settings.

Henke spotted another steamer the next evening and immediately set out in pursuit. For once, however, an energetic chase was not enough. After a nine-and-one-half-hour pursuit at full speed, the U-Boat had not attained favorable conditions for an attack and the engines had begun to overheat. Reluctantly, Henke abandoned pursuit and resumed a westerly course.[3]

At this point Dönitz's New York plan was overtaken by developments. To try to keep the planned force of Type IXC boats together, *U–515* and two other boats already west of the Azores were slowed to allow the

other three boats to catch up. Then on 9 March, the German B-dienst—
operating at peak efficiency in the decryption of Allied convoy codes—
intercepted the radio signals of the fast Mediterranean-bound Convoy
UGF 6 that had just departed New York. As the convoy's course brought
it toward the U-Boats, Dönitz called off the dangerous coastal operation.
The next day, additional decrypts revealed the course and destination
of the slower Convoy UGS 6 as it left New York, leading to another
change in Dönitz's plans. The six boats would form a wolf pack—Group
Unverzagt—to operate against the slower convoy, giving the submarines
maximum time to prepare their ambush west of the Azores. A second
group of U-Boats would be deployed to the east in support. Unknown
to Dönitz, however, the ULTRA intercepts of German signals in turn
allowed the Allies to divert the convoy slightly to the north, to avoid
the heaviest submarine concentration.

Thus, for the first time *U–515* would participate in a set-piece convoy
battle. Six veteran U-Boats, with six others in support, would engage a
slow convoy of forty-three merchant ships and its escort of seven U.S.
Navy destroyers. The latter carried the latest type of radar, capable of
revealing a submarine's conning tower at a range of 10,000 meters; but
the destroyers lacked the HF/DF (high frequency/direction-finding)
equipment that disclosed the position of a radio-transmitting U-Boat in
the vicinity. With no Allied aircraft available, and with both sides making
use of communications intelligence, the combatants appeared evenly
matched.[4]

The first U-Boat to contact the convoy, *U–130* (Oblt. Siegfried Keller),
fell victim to the USS *Champlin* in the early hours of 13 March. At approximately the same time, *U–515* spotted the lights of a destroyer on
the darkened eastern horizon. Correctly assessing the warship as a part
of the starboard screen of the convoy, Henke sought to slip in behind
her when the Metox warned of radar contact. The destroyer turned and
attacked with shellfire as Henke submerged. The cascade of depth-
charges that followed could not mask the sounds of the convoy passing
directly overhead. The U-Boat eluded her pursuer and surfaced, but
immediately came under fire before Henke could transmit a message.
Again forced under and depth-charged, *U–515* could only wait it out
while the convoy escaped.

When Henke finally resurfaced, ten hours had passed since his initial
contact. He set off to the east in pursuit. That day three other boats of
the pack established contact with the convoy, but all were driven off at
a net cost to the Allies of only one straggling merchant ship sunk.

U–515 spent the 14th of March searching the horizon and following developments as reported over the radio. Three submarines did find the convoy that day, but the escorts kept them at bay. At midnight, Henke's Metox again picked up the radar pulses of one of the outlying destroyers. As no pursuit followed, however, it became apparent that the U-Boat had not been detected: Either the radar operator or his captain lacked experience. After a hurried conference with his officers and the radio operator, Henke found he could take bearings on the destroyer's radar pulses to guide him to the convoy. Within ninety minutes, Henke's lookouts had spotted the vessel, indicating the convoy was close by. At 0230, the appearance of shadows and masts on the starboard horizon betrayed the presence of UGS 6, slowly moving northeast. Henke immediately radioed BdU the convoy's position, course, and speed. Remaining at the limit of visibility, he drove forward to place himself in an advantageous attack position.

U–515 had nearly reached the head of the convoy when the Metox apparatus again detected probing radar pulses. This time, the operator at the other end of the set immediately recognized the image on his scope. A blast of shellfire announced the presence of the USS *Wainwright*, forcing the U-Boat to crash dive. A well-laid pattern of depth-charges followed, severely shaking the submarine. Mahnken's rapid assessments revealed damage to the diesel engines and a completely inoperative hydrophone system. Despite this condition, Henke doggedly set off in pursuit the next morning, notifying Dönitz of his situation.

Toward evening, Henke met *U–106* (Kaptlt. Hermann Rasch) and exchanged observations via signal lamp. Where Rasch preferred to get ahead of the convoy for an attack the next morning, Henke signaled his intention to try again that night. At 0200 the next morning he did regain contact, but once again the Metox warned of a destroyer that had locked on to the U-Boat's location. Another emergency dive and heavy depth-charging followed.

Henke's subsequent decision demonstrates his recognition of the difference between daring and recklessness. Without hydrophones, he could not hope to home in on potential targets for a submerged daylight attack; nor could he rely upon uncertain diesel engines for high-speed pursuit or night surface attacks. Reluctantly, he abandoned the action. *U–515* remained submerged for several hours while the engine-room staff worked to repair the diesels. When the boat surfaced that morning, Henke again reported his condition to BdU, requesting further orders and a replacement part for the hydrophones.[5]

The battle of Convoy UGS 6 continued until 19 March, when the intervention of land-based Allied aircraft and the exhaustion of his crews induced Dönitz to abandon the effort. On a couple of occasions, submerged U-Boats penetrated the destroyer screen to sink a total of three ships (the attackers claimed five). Though only one submarine was lost, most could not fight their way through the escorts. None had been able to execute a night surface attack, the preferred tactic in convoy actions. Without any air support, radar-equipped convoy escorts frustrated a wolf pack. The concurrent battles taking place on the North Atlantic lifelines claimed greater attention, but this smaller action demonstrated how technology and experience had begun to tip the balance of the Battle of the Atlantic to the Allies' advantage.[6]

For *U–515*, the frustrations and exhausting work did not end with the conclusion of the action. After extensive repairs to the engines and the engine clutches, the U-Boat again rendezvoused with the homeward-bound *U–106* to take on fuel and provisions. The refueling, the first for *U–515*, required sixteen difficult hours in moderate seas to complete. BdU then ordered the boat to join another convoy operation near the Canary Islands. A two-day running fight resulted only in constant submergings due to aircraft and escorts, without even the opportunity of a shot at a target. Another arduous refueling with *U–67* (Kaptlt. Günther Müller-Stockheim), lasting over seventeen hours, followed as *U–515* received fuel oil, food, and a hydrophone replacement part. This completed, Henke proceeded as directed by his latest orders to the West African port of Dakar.[7]

The strain of the patrol had begun to tell upon *U–515*'s crew. A long-standing personality conflict between the chief engineer and one of the senior machinists, doubtless exacerbated by the continued troubles with the diesels, gradually developed into a rift within the engineering staff, with the potential for an explosive confrontation.

No significant change of fortune accompanied the boat's arrival off Dakar, principal port of the French colony of Senegal. The collapse of Vichy and the declaration of French African colonies for De Gaulle yielded little in the way of easy pickings. *U–515* spent eight days cruising outside the harbor entrance, continually forced to submerge by aircraft during the day and by land-based radar contact at night. The limited ship traffic afforded few opportunities for attacks. Only once did Henke catch a vessel within easy range of his torpedoes, dispatching the French motorship *Bamako* (2,357 tons) with two shots in the early hours of 9 April. Three days later he set off after a southward-bound convoy, but a seventy-two-hour pursuit accomplished nothing beyond the consumption of fuel. New orders then directed Henke to the area southwest of Freetown, in the hope of intercepting Allied shipping as it rounded the bulge of west Africa.[8]

This stretch involved crossing the equator, an event traditionally accompanied by a rite-of-passage ceremony among sailors. The occasion also offered the crew a badly needed opportunity to put aside the strains and disappointments of the previous two months. The veterans of the crew who had crossed the equator earlier in their careers prepared to "baptize" the novices making their first passage. On 22 April, the moment arrived. One of the initiates, *Matrosenobergefreiter* Hans Hahn, describes the event:

> A red carpet was laid out on the afterdeck. A rubber life raft, filled with water, was placed over the side. Now came crewmen attired as Neptune, his daughter Thetis, and two attendants—these were the veterans. Each initiate was individually called. First we were placed in the raft and soaped up, then the attendants held us while an old cleaning brush was thrust into our mouths to "brush our teeth." We had to swallow pills made of salt, pepper, and fat to make us "healthy" for the crossing. Then we were washed off with a hose, put back into the raft, and held under the water for a considerable time. Finally we had to crawl along the carpet to King Neptune, whose feet had been smeared with engine grease. Naturally, we had to kiss his feet. Afterward, we cleaned ourselves off in the raft and received a drink of schnaps, together with a "baptism" certificate.[9]

Following the ceremony, *U–515* entered another of those interludes on patrol when the war vanished. For more than two weeks, not a single Allied ship or plane was seen. The enemy became the heat that reached over 100-degrees Fahrenheit below decks, and even more in the engine-room spaces. All hands, including Henke, stripped down to shorts, but nothing helped against the oppressive heat and humidity. April also marked the beginning of the rainy season, when severe thunderstorms and squalls could develop quickly, drenching all on deck in seconds.

On the morning of 25 April, the war returned with the sighting of a British Sunderland flying boat. Henke dived, but was not observed. Later that morning, another Sunderland could be seen in the distance. The presence of Allied aircraft usually signified the end of U-Boat action against convoys, Henke reasoned; why should it not work the other way around? A shouted exchange of orders and confirmations headed *U–515* toward the position and course of the aircraft, closer in toward the coast.

Henke's strategy paid off. On 27 April, the smoke of a merchant steamer about twenty miles away enticed Henke into another full-speed chase, but a Catalina aircraft forced *U–515* to dive and lose contact. The next morning, after the submarine had routinely submerged to avoid morning air patrols, a series of depth-charges suddenly detonated in the near distance. Within an hour the radioman operating the hydrophones picked up the propellors of several fast ships nearby. More depth-charges followed as a destroyer passed directly over the U-Boat's position. Henke came to periscope depth to observe a cruiser, four destroyers, and two troop-laden passenger liners steaming northwest.

For the first time in months, *U–515* prepared to launch an underwater torpedo attack. At a distance of 5,000 meters, the Allied ships lay at the extreme range of the U-Boat's torpedoes, but even a slim chance had to be tried. Aiming at the overlapping targets of the cruiser and one of the liners, Henke fired a double shot. Eight minutes later, two distant explosions marked the torpedoes' harmless detonations at the end of their runs. Henke surfaced as the vessels disappeared toward Freetown. *Fünffünfzehn*'s bad luck, it seemed, would not end.

The next day, however, fortune turned when the submarine experienced its narrowest escape. In the early afternoon a Catalina flying boat of the RAF's 270 Squadron, emerging suddenly from the cover of some passing dark clouds, surprised *U–515*. There was no time to submerge; a guncrew quickly manned the 20mm mount on the conning tower as the submarine swung a tight circle to starboard. At a range of 300 yards, the 20mm opened fire, scoring several hits on the plane's underside. The hits and the submarine's turn spoiled the Catalina's aim, as the stick of 6 Torpex depth-bombs fell harmlessly 50 feet aft of the U-Boat. While the flying boat banked, the German sailors scampered back through the hatches and *U–515* crash dived to safety.[10]

While the crew rightly congratulated the flak gunner on his marksmanship, they never suspected how fortunate they had been. The Catalina's appearance had not been accidental. When Henke radioed the report of his abortive attack the previous day, Allied radio direction-finders picked up the transmission and fixed the U-Boat's general position.[11] The Catalina and other aircraft were specifically sent to the area to look for a submarine, and they did not give up after the first attack. Twice more during the evening of 29 April, *U–515* submerged to avoid prying Catalinas.

Most of the next day, 30 April, passed quietly underwater for the submarine. When she surfaced in the afternoon to "air out" the interior, lookouts noted the severe thunderstorms and a line of squalls passing through the area. The boat returned to the safety of the depths for the rest of the daylight hours. At 2041 hours, *U–515* came to the surface for a look around in the last half-hour of daylight. Twenty-one minutes later, lookouts observed smoke plumes about fifteen miles to the southeast. In the fading light, the plumes gradually revealed a formation of several columns of ships.

From the moment it had left Takoradi on the Gold Coast (now Ghana) on 26 April, Convoy TS 37 had not engendered much confidence among the merchant captains who had entrusted their ships to the voyage. Bound for Freetown, they would traverse a stretch long known as a U-Boat hunting area with only four escorts—a corvette and three trawlers—for eighteen merchant vessels. Everything depended on adequate air cover from the several Allied airfields on the West African coast. But all recognized that with the onset of the rainy season, air cover could not be guaranteed.

Nevertheless, continuous air escorts for four-hour intervals at dawn and dusk ensured an uneventful passage until midday on 29 April, when news of Henke's monitored radio transmission alerted the convoy to the threat. All necessary precautions were taken. Around noon on 30 April, the naval escort commander chased and depth-charged what he believed to be a submarine: In fact, it was merely a false contact. When the air escorts arrived at 1507 hours (Greenwich mean time, two hours behind *U–515*'s chronometer), the escort commander diverted the flight to follow up his attack on the "presumed damaged" U-Boat. The planes searched fruitlessly for an hour, then returned to the convoy just as the latter entered a line of squalls and electrical storms. The turbulent weather forced the planes to abort their mission and, at 1620 hours— twenty-one minutes before Henke surfaced—they began their return to base.

As the last planes banked, the convoy's naval escort commander visually signaled that a submarine's radio transmissions had been detected in the vicinity, requesting the aircraft to forward a request for reinforcements to British forces in Freetown. British authorities later wondered why the escort commander adamantly maintained radio silence instead of immediately calling for help, as the aircraft could not pass along the message until after its return to base. To the ill-timed intervention of bad weather, TS 37's misfortunes now added questionable judgment of its escort commander.[12]

Aboard *U–515*, Henke and his officers reckoned the convoy to include fourteen merchantmen, three destroyers, and five smaller escorts. In the darkness, the convoy did not zigzag but followed a steady north-westerly course. The Metox set soon indicated the presence of radar probes, so the submarine moved out of range and took cover in a line of showers. Overestimating the number of escorts, Henke judged it best to avoid the front and flank of the convoy and unobtrusively slip into the rear. Nearly two hours of careful maneuvering brought him unobserved into the middle of the convoy, with stern tubes bearing on the last ships in the port columns and bow tubes aiming at the first ships in the starboard columns.

The moonless, showery night permitted only limited visibility, aided occasionally by lightning flashes and a moderate sea. At 2256, *U–515* began her attack. In 5 minutes of shouted commands and twisting maneuvers, the submarine fired 6 torpedoes—all with magnetic detonators, set at 5 meters—at 6 separate targets. In the excitement and confusion, Henke believed that all had struck home. In fact, the stern shots missed their marks, but each of the 4 forward torpedoes claimed a victim: freighter *Corabella*, 5,682 tons, carrying a cargo of manganese, sunk in 17 minutes; the 7,295-ton Dutch freighter *Kota Tjandi*, with a cargo of potash and tin, sunk in 10 minutes; the 6,551-ton steamer *Nagina*, carrying nearly 3,000 tons of pig iron, sunk in 3 minutes; and British freighter *Bandar Shahpour*, 5,236 tons and loaded with manganese ore, exact time of sinking unknown.

With star shells bursting overhead, Henke saw what he believed to be a destroyer heading straight for him, and immediately ordered a crash dive. At a depth of 170 meters, the crew began reloading the torpedo tubes as the corvette's depth-charges exploded harmlessly above them. After more than two hours, *U–515* surfaced to a sea covered with wreckage. Henke spotted one of the escorts, a trawler, recovering survivors, and immediately made for her. For reasons not clear, the attempt to attack the escort miscarried; and with no other targets in sight, Henke set off in pursuit of the convoy.

At 0513, Henke's lookouts regained contact. Despite its losses, the convoy held course and formation as before. The submarine drove across the convoy's rear and established position on the starboard side, where

Henke could fire into the heart of the formation. At 0540, he and Sauerberg released three torpedoes at three targets. This time, Henke did not err when he observed all strike home.

The 4,996-ton Belgian freighter *Mokambo*, bearing a cargo of copper, cotton, copal, and palm kernels, received the first hit at 0528 (0328 Greenwich mean time). The blow ignited a fire that spread to the cargo holds, yet the ship remained afloat for nearly 2 days before capsizing while under tow. British steamer *City of Singapore* (6,555 tons), carrying 2,700 tons of pig iron and over 6,000 tons of Indian nuts and produce, took a torpedo on the starboard quarter two minutes after *Mokambo*, and sank within 7 minutes. Finally, the 6,940-ton freighter *Clan Macpherson*, also loaded with 2,700 tons of pig iron, was struck on the starboard beam and abandoned within 10 minutes. As she remained afloat, the crew later reboarded her, but the flooding could not be stopped and she sank that morning.

The convoy's corvette and a trawler finally spotted *U–515* and attacked. Henke submerged, but discovered that the water depth stood less than 250 feet, dangerously shallow when pursued by sonar and depth-charges. By creeping along the bottom toward deeper water, and taking full advantage of the varying density layers that confounded sonar, Henke made off to the southwest as the sound of depth-charges faded in the distance.[13]

For one night, Werner Henke and his crew had turned back the clock to the U-Boat "happy times" of 1940. A single U-Boat in a night surface attack had savaged a weakly escorted convoy lacking air cover. Henke's seven sinkings during the night of 30 April–1 May 1943 matched the performance of Joachim Schepke and *U–100* against Convoy SC 11 in November 1940, and exceeded Otto Kretschmer's accomplishment (six sinkings, one damaged) against Convoy SC 7 in September 1940.[14] The new Pi–2 magnetic detonators contributed greatly to this success: Seven hits in nine shots with seven sinkings offered a sharp contrast to the pattern of his first patrol, when twenty-three torpedoes and eighteen hits were required to sink ten ships.

Remarkably, the loss of life aboard TS 37's sunken vessels was light. Only 22 of 611 crewmen and passengers (less than 4%) died in the attacks, a total that would have been much greater had Henke succeeded in sinking the escort vessel picking up survivors. The loss of the ships and their precious cargoes of raw materials, however, greatly embarrassed the British government. Prime Minister Winston Churchill described the incident as "deplorable," and the War Cabinet demanded a report from the Secretary of State for Air on the lack of proper air cover for the convoy.[15]

The remainder of *U–515*'s patrol, however, gradually dissipated the enthusiasm and high morale resulting from the action. For more than a month the boat patrolled the area between Togo and Liberia, dodging constant air patrols while encountering little merchant traffic. In the predawn hours of 9 May the U-Boat found the Norwegian fighter *Corneville* (4,544 tons) en route from Capetown to Takoradi with a load of silk, tea, and pig iron. Two contact torpedoes sent her to the bottom, though the entire crew got off safely. On 13 May, BdU ordered Henke to rendezvous with *U–460* (Kaptlt. Ebe Schnoor), a Type XIV "milk cow" supply submarine, to receive more fuel, food, and torpedoes to extend their patrol.[16]

During the refueling on 22 May, the smoldering conflict between Chief Engineer Mahnken and his senior machinist finally exploded. The fuel oil intake line loosened from its intake valve, spraying the contents onto the deck. Mahnken accused his antagonist of sabotage, adding other charges from incidents earlier in the patrol. Henke backed his subordinate and transferred the machinist under arrest to *U–460*. There he was confined in a narrow compartment for the voyage home. Many of *U–515*'s engine-room personnel considered the punishment unjustified and held Mahnken equally culpable in the conflict. After nearly fifty years, the memory of this incident still rankles *U–515* veterans.[17]

Other events carried more worrisome implications. While pursuing a convoy west of Liberia during the night of 1 June, destroyers twice surprised Henke without prior warnings from the Metox radar detector. During the second attack, well-placed depth-charges inflicted damage on the boat at a depth of 180 meters (nearly 600 ft.). A similar experience occurred less than a week later, this time knocking out torpedo tube IV. The incidents added to a growing body of evidence that the Allies now employed a new type of radar, one that employed centimeter wave lengths too short to be detected by Metox.[18]

Even more significant, though unrecognized by those aboard *U–515* at the time, was the growing contribution of ULTRA intelligence. On 11 June, shortly after turning back, Henke radioed a lengthy message to BdU with all his observations and recommendations on shipping and defenses in the area, for the use of the next boats to operate there. The message, duly intercepted and decrypted by Allied intelligence, aided the British in preventing any repeat performance by submarines off Freetown.[19]

The immediate concern to Henke at this time centered on the damage suffered in the recent attacks, complicated by continued problems with the engine clutches: malfunctions here might not allow the boat to submerge. The extent of damage convinced Henke to take the risk of all-day surface cruising to return to port as quickly as possible. Swinging wide to the west of Gibraltar and its strong air cover, U–515 angled back to the northwest tip of Spain, hugged the Spanish coast into the Bay of Biscay, then cut a diagonal straight across to Lorient. Escorted by three torpedo boats, the submarine docked on the afternoon of 24 June.

Thus ended one of the most remarkable U-Boat patrols of World War II. In 124 days, U–515 traveled 20,383 nautical miles, sank 10 Allied merchant ships totalling nearly 58,500 tons, and endured 9 depth-chargings, one air attack, and 43 crash dives to avoid aircraft. (By contrast, the longest American submarine patrol of World War II—by USS *Guitaro*, December 1943–March 1944—lasted 83 days; and only USS *Tang* sank as many as 10 ships on one patrol, in June–July 1944.)[20] By any standard, the patrol constituted an extraordinary feat of endurance and accomplishment.

But for the men of *Fünf-fünfzehn*, the patrol's numbers boiled down to physical and mental exhaustion—of lookouts straining for ships and planes on the horizon, of machinists struggling with diesel engines in 100-degree heat, of radiomen constantly scanning through the squawks and whistles of the Metox set for the trace of a radar pulse. Mahnken's conflict with his machinist, and the eventual arrest of the latter, left a bitter memory. The strain was made worse by extended periods of tedium—on seventy-three complete days of this patrol, not a single ship or plane was seen. So long accustomed to the rhythm of the deck and the sea, the mens' legs collapsed on contact with the unyielding hardness of dry land, and escorts had to help each onto shore.

Not until long afterward would they realize that, during their patrol, the U-Boats had lost the Battle of the Atlantic.

NOTES

1. For a succinct discussion of German torpedoes at this time, see Robert C. Stern, *Type VII U-Boats* (Annapolis, MD: Naval Institute Press, 1991), 78–84.

2. *U–515* KTB; KTB BdU, 27 February, 5 March, and 5 May 1943, T1022/4064/ PG 30318–19, 30323; Jak P. Mallmann Showell, *U-Boat Command and the Battle of the Atlantic* (Lewiston, NY: Vanwell, 1989), 137–48; and Jürgen Rohwer, *The Critical Convoy Battles of March 1943* (Annapolis, MD: Naval Institute Press, 1977), 49, 212–13. Examples of intercepted messages to and from Henke on 27–28

February, decrypted and read by Allied intelligence on 1 March, are reproduced as SRGN nos. 12520, 12551, and 12586, SRGN Collection, RG 457, NA.

3. *U–515* KTB; "Report of an Interview with the Master, Captain S. Foulkes, SS *California Star*," 19 April 1943, file ADM 199/2144 (XC009458), PRO.

4. KTB BdU, 9–10 and 12 March 1943, T1022/4064/PG 30319; Rohwer, *Convoy Battles*, 79–81. On the radio intelligence aspects of the period, see also Heinz Bonatz, *Seekrieg im Äther. Die Leistungen der Marine-Funkaufklärung 1939–1945* (Herford: E. S. Mittler & Sohn, 1981), 241–43.

5. *U–515* KTB; *U–106* KTB, 14–15 March 1943, T1022/3034/PG 30102; "Report of Proceedings-Convoy UGS6," 12 May 1943, in Tenth Fleet Routing and Convoy Files, OpArchives; and SRGN intercept nos. 13239, 13245, and 13318, RG 457, NA. Rasch's war diary provides an interesting contrast to Henke's; he recorded all radio messages and many details not found in Henke's more laconic entries.

6. See Rohwer, *Convoy Battles*, 82–86; and Günter Hessler, *The U-Boat War in the Atlantic 1939–1945* (London: Her Majesty's Stationery Office, 1989), pt. 2, 97–98.

7. *U–515* KTB (18 March–2 April 1943); KTB BdU, 29–31 March 1943, T1022/4064/PG 30320; and *U–67* KTB, 1–2 April 1943, T1022/3030/PG 30064 (Müller-Stockheim's account of the refueling is far more detailed than Henke's).

8. *U–515* KTB; KTB BdU, 11–12 and 19 April 1943, T1022/4064/PG 30321–322.

9. Letter of Hans Hahn to author, 1 July 1991.

10. *U–515* KTB; ASW Assessment Incident no. 5014, "Catalina 'D' of 270 Squadron, attack of 29 April 1943, time 1133Z," in Tenth Fleet ASW Analysis and Statistical Section, OpArchives. The Catalina acknowledged only one hit by the U-Boat's gunners.

11. A copy of the message cannot be identified, as the radio appendices to Henke's war diary do not include this patrol, and Henke did not record messages in the text of the war diary; a search of the SRGN radio intercepts in RG 457 reveals a gap for the period 27–30 April 1943, possibly an interval when decryptions were temporarily unobtainable. Nevertheless, Henke's sighting and attack called for a report, and a transmission was monitored (noted in the Minute from the Secretary of State for Air to the Prime Minister, "The Air Protection of Convoys," 8 May 1943, file "Anti-U-Boat Warfare Committee, War Cabinet, May–June 1943," CINCUS/COMNAVEU subject files, RG 38, NA).

12. The story of the air escorts is taken from the Minute of the Secretary of State for Air, "Air Protection of Convoys"; other criticisms and the anecdote regarding the visual signal to the aircraft appear in Chief of Naval Operations, "Summary of Statements by Survivors of SS *Clan Macpherson*," 12 June 1943, WWII Command Files, OpArchives. The latter is also noted in Stephen W. Roskill, *The War at Sea 1939–1945* (3 vols. in 4 pts.; London: Her Majesty's Stationery Office, 1954–61), vol. 2, 371–72. The possibility remains, however, that *U–515* was picked up on the corvette's radar, as noted in Henke's war diary, rather than by radio transmissions.

13. *U–515* KTB; summaries of statements by survivors for all seven ships in World War II Command Files, OpArchives; and equivalent interviews of survivors of the same vessels among the records of the Shipping Casualties Section-Trade Division, file ADM 199/2145 (XC009488), PRO.

14. Letter from Dr. Jürgen Rohwer to author, 4 October 1988. In addition, Kretschmer sank six ships from Convoy HX 112 in March 1941 before his own *U–99* was lost. *Kapitän zur See* Karl Neitzel and *U–510* actually torpedoed eight ships of Brazilian Convoy BT 6 in March 1943, but five survived to sail again.

15. Roskill, *War at Sea*, vol. 2, 372; War Cabinet, Anti-U-Boat Warfare, minutes of 17th and 18th Meetings, 5 and 12 May 1943, in CINCUS/COMNAVEU subject file "War Cabinet May–June 1943," RG 38, NA.

16. *U–515* KTB; "Summary of Statement of Survivors of MV *Corneville*," 9 July 1943, WW II Command Files, OpArchives; radio messages of BdU to *U–460*, 16 May 1943; and Henke to BdU, 18 May 1943, SRGN intercept nos. 18320 and 18451, RG 457, NA.

17. Interestingly, the KTB of *U–515* makes no reference whatsoever to this incident; a description of its final stages can be found in the KTB of *U–460* for 23 May 1943 (T1022/2888/PG 30513). According to Carl Möller, a subsequent court-martial in which all the officers and most of the engine-room staff gave testimony resulted in the machinist's loss of rank and assignment to a punishment battalion (letter to author, 21 November 1987; and interview with author, Hamburg, 30 August 1989). The incident was the subject of a lively discussion at the May 1992 reunion in Lübbenau.

18. *U–515* KTB; Stern, *Type VII*, 124.

19. Henke's message is reproduced in the KTB BdU, 1 June 1943 (T1022/4064/PG 30325); and as SRGN intercept nos. 19677–678, RG 457, NA. On Allied countermeasures in the area, see the U.S. Navy's Op-20-G report, "Battle of the Atlantic, vol. 2: U-Boat Operations (Dec. 1942–June 1945)," 166–66b, Study no. SRH–008, RG 457, NA.

20. Clay Blair, Jr., *Silent Victory: The U.S. Submarine War Against Japan* (New York: Bantam Books, 1976), 952, 966.

13

Such Things at Home

The interval from June to August 1943 gradually brought home to the crew of *U–515* the true state of Germany's military situation. The education began in their home port of Lorient.

Before departing on their third patrol, most of the crew experienced the heavy RAF and U.S. Army Air Force raids from 14 January to 17 February 1943 that gutted the former French naval base and most of the city. Previously quartered with other Tenth U-Boat Flotilla personnel in the former music school known as the Hundius Kaserne, Henke's men had been forced to improvise when the buildings suffered severe damage. Now, as they returned to their home port, they could see that very little remained standing. Another large-scale American attack on 16 April had finished the destruction. Gone for the duration were the cafés, brothels, and the lavishly furnished *U-Heim* (U-Boat recreation center) that had provided so many comforts in the past. Of the officers' lounge in the *Prefecture*, where Henke had listened to the tales of U-Boat aces in 1940–41, nothing remained.

Ironically, the principal Allied targets, the U-Boat pens, emerged virtually unscathed because of the tremendous strength of the concrete bunkers protecting them. *U–515* normally tied up in either the Scorff bunker or one of three Keroman bunkers, the walls of each of which measured up to 11.5 feet thick. As Dönitz remarked of the destruction of St. Nazaire and Lorient, "Not a dog is left in these towns. Nothing remains—but the U-Boat shelters."[1]

The crew found themselves trucked to temporary new quarters at Kerneval, the former site of Dönitz's headquarters outside Lorient. Separate bunkers there housed the officers, petty officers, and enlisted personnel of the Tenth Flotilla until the permanent facilities at Lager Lemp near Pont Scorff, about sixteen miles north of Lorient, could be completed. The latter camp promised to provide complete living and recreational facilities for the personnel of both the Tenth and Second U-Boat Flotillas stationed in Lorient. Doubtless the well-camouflaged complex of wooden and concrete barracks impressed the crewmen, but it equally underscored the acknowledgment of a long-term struggle.[2]

Nevertheless, the immediate period after *U–515*'s return did not diminish the festivities that accompanied the completion of a long and successful patrol. A special surprise also awaited them: From his Flotilla Chief, Kaptlt. Günther Kuhnke, Henke learned that his actions had earned him the coveted Oak Leaves Cluster to his Knight's Cross of the Iron Cross, to be awarded by the führer himself.

In Lorient the flotilla celebrated the victorious submarine's accomplishments with a formal review and all due ceremonies. Many crewmen received the Iron Cross, First Class, for their performance during the patrol. A reception followed with lunch and the division of letters and packets from German civilians, distributed at large to U-Boat crewmen upon return from long patrols. Carl Möller recalls that at one time he was answering the letters of three "pen pals" from different parts of Germany.[3]

Completely unknown to the crew at this time was the extent of the horrific U-Boat losses suffered during the course of their long patrol. Forty-one submarines had been sunk in May 1943 alone, the first time in more than three years that the total lost exceeded the number commissioned. At the same time, the rate of sinkings of merchant ships declined to its lowest rate of the war, a mere sixty-four tons per U-Boat per day at sea.

During her patrol *U–515* had encountered some of the reasons for the Allied victory. The new 10-centimeter radar installed aboard convoy escorts and aircraft could not be detected by the Metox search receivers, exposing many surfaced U-Boats to attacks for which they were not prepared. More long-range Allied aircraft had now joined in the campaign, effectively closing the "air gap" that had benefited submarines in the central North Atlantic. The increased production of escort vessels moreover allowed convoy escorts to assume the offensive against attacking U-Boats without endangering the convoys.

The reality, if not the exact figures, could not be evaded among the Type VIIC crews who bore the brunt of these losses in the North Atlantic convoy battles. The crews at Lorient, however, manned the Type IXCs that largely escaped the May massacre. Of the twenty-nine submarines that comprised the Tenth Flotilla on 5 March 1943, for example, only two were lost in May 1943, and none at all in June. Lacking contact with other submariners, the Lorient crews would have to wait their turn to feel the full weight of Allied supremacy at sea.[4]

Thus, when *U–515*'s men left on home leave they did not comprehend how badly the war was going until their trains brought them to Germany. The devastation wrought by Allied air raids, particularly in the Ruhr, provided them with a rude awakening.

Crewman Gerhard Fehling, not quite 19, journeyed home to visit a widowed mother living in Wuppertal-Barmen. Two massive night raids by the RAF on 29–30 May and 24–25 June 1943 leveled the twin cities, killing approximately 5,200 inhabitants, injuring several thousand others, and destroying nearly 7,000 homes. Fehling doubtless spent his leave assisting his mother in the salvage of belongings and the repair of what could be mended.

Bruno Deussen was less fortunate. He returned to Düsseldorf to find his father and sisters among the 1,300 killed by the raid of 11–12 June that burned out 130 acres of the city's center. During his furlough he settled his wife in a small town in Alsace, out of the bombs' path. Carl Möller and Heinrich Lamprecht had just completed their furloughs in Hamburg and returned to base when RAF incendiary attacks on 27–28 July produced a raging firestorm in the aged port, leaving over 40,000 inhabitants dead. Both crewmen faced the prospect of returning to combat without knowing whether or not their families were still alive.[5]

The crewmembers not directly affected by these raids perceived that it might only be a matter of time before the same rain of destruction visited their own towns and cities, a fear all too often realized by the time they next returned home in January 1944. Little could be accomplished in the course of an ordinary furlough, and the recognition that several months would pass before the next possible leave only increased the general feeling of impotence. It was one thing to sweat out a depth-charge pounding at sea, quite another to realize your family stood more vulnerable to enemy attack than you.

German military and naval authorities exacerbated this situation by a strict adherence to regulations and standard bureaucratic procedures consistent with peacetime conditions, but hardly suited to wartime realities. Whether on duty in Lorient or at home on leave, U-Boat crewmen remained subject to a mass of regulations, standing orders, and special orders whose relevance grew daily more questionable. Precise rules governed such issues as the carrying of sidearms and ammunition on leave, the proper use of separate leave and transportation passes, "unsoldierly" lengths of hair and sideburns, fines for lost items of clothing and equipment, and the strictly defined eligibility of personnel on leave to take home supplementary rations to their families.[6]

Responsible for enforcing these policies were two categories of personnel who especially antagonized U-Boat crewmen: the Feldgendarmerie (military police), more popularly known as *Kettenhunde* (watchdogs), and navy officers who took it upon themselves to safeguard the standards of conduct of noncommissioned and enlisted ranks on shore. These officers generally represented administrative or technical specialists who wore silver braid to distinguish them from gold-braided line officers. The disparaging term *Silberlinge* (silverlings) thus came into use by combat veterans to describe them.

U–515's crewmen fell afoul of both categories of authority during their stays in port. As with other top crews, however, they shared the advantage of a captain who stood behind his men. Harsh disciplinarian though he might be on board, Henke regularly supported his crew in conflicts with shore-based officials, at some risk to himself.

En route home with the BdU-Zug (the train that carried U-Boat crewmen home on leave and their commanders to BdU headquarters in Berlin), the usual stopover in Paris resulted in Henke and several of the men taking in a floor show at the opera. The boisterous behavior of the crewmen drew the attention of one *Silberling*, who remonstrated with Henke to quiet his men. Henke ignored him. The official returned with several military policemen who compelled them all to leave, though not before a heated exchange between the U-Boat commander and the official. The crewmen afterward learned that the incident had been reported to higher authority, with strong criticism of Henke.

Carl Möller recalled Henke's personal intervention on his behalf on a number of occasions. On a trip to Rennes with another crewman to pick up some needed machine parts, the two submariners stopped off in a cafe for a drink. Military policemen followed them in and, upon determining that the sailors had no authorization for refreshment, arrested them. Henke secured their release. Another time Möller was arrested and held for three days in Lorient for "conduct unbecoming a representative of the Wehrmacht in occupied territory." Within twenty-four hours, Henke approached the flotilla chief to reduce his machinist's punishment to time served and return him to the submarine.[7]

Thus Henke's status allowed him some freedom to mitigate the influence of external authority on his crew. But what would happen if Henke himself fell victim to such forces?

For Werner Henke, this home leave proved the most eventful of his career. First he traveled to Berlin to make his report to U-Boat Headquarters, which in March 1943 had relocated from Paris to Steinplatz in Berlin-Charlottenburg. There he doubtless learned of the massive defeat suffered on the convoy routes in May 1943. Very likely he was briefed on the heightened significance of his own long-range, solo operations as a holding action in the Battle of the Atlantic until improved weaponry and new models of submarines could reverse the scales in Germany's favor.

Henke then headed on to the führer headquarters, designated the *Wolfsschanze* (wolf's lair) located east of Rastenburg in East Prussia (now Poland). When Henke arrived on 4 July, the dense forests and marshland probably reminded him of his native Thorn, and of the long path he had taken to this moment, the apogee of his career. That afternoon he and several other navy officers entered one of the barracks at the complex and stood at attention as Adolf Hitler personally presented each with his decoration. Henke received a black-hinged case containing the Oak Leaves device to attach to his Knight's Cross, with the personal thanks of the führer. As only the 257th recipient of the decoration, and only the thirty-third naval officer, Werner Henke had joined a truly select company.

No textual records accompany the photographs that document the event; therefore, the precise remarks and impressions have been lost. It would not have been uncommon for Hitler to have invited his navy guests to lunch or a tea, as he had shortly before with other decorated U-Boat commanders. If so, he doubtless solicited their views on weapons and tactics, as Hitler always preferred observations of front-line soldiers over staff officers. He also would have discussed with them the latest information on the U-Boat models under development, which he promised to accord top priority in production. Four days later, in meetings with Dönitz and Reich Armaments Minister Albert Speer, Hitler kept his promise. The prospect of a new generation of submarines buoyed Hitler in his talks with military and political leaders for the next several months.[8]

Now one of the highest decorated heroes of the National Socialist state, Henke left for a brief vacation to the Tyrol. There he immediately plunged into conflict with the Gestapo.

In the last years of peace, Henke had grown fond of Innsbruck as a vacation spot. Not only did he enjoy the skiing opportunities there, he had also formed friendships with residents of the area. Among these he counted the Proxauf family, who operated a small drapery store in the town. When he stopped by to visit, he learned that the family had recently endured questioning and rough treatment at the hands of the local Gestapo on some issue (the available documents do not record the subject of interest). The youngest daughter in particular was verbally browbeaten and physically threatened.

Henke wasted no time. On the morning of 19 July, two weeks after leaving Hitler's chambers, the U-Boat war hero visited the offices of both *Gauleiter* Franz Hofer, Nazi governor of the Austrian Tyrol and the Vorarlberg, and the Innsbruck Gestapo. According to the latter's report

> Kaptlt. Henke inquired in a very irritated manner about the status of the Proxauf affair. He considered the Gestapo's handling of the case an injustice, as he knew the Proxauf family to be one of the finest in all of the Reich. It was a disturbing feeling for him to serve at the front when decent families were so callously and brutally treated in the rear.

The SS *Sturmbannführer* calmed Henke with assurances that no injustices had been committed and that the entire matter had been turned over to local authorities for a decision. Henke allegedly left in a quiet and friendly manner.

Four days later, however, he returned to the *Gauleiter's* office in a white-hot anger. Without stretching the imagination, one may infer that some local authority intimated to the Proxaufs what might happen to them once their decorated protector returned to the front. Henke demanded to see Hofer or his deputy, both of whom refused. The U-Boat ace could only vent his anger on the receptionist, one Frau Leuk, who recorded his words precisely: "It is unacceptable for Gestapo officials, who leave the impression of the Soviet secret police and who look like gangsters, to treat decent people in the manner in which the Proxauf ladies have been treated. . . . You can't expect me to hold my head up at the front when such things happen at home."

Frau Leuk again tried to inform Henke that the Proxaufs had misrepresented their case to him, but Henke would have none of it. Promising to take up the matter with higher authorities in Berlin, he "left the room in a rage, slamming both doors loudly behind him."[9]

Against the sea of crimes committed by National Socialism, this incident is all but imperceptible. No atrocities were involved, merely one of the routine, petty brutalities of a police state. What distinguishes the case is Henke's involvement: an instinctive reaction to seeing friends pushed around by the arbitrary power of the state, and by a decorated and honored officer of the state. Henke's action cannot be seen as a conscious act of political opposition, yet to the Gestapo it signified something potentially very dangerous. It was for this reason they so precisely noted Henke's words and actions, and so promptly notified the navy to take corrective action.

While the paperwork wound its way through the bureaucracy, Henke returned to his family home in Scharnebeck near Lüneburg. With his brother Albrecht home on convalescent leave for a mouth infection, the entire Henke family was reunited for the first time in two years. For a few days, the war disappeared as all celebrated past memories and Werner's current success. When Werner packed and left for Lorient, the last reunion of the Henke family was over.[10]

Already the object of attacks from the authorities in Paris over the opera incident, and the Innsbruck Gestapo over the Proxaufs, Henke promptly used a party in his honor at the flotilla headquarters in Lorient to antagonize a superior officer. Among the officers attending the party to congratulate him, Henke noted one of his previous commanding officers who had punished him with a disciplinary action—as more than one individual fits this description, his precise identity is not known. In one of his most spiteful acts, Henke refused to acknowledge his presence and kept turning his back to the individual whenever the latter tried to approach and congratulate him. The officer allegedly complained to Dönitz of this deliberate snub, placing Henke in even hotter water.[11]

As *U–515*'s crew reassembled in Lorient, the sobering effects of their home leaves received additional reinforcement by developments at the front. The turn of the Type IXCs, spared the slaughter of May 1943, had come in July. Ten Lorient-based submarines, together with one other boat en route to the port, were sunk that month alone.

The Allies, no longer satisfied with the extended protection of convoys as the best means of killing submarines, had now developed antisubmarine task forces for the express purpose of hunting down U-Boats. These task forces, built around the escort aircraft carrier, swept the central Atlantic from the Bahamas to Casablanca. Their natural targets were the Type XIV supply U-Boats (*Milch-kuhe*, "milk-cows") so necessary for long-range operations, and the Type IXCs outward-bound or returning home from distant missions.[12]

Seven of the submarines lost in July belonged to the Tenth Flotilla.

The absence of more than 350 familiar faces and voices at the mess hall drove home the extent of the loss, and forecast their own likely fate. Together with the experiences and observations of the bombings of German cities, the period in port from June to August 1943 underscored the desperate condition of Germany's situation in a way that the most harrowing patrol could not. Yet there was nothing to do but go on.

For Henke, the paperwork began to catch up to him in early August. With the preparations for *U–515*'s next patrol already at an advanced stage, no major action could be taken. Admiral von Friedeburg, however, apparently decided to end the preferential treatment previously accorded Henke in allowing him to keep his crew intact. Orders were issued for the replacement of 12 men, 20 percent of the crew. Moreover, Henke was ordered to allow anyone who wished to do so to transfer to another submarine.

How Henke evaded this order further attests to his ingenuity. He paraded the crew and explained the order before announcing: "Whoever no longer wishes to serve with me may step forward." Without pausing to catch his breath, and before any man could move a muscle, he continued: "Thank you all very much. I knew I could count on you. Dismissed."[13]

Whatever fate held in store for them, Henke and his crew would face it together.

NOTES

1. Sönke Neitzel, *Die deutschen Ubootbunker und Bunkerwerften* (Koblenz: Bernard & Graefe Verlag, 1991), 51–64, 214 (photos of *U–515* on 54–55); Dönitz quote in Terry Hughes and John Costello, *The Battle of the Atlantic* (New York: Dial Press/James Wade, 1977), 298.

2. Air raids detailed in Martin Middlebrook and Chris Everitt, *The Bomber Command War Diaries. An Operational Reference Book, 1939–1945* (London: Viking, 1985), 343–55, and Roger A. Freeman, *Mighty Eighth War Diary* (New York: Jane's, 1981), 34, 54; Lorient data in file "U-Boat Bases," 15 July 1943, Op-16-Z files, RG 38, NA.

3. Group interviews at Steinhude, 25 May 1991; letter of Carl Möller to author, 8 February 1990.

4. V. E. Tarrant, *The U-Boat Offensive 1914–1945* (Annapolis, MD: Naval Institute Press, 1989), 115–19, and the listing of Tenth Flotilla U-Boats reproduced on T1022/2151–52/PG 36678.

5. Based on crew list with family addresses, ca. August 1943 (U-Boot-Archiv); U.S. Army interrogations of Deussen, RG 165, NA; Carl Möller letter of 8 February 1990; and Middlebrook and Everitt, *Bomber Command*, 394–97, 401, 413–14.

6. Examples are strewn throughout the issues of the *Marineverordnungsblatt*; others are provided in the *Dauernder/Laufender Flottillenbefehle* of the 2d U-Boat Flotilla, February 1943–May 1944, file F-6-e, 24309-V, formerly secret naval attaches' correspondence, RG 38, NA.

7. Group interviews in Steinhude, 25 May 1991, and interview with Carl Möller, Hamburg, 30 August 1989.

8. See John R. Angolia, *On the Field of Honor: A History of the Knight's Cross Bearers*, vol. 2 (San Jose, CA: Roger J. Bender, 1978–80), 14–16, 221; David Irving, *Hitler's War* (New York: Viking, 1977), 278–79, 536, 592–96; and Erich Topp, *Fackeln über dem Atlantik. Lebensbericht eines U-Boot-Kommandanten* (Herford: E. S. Mittler & Sohn, 1990), 106–7.

9. Gestapo/Staatspolizeistelle Innsbruck to Abwerstelle Wehrkreis XVIII, "Eichenlaubträger Kaptlt. Henke. Vorsprache beim Gauleiter in der Angelenheit Proxauf," 5 August 1943, T175/33/frames 25416600662.

10. Albrecht Henke interview, Lüneburg, 19 September 1987.

11. Albrecht Henke interview, Lüneburg, 19 September 1987, and letter to author, 6 May 1988, citing the statements to him of a *Crewkamerad* of his brother's; Albrecht identifies the individual as one Admiral Stange, but there is no corroborating evidence.

12. Tarrant, *U-Boat Offensive*, 123–24; Samuel E. Morison, *The Atlantic Battle Won, May 1943–May 1945* (Boston: Little, Brown and Company, 1975), 108ff.

13. Carl Möller interview, 30 August 1989.

14

The Net Tightens

The approach of their fourth patrol allowed Henke and his crew the opportunity to take some action, to strike back at the circumstances beginning to engulf them. Success at the front offered the best means of retaliation, of vindication.

That success, however, had become more difficult than ever to achieve. During Henke's eventful furlough of July 1943, the Kriegsmarine lost nearly as many submarines as in the disastrous month of May 1943. The thirty-seven U-Boats that never returned included most of the "milch kuhe" tankers and many Type IXCs. A shift of the operational focus to the Central and South Atlantic could not stop the bleeding of the fleet as the U.S. Navy's newly introduced escort aircraft carriers, guided by the latest intelligence furnished by ULTRA, sealed the last "air gap" between the continents. These carrier task forces or "hunter-killer" groups, unassociated with any convoy duty, marked a major change in Allied strategy in actively hunting down U-Boats.

Many other losses resulted from Dönitz's faulty strategy in challenging Allied air power in the Bay of Biscay with greater flak armament and daylight group sailings, a policy abandoned on 2 August. As a result, U-Boat losses declined from ten in the month's first week to fifteen for the remainder of August. In return, however, only twenty merchant ships fell victim to submarines, less than half the previous month's total.[1]

The extensive preparations for Henke's patrol reflected the frantic stopgap measures to counter Allied supremacy. The rear of U–515's bridge had been expanded and altered as an antiaircraft platform (termed *Wintergarten* by U-Boat sailors), supporting two single 20mm guns forward and a quadruple 20mm mount aft. In addition, a 37mm flak piece replaced the 105mm deck gun forward of the bridge. This new armament not only required additional target practice and maintenance, but necessitated several test and trim dives to determine adjustments for the added weight and new configuration.[2] A new radar search receiver, the W. Anz G1 (quickly dubbed "*Wanze*," German for "bed bug") replaced the Metox radar detector, whose radiation emissions were erroneously believed to betray submarines' positions to Allied radar. Another innovation introduced consisted of several radar decoys designated Aphrodite, hydrogen-filled balloons, each of which deployed three thirteen-foot aluminum foil strips to simulate the radar echoes of a surfaced submarine.

Henke also received four of the eighty brand-new acoustic torpedoes distributed to twenty submarines in France, the T–5 *Zaunkönig* (translated as "wren," but more generally known by its Allied designation "gnat"), specifically intended for use against Allied escort vessels. Designed to hone in on the noise generated by a destroyer's propellers, the T–5 aroused high expectations in Dönitz's headquarters for restoring the U-Boat's "punch" in convoy battles.[3]

Both the Wanze search receiver and the T–5 torpedo reflected the technological haste with which the Kriegsmarine sought to keep pace with the Allies. The Wanze, or Hagenuk after the manufacturer, marked an advance over the Metox in an automatic frequency search that relieved the operator of constant tuning, yet it still lacked the ability to detect the centimeter-length pulses of Allied radar. Moreover, German testers failed to note that the apparatus emitted the same radiation that caused withdrawal of the use of Metox (based on the false premise that Allied radar detected and honed in on the source of the emissions). The T–5 torpedo suffered from a short arming range that could leave the U-Boat's own propellers as the strongest sound to attract its deadly warhead. Two U-Boats and their crews probably met their ends because of their own acoustic torpedoes.

For Henke, however, the worst development concerned the turnover in his crew. As noted earlier, Admiral von Friedeburg revoked the special dispensation that Henke had heretofore enjoyed in crew selection. Twelve new crew members had to be integrated within the tightly knit team that had been forged through three patrols. Henke disliked losing any of his old hands, though at least five of the new men were also U-Boat veterans. In this regard, the training required by the new equipment provided the means for a more rapid assimilation.

Henke's concern to keep his remaining crew intact revealed itself in a particular personnel matter prior to departure. In the aftermath of the devastating air raids on their city in late July, Hamburg residents Heinrich Lamprecht and Carl Möller approached Henke with a request for emergency leave to look after their families. The captain merely shook his head, saying: "Men, I need you both here on the boat. But we'll show these Englishmen something, that I promise you." Then, taking each petty officer by the arm, he added: "It's a shitty war, but what can you do?"[4]

One change that caused no problems involved the promotion of Lt. Heinrich Niemeyer to first watch officer. Niemeyer, less than a year Henke's junior, had sailed with Henke in 1926 aboard the training ship *Grossherzogin Elisabeth*. After thirteen years in the merchant marine, Niemeyer and the whaling vessel he captained were requisitioned together by a Kriegsmarine desperate for experienced mariners and vessels. Two years of duty aboard subchasers and patrol craft ended with a severe throat wound inflicted by a strafing Spitfire. Recovery brought a transfer to the U-Boats and assignment to *U–515* as the second watch officer in February 1943. With common backgrounds and a wealth of shared experiences, Henke and Niemeyer worked well together.[5]

Preparations complete, *U–515* departed Lorient on the evening of 21 August 1943. Her first deep-dive test, however, resulted in numerous leaks and breakdowns in the forward hydroplanes and the sounding gear. After a return to port and additional repairs, Henke slipped out of the massive Scorff bunker at 1800 hours on 29 August. The delay worked to Henke's advantage, as the new moon period helped conceal the boat's movements: With a nine-man bridge watch and flak guns manned and ready, Henke ran at night on the surface and traversed the dangerous Bay of Biscay without a single enemy contact. Late in the evening of 4 September, Henke received orders to proceed to a refueling rendezvous with two other Type IXCs in quadrant CE 40, roughly 450 miles west of Portugal.[6]

Though no copies of operational orders for this patrol are available, Dönitz likely intended Henke to return to the scene of his previous triumphs off Freetown. None of Henke's successors had matched his success in this operational area since May. With his proven ability and familiarity with the area, *U–515*'s captain could be expected to wrack up enough tonnage to tie down Allied escorts that might be used in the North Atlantic, where Dönitz now planned (September 1943) to return to convoy warfare.[7]

But long before Henke approached Freetown, he himself became involved in a convoy action. The morning after receiving BdU's signal, Henke's lookouts spotted numerous masts on the northwest horizon. At a distance of ten miles, he estimated the convoy's size at about twenty-five merchantmen with numerous escorts, heading south toward Gibraltar. There was no question of his course of action. Henke immediately gave chase.

In fact, Henke had spotted a combined convoy: OS 54, laden with cargoes for Freetown, accompanied by North Africa-bound KMS 25 as far as Gibraltar. A total of fifty-four merchant ships comprised the convoy, escorted by at least fifteen warships. Except for one torpedoing in mid-July, this convoy route had enjoyed immunity from submarine attack since 2 April, when Henke's old boat, *U–124* under Jochen Mohr, sank two vessels from Convoy OS 45 before being destroyed by the escorts. Ironically, Mohr had also been bound for the Freetown area when he encountered OS 45, and had met his fate in the same area in which Henke now stalked his game.[8]

Henke spent the day of 5 September positioning himself for an attack, maintaining a distance of fifteen nautical miles from the slow-moving convoy despite being driven under twice by aircraft sightings. The planes had not seen him, however, as no escorts inquired in his direction. Aware that his was the only boat in the immediate area, and justifiably fearful that a radio signal would betray his presence, Henke did not communicate his find to BdU. He would attack first and report later.

A surface run at dusk could not be attempted because of the dark silhouette of the high conning tower—Henke again determined to paint the tower a lighter gray to reflect, rather than absorb, light. He resolved instead upon the tactics that had served so well against TS 37, a midnight attack into the convoy's rear.

U–515's chronometer read 2330 hours as she closed on her target. On the bridge Henke fastened his binoculars on the convoy escorts, counting eight to ten corvettes, four destroyers, and one cruiser ahead and on the flanks, with another cruiser and destroyer trailing behind. The convoy was not zigzagging, nor was there any indication of night air cover. Approaching from the rear starboard quarter, Henke aimed to slip through a widening gap between the right flank escorts and the columns of freighters. To his left and just behind him, *Oberleutnant* Heinrich Niemeyer locked the *U-Boot-Zieloptik* into position. This would be the new first watch officer's first surface torpedo attack, but Niemeyer's extensive service in the merchant marine and in navy patrol craft diluted his excitement. Neither he nor Henke would be rushed.

With a starless sky and cloud-covered moon, and traveling at slow speed to diminish their wash, they believed they could not be seen. Henke's course cut diagonally across the convoy's trail and into its center where, at the prescribed night range of a few hundred meters, he could savage the convoy's vitals in the same manner as he had done in May.

U–515 had already passed the tail of the first column of merchantmen when the deck and surrounding sea perceptibly brightened. The clouds had parted to reveal the first-quarter moon low on the horizon. "Stop all engines!" commanded Henke. Had they been seen?

The answer came immediately. Alert crewmen on the freighter SS *Gascony* spotted the submarine 1,100 yards off their starboard quarter and brought their four-inch gun to bear. As they fired, star shells burst over the convoy and the closest escort veered sharply toward them.

"ALARM!"

In seconds Henke completed the transformation from greedy hunter to cautious prey. Turning away from his former targets as he dived, Henke directed his chief engineer to descend to 170 meters (nearly 560 feet). He abandoned all hope of attacking the convoy, but at least believed that his boat would be safe from depth-charges—there was no sense pressing one's luck with the structural changes that had just been made. The boat descended silently to the prescribed depth while the hydrophones tracked the propellers of what sounded like two destroyers overhead. As the first depth-charges detonated in the distance, Henke's thoughts likely returned to the too-dark color scheme of his conning tower, a problem he resolved to correct immediately upon return to base.

Suddenly, a sound like that of gravel being flung against the hull announced that the boat's location had been pinpointed by Asdic. Henke ordered a change in course and speed, but within seconds the submarine shuddered violently from a series of depth-charges that exploded just outside the hull. Lights burst and streams of sea water shot into compartments as the boat began to sink by the stern. The needle of the depth gauge swept past 200 meters as U–515 continued her plunge.

Only by blowing all ballast tanks that still responded to control did Mahnken finally halt the descent at the incredible depth of 250 meters (820 feet)—one of the deepest dives recorded by a U-Boat.[9] Here the experience of the crew proved decisive as they coolly and quickly effected the most basic repairs in the half-light and rising water. As the leaks were stopped and the boat slowly ascended, one question dominated everyone's mind: Would an Allied escort vessel or aircraft still be awaiting them on the surface?

Fünf-fünfzehn's luck still held: only darkness and a clear horizon greeted the submarine. A mere ninety minutes had passed since she had been spotted, but it seemed to the crew an eternity. Mahnken inventoried the damage and reported to Henke that one of the aft diving tanks had been ripped open, two-thirds of the battery cells had been cracked, the main bilge pump was damaged, and the hydraulic system had been punctured in several places. The six torpedo containers stored between the pressure hull and the deck had been smashed as well. Several hours of repair work restored the submarine's ability to submerge, but the damage proved too extensive to continue the patrol. Before dawn, Henke radioed BdU that he was returning to base.

None aboard realized how fortunate they had been. Their assailant had been HMS *Tavy*, commissioned only five months earlier as one of the new *River*-class frigates. Intended to replace the slower corvettes on convoy escort, these frigates were fast, durable, and armed with some of the latest antisubmarine equipment and weaponry. The latter included the Hedgehog, a mortarlike device which fired a pattern of 24 projectiles up to 250 yards ahead of the warship. These projectiles, each loaded with 32 pounds of the deadly explosive Torpex, would detonate only on contact with a submarine, allowing a steady sonar contact during the pursuit. Yet that night *Tavy* lacked the otherwise-standard item of an operational radar set.

Tavy locked on to her submerged target and released a pattern of ten conventional depth-charges set for 550 feet—less than 10 feet from U–515's actual depth, a testament to *Tavy*'s sonar gear. But the frigate's greenness betrayed her. Nineteen minutes after her devastating attack on her quarry, *Tavy* regained what she believed to be sonar contact and fired her Hedgehog projectiles, without effect. In all probability, the regained contact represented one of the many phenomena that often deceived sonar—a dense layer of salinity, a school of fish. Suddenly contact was lost, and shortly thereafter the Asdic equipment broke down.

Without radar, she could not detect surface movement. By the time the radar-equipped corvette HMS *Geranium* arrived on the scene, they were looking in the wrong area for a submerged submarine. Henke surfaced a mere five minutes before his pursuers received orders to rejoin the convoy; U–515 must have lain, helpless, just outside their radar range. The antagonists then departed in opposite directions, never to know how close they had come to a second and decisive encounter.

The return trip took five days, following the same pattern of daylight submergings and evening surfacings as the outbound trip. Dodging

Allied air patrols, *U–515* staggered into Lorient in the early hours of 12 September.[10]

For the first time, Henke and his men had returned empty-handed from a patrol. The narrowness of their escape, however, brought home to them what other U-Boat crews had learned earlier: victory lay now in survival rather than sinkings. Henke's midnight charge into a convoy had still worked in May 1943, but only under very favorable conditions. Such tactics increasingly belonged to a bygone era of the Atlantic campaign; both BdU and the British felt Henke would have done better to fire a spread of torpedoes earlier in his run. On the other hand, Henke's caution in using the radio may have been more important to the safety of the submarine than even he realized. Every message he received or sent during the patrol was intercepted and decrypted by Allied cryptanalysts.[11]

The veteran skipper and his crew also benefited from the Allies' inexperience with their own new weapons. When Hedgehog came into general use in the second half of 1943, British vessels achieved a "kill" rate of only 7.5 percent with its use; by the first half of 1944 this had improved to 15.4 percent, and by the latter half of 1944 to 28.1 percent. By contrast, the relative lethality of depth-charges—even those with increased explosive power—remained constant throughout this period, between 4.0 percent and 6.4 percent. *Tavy* would prove the value of her experience in July 1944, when together with HMS *Wanderer* she sank *U–390* (Oblt.z.S. Heinz Geissler).[12]

Henke detailed his experiences to Admiral Godt, head of U-Boat operations, who did not fault any of the actions taken on the patrol. When Godt ordered Henke to report to Admiral von Friedeburg, however, the U-Boat captain found himself facing a different kind of ordeal. The Gestapo's complaint of Henke's conduct in Innsbruck, forwarded to von Friedeburg after *U–515*'s departure, now confronted the impetuous officer.

Though we have no record of Henke's interview with von Friedeburg, or of his subsequent discussion with Dönitz, the result is apparent enough in von Friedeburg's letter of apology directly to *Reichsführer* Himmler on 19 October 1943. While not excusing Henke's behavior, the admiral offered the curious explanation that "U-Boat commanders whose nerves, burdened by day- and night-watches and by ceaseless attacks by aircraft and depth-charges, are not up to the level of the average German citizen"—in obedience to authority, apparently. "The sharpness, with which both I and *Grossadmiral* Dönitz reproved (Kaptlt.

Henke)," continued von Friedeburg, "achieved the desired effect. . . .
He realizes that he acted inappropriately and regrets his statements."[13]

The truth of the last statement may be doubted. It was out of character
for Henke, and the absence of a letter of apology from the quick-tempered captain suggests one was neither required nor offered. As will be
seen, Henke retained his independence with respect to party officials.

But Henke's personal feelings were immaterial, a point doubtless
made clear to him by his superiors. The issue concerned the relationship
of the navy with the SS and police authority, and by extension with the
National Socialist regime itself. Henke's offense could not have been
worse timed, for by autumn 1943 that relationship had acquired an
ideological dimension.

Throughout August 1943, *Grossadmiral* Dönitz met constantly with
Hitler to discuss the imminent Italian collapse, the precarious U-Boat
situation and the effect of Allied bombing on production. The führer's
influence on his navy commander in chief in these discussions, as it had
with so many other individuals, left its mark. After one conference on
11 August, Dönitz noted "The enormous strength which the Führer
radiates, his unwavering confidence, and his far-sighted appraisal of the
Italian situation have made it very clear in these days that we are all
very insignificant in comparison with the Führer. . . . Anyone who be-
lieves he can do better than the Führer is silly."[14]

Dönitz, alert to the drop in morale as Germany's situation worsened,
determined that the navy would not experience another 1918. In September, he issued an "Order Against Habitual Criticism and Grum-
bling," threatening chronic complainers and rumor-mongers in the navy
with court-martials—though, significantly, the order acknowledged the
right of front-line sailors to "let off steam."[15] More appropriate to Henke
were Dönitz's opening remarks to an assembly of Kriegsmarine officers
at Weimar on 17 December, when the admiral stressed the need for
ideological conviction among his officers. "It is nonsense to say that the
soldier or officer must be non-political. The soldier embodies the State
in which he lives, he is its representative, the outspoken advocate of
the State. Therefore he has to stand behind this State with all his
might."[16]

That Dönitz meant what he said was revealed in the case of Oblt.
Oskar Kusch, commander of *U–154*. During his two operational patrols,
Kusch had strongly criticized Hitler's leadership in the presence of his
officers, observing that the "German people's only hope for peace and
a cultural rebirth lay in the collapse of Hitler and the Party." Among
other "defeatist" statements, Kusch allegedly told one crewman, "Why

do we have this war? Only because the Madman wants to swallow up all Europe! Why haven't we ended this war?"

Upon *U–154*'s return to Lorient in July 1943, Kusch's first watch officer reported his captain's statements to naval authorities. The orders for Kusch's arrest and Henke's own Gestapo report probably crossed the same desks at the same time. At the court-martial in January 1944, the prosecutor proposed a lengthy prison term for Kusch, but the navy court sentenced him to death. Both von Friedeburg and Dönitz confirmed the sentence in view of the "fundamental significance" of the case. On 12 May, a firing squad executed Kusch outside Kiel.[17]

There can be little doubt, therefore, that Henke received a stern rebuke in his audience with his commander in chief. Yet he received no other punishment. Perhaps, as he had executed Kusch for a breach of faith, so Dönitz stood by Henke for a lapse in judgment. Moreover, the navy's acknowledgment of SS supremacy paid off for the Proxauf family: Before the end of October Himmler accepted von Friedeburg's apology and notified *Gauleiter* Hofer and the local Gestapo that the incident was closed. The *Reichsführer* even went so far as to issue a warning to the Innsbruck office regarding its handling of the affair.[18] Henke had actually accomplished something by his protest, if only indirectly.

This minor incident, however, revealed much of the nature of power in National Socialist Germany, and how it had changed since the beginning of the war. The hasty remarks of a quick-tempered but highly decorated submarine commander, criticizing not a policy matter but simply one of the petty brutalities of the police state, required the personal intervention of the navy commander in chief and another officer of flag rank with *Reichsführer-SS* Himmler to avoid punishment. Only four years earlier, Henke as an anonymous junior officer had struck down an SS officer and received an apology in return. Daily life in Germany had begun to mirror the U-Boat war: an existence of isolation, unexpressed fear, and constant vigilance against the false step that separated the living from the disappeared.

For Henke, at least, a return to the front meant he could fight back on his own terms. But he was once again on probation, and in desperate need of successes to balance his account—while the prospects for success grew ever more dim.

NOTES

1. See Alfred Price, *Aircraft versus Submarine: The Evolution of the Anti-Submarine Aircraft 1912 to 1972* (Annapolis, MD: Naval Institute Press, 1973), 144–

68; William T. Y'Blood, *Hunter-Killer: U.S. Escort Carriers in the Battle of the Atlantic* (Annapolis, MD: Naval Institute Press, 1983), 62ff.; and V. E. Tarrant, *The U-Boat Offensive 1914–1945* (Annapolis, MD: Naval Institute Press, 1989), 120–24.

2. Details of flak armament are taken from the "U–515 Final Interrogation Report," RG 38, NA; for information concerning the design of bridge "platforms," see Eberhard Rössler, *The U-Boat. The Evolution and Technical History of German Submarines* (Annapolis, MD: Naval Institute Press, 1981), 188–95.

3. See Günter Hessler, *The U-Boat War in the Atlantic 1939–1945* (London: Her Majesty's Stationery Office, 1989), Vol. 3, 21–24; Rössler, *U-Boat*, 196; and Robert C. Stern, *Type VII U-Boats* (Annapolis, MD: Naval Institute Press, 1991), 87–90, 124–25, 132–33; additional data on the T–5 is located in Eberhard Rössler, *Die Torpedos der deutschen U-Boote* (Herford: Koehler, 1984), 142–53, and Jak P. Mallmann Showell, *U-Boat Command and the Battle of the Atlantic* (Lewiston, NY: Vanwell, 1989), 178–80.

4. Crew data is taken from the crew lists for *U–515* from the U-Boot-Archiv, Cuxhaven (additional information appears in chapter 6); letter from Carl Möller to author, 21 November 1987.

5. Letter from Heinrich Niemeyer to author, 16 December 1990.

6. *U–515* KTB.

7. See Hessler, *U-Boat War*, vol. 3, 17–18.

8. Convoy data is taken from the U-boat Assessment Committee report, "Précis of Attack by HMS *Tavy*," 5 September 1943, copy furnished by the British Ministry of Defence (hereafter cited as "HMS *Tavy* Report"); information regarding the OS convoys and *U–124* appear in J. Rohwer and G. Hümmelchen, *Chronology of the War at Sea, 1939–1945*, trans. by Derek Masters (New York: Arco Publishing, 1972–74), vol. 2, 314, 329; and E. B. Gasaway, *Grey Wolf, Grey Sea* (New York: Ballantine Books, 1970), 1–6.

9. The record depth attained and survived by a U-Boat is not clear, in view of the dire conditions prevailing in such situations. The earliest record seems to have been established in November 1941 by Oblt.z.S. von Tiesenhausen in *U–331* (Type VIIC) at 266 meters (Jochen Brennecke, *Jäger-Gejagte: Deutsche U-Boote 1939–1945* [Munich: Wilhelm Heyne Verlag, 1986], 130). Herbert Werner claims his *U–230* (another VIIC) descended to 280 meters during a depth-charge attack in May 1943 (Werner, *Iron Coffins: A Personal Account of the German U-Boat Battles of World War II* (New York: Holt, Rinehart & Winston, 1969), 123–26. Martin Middlebrook, based on unspecified interviews, cites 270 meters (885 ft.) as the maximum attained by a Type VIIC and 310 meters (1,020 ft.) by a Type IXC (Middlebrook, *Convoy* [New York: William Morrow and Company, 1976], 69).

10. Except where otherwise noted, the story of this patrol derives from Henke's war diary, 21 August–12 September 1943 (T1022/3067/PG 30553/4); and the report of the Admiralty's U-boat Assessment Committee, "Précis of Attack by HMS *Tavy*, 5 September 1943," furnished by the Ministry of Defence, London. Details of HMS *Tavy*'s equipment and armament are taken from Peter Elliott, *Allied Escort Ships of World War II: A complete survey* (Annapolis, MD: Naval Institute Press, 1977), 211–22.

11. The BdU and British assessments appear at the end of the war diary and

in the Précis, respectively, as cited in note 8; U.S. Navy translated intercepts of Henke's messages are reproduced as items SRGN 22982, 23093, and 23107, RG 457, NA.

12. Operations Evaluation Group (OEG) Report 51, "Anti-Submarine Warfare in World War II, Part 2: Anti-Submarine Measures and their Effectiveness," n.d. (ca. 1946), located among the general records of the OSRD, Records of the Office of Scientific Research and Development, RG 227, NA.

13. Admiral von Friedeburg to *Reichsführer* Himmler, 19 October 1943, on T175/33/2541663–666.

14. *Fuehrer Conferences on Naval Affairs 1939–1945*, foreword by Jak P. Mallmann Showell (Annapolis, MD: Naval Institute Press, 1990), 360.

15. The order is reproduced in Michael Salewski, *Die deutsche Seekriegsleitung 1935–1945, Bd. II: 1942–1945* (Munich: Bernard & Graefe Verlag, 1975), 638–39.

16. Dönitz's "Schlussansprache auf der Tagung für Befehlshaber der Kriegsmarine in Weimar am Freitag, dem 17. Dezember 1943," is reproduced as Document 443-D in *Trial of the Major War Criminals Before the International Military Tribunal, Nuremberg 14 November 1945–1 October 1946* (Nürnberg, 1947–49), vol. 35, 106–16.

17. See Heinrich Walle, "Individual Loyalty and Resistance in the German Military: The Case of Sub-Lieutenant Oskar Kusch," in Francis R. Nicosia and Lawrence D. Stokes, eds., *Germans Against Nazism: Nonconformity, Opposition and Resistance in the Third Reich. Essays in Honour of Peter Hoffmann* (New York/Oxford: Berg, 1991), 323–50. A differing viewpoint is offered by Karl Peter, "Der Fall des Oberleutnants zur See Kusch. 'Wider besseres Wissen zum Tode verurteilt'— Stimmt das?" (typewritten, n.d. [ca. 1985]), in the custody of the U-Boot-Archiv, Cuxhaven.

18. Himmler's letter to von Friedeburg and internal SS memoranda, 26–29 October 1943, are reproduced on T175/33/2541653–658.

15

Drawing Fire

The pattern of the previous layover in port repeated itself after *U–515*'s fourth patrol. More bombed-out cities greeted crewmen on leave; fewer familiar faces could be seen in the Lorient mess; and yet more hours were devoted to hurried instruction on new equipment and armament in a losing race with Allied weaponry.

Symptomatic of the improvised desperation was the replacement, after only one patrol, of the quadruple-mount 20mm antiaircraft mount. Based upon the German Army's standard model, the weapon proved too cumbersome, too weak in punch, and prone to problems from sea-water immersion. A total of three twin-mount 20mm pieces, sturdier and easier to operate, replaced the quadruple mount and the two single mounts on the expanded conning tower. In an appendix to his war diary, Henke himself had pointed out the limitations of existing flak armament and suggested instead the use of a 30mm twin-mount and a 50mm piece, though these recommendations were not followed up.

Similarly, the Wanz G1 radar search receiver was now dropped after one patrol, with the belated discovery that it also radiated (supposedly) detectable energy waves. Not one, but two separate devices in combination replaced it to provide adequate radar detection: the Wanz G2 search receiver, to cover the meter-length radar waves previously covered by Metox, and the Naxos FuMB 7, which at last scanned the centimeter-length radar waves of the latest Allied sets. The Wanz G2 was so new that sufficient quantities had not yet reached Lorient; the crews shared training on available models.[1]

In addition to these improvements, *U–515* received new electrical batteries and a coat of gray-white paint to reduce her visibility. The officer complement also underwent changes, as Oblt. Hans Schultz replaced Lieutenant Harmeln as second watch officer and *Stabsarzt* (staff surgeon) Erdmann Priewe joined the crew as their first regular doctor. A new engineering officer in training also joined the crew, a man destined to play a major role in the rest of *Fünf-fünfzehn's* story.

Günther Altenburger, a twenty-nine-year-old Thuringian, was a *Volksoffizier*, an officer risen from the ranks. A member of the U-Boat arm of the navy since his entry in January 1936, he had already served on twelve U-Boat patrols in the North Atlantic and eastern Mediterranean, with steady promotion the reward for outstanding performance. He joined *U–515* as Mahnken's assistant on a "confirmation" voyage that would qualify him as an engineering officer in his own right. Henke, convinced that an officer's duties should be accompanied by an officer's pay, promoted Altenburger on the spot from the rank of *Oberfähnrich (Ing)* (senior officer candidate, engineering), to *Leutnant (Ing)*.[2]

The technological race even forced a detour at the beginning of the patrol. *U–515*, accompanied by *U–508* (Kaptlt. Georg Staats), left Lorient on 1 November 1943 for St. Nazaire to pick up the Wanz G2 radar search receiver and six T–5 acoustic torpedoes. As the latter represented antiescort weapons, and with the inclusion of three of the new "FAT" torpedoes (*Federapparat Torpedo*, spring-operated torpedo) that could be set to run back and forth through a convoy formation, it was obvious to all aboard that *U–515* was again headed for convoy actions.[3]

Dönitz's strategy behind this commitment reflected both a dogged refusal to acknowledge defeat and a fatalistic rationalization. Despite catastrophic losses, Dönitz believed that the improvements in flak, radar protection, and torpedoes at least permitted his submarines to hold their own in a delaying action while waiting for the new Type XXI submarines. This belief was buttressed by the supposed effectiveness of the acoustic torpedo against convoy escorts: By June 1944, the BdU staff reckoned that this weapon had sunk 128 Allied warships, when the actual total amounted to perhaps twenty. Moreover, in mid-November 1943 a number of long-range Junkers 290 reconnaissance aircraft became available for the first time in searching for Allied convoys.

Yet Dönitz apparently understood that, to the average U-Boat sailor, the fight had grown increasingly futile; perhaps he even grasped that the common sailor was right. But if so, there remained yet one appeal. In a radio message to all submarines on 13 November, Dönitz presented all of the above arguments as justifications for continuing the fight. He closed, however, by invoking a seemingly inescapable logic: "Your actions have tied down much of the enemy's air and sea forces. These forces must not be freed for use against Germany. Thus you defend your homeland, even though the struggle at the moment seems hopeless to you."[4]

Even before receiving this message, Henke and his crew experienced some of the problems that accompanied Dönitz's new weapons. Departing from St. Nazaire with U–508 on 9 November, U–515 immediately encountered problems with the Wanz G2 receiver. Unable to obtain clear signals, Henke opted to forego the dangerous route across the Bay of Biscay and instead take the longer but safer route along the French and Spanish coasts. The Naxos detector meanwhile provided several warnings of radar-equipped aircraft, but the range of the device proved too limited: the lack of proper warning time compelled Henke to report the problem to BdU immediately.

Thus, U–515 would have to conduct her fifth patrol with unreliable radar-detection gear. But the men aboard were already more fortunate than their comrades aboard U–508, all of whom were lost with their submarine in a predawn air attack on 12 November.[5]

On the evening of 16 November the boat took up position with group *Schill 1*, deployed in a rough line 450 miles west of Portugal to intercept a large northbound convoy from Gibraltar. Allied air cover was stronger than ever, with air bases available in the Azores for the first time in October. In recognition of this, *Schill 1* remained submerged by day and looked to make contact on the surface during the night of 18–19 November. Reconnaissance aircraft tracking the convoy, however, reported the Allied formation veering eastward as it approached the U-Boat line.

On the morning of 18 November, U–515 submerged and proceeded on the southwest jog of its search pattern. At 1137, the radioman picked up distant propeller noises on the hydrophone. Henke came to periscope depth for a look around. At a distance of seven to eight miles, Henke could see escorts and merchant ships heading straight for him. By pure chance, *Fünf-fünfzehn* found itself squarely in the path of the convoy they were seeking.

They were not alone. Kaptlt. Peter "Ali" Cremer's U–333, stationed just to the east of Henke, had spotted the convoy a mere seven minutes before Henke. Cremer enjoyed an even better view of joint Convoy SL 139/MK 30: fourteen columns with sixty-seven merchant ships, including eleven landing ships, tank (LSTs) destined to serve in the Normandy invasion, screened by a total of twenty-eight escorting destroyers, frigates, and sloops. Before Cremer could slip into the formation, the frigate

HMS *Exe* ran down his periscope and badly damaged the submarine with depth-charges. Cremer was barely able to limp home.[6]

Henke, unaware of Cremer's proximity, heard only the detonation of depth-charges in the distance. He moved off to the west and surfaced at 1502 about twelve miles distant from the convoy, intending to radio the latter's position to the rest of *Schill 1*. But an approaching Allied plane forced the boat down before the message could be sent. At periscope depth, Henke sighted two warships headed toward his position. Commands passed from the conning tower to the torpedo rooms to load the T–5 torpedoes.

HMS *Chanticleer* had been sweeping astern the convoy with another sloop, HMS *Crane*, looking for the damaged submarine attacked earlier in the day, when her lookouts spotted *U–515* diving at a range of about six miles. Both warships moved toward the location, unaware they were in Henke's sights. The U-Boat fired a T–5—but Henke had miscalculated his opponents' speed, and the acoustic torpedo missed its mark. Neither of the British ships realized they had been attacked, but conducted a routine search for what they still believed to be a damaged submarine.

After an hour, Henke decided he could wait no longer. The convoy was getting away, and he could only report its course and speed to BdU by taking on the escorts still searching for him. He came to periscope depth again and readied another T–5.

Chanticleer sighted the periscope 2,000 yards away on its starboard bow and immediately turned toward it. The warship quickly gained Asdic contact and prepared a pattern of ten depth-charges for firing. At the command, the first two charges were launched and in the air when a terrible explosion suddenly rocked the sloop. Petty Officer (Gunnery) Ernie North, a ten-year Royal Navy veteran on station as Officer of the Quarters, was just running aft to ready the "X" gun mounting for a possible target when the torpedo struck. He later described the scene:

> With a tremendous roar, it appeared that the whole quarter deck just disintegrated upwards in a jumbled mass, and a wave of pressure and heat hit me. . . . The ship's rudder, which I supposed weighed between 30 and 50 tons, had flown up into the air and had come down like a butcher's cleaver, and was knifed into the upper decks. Both the after Oerlikon (flak) mounts together with the upper deck had gone and the cabins and offices below were open to the sky and sea.

Over thirty crewmen were killed by the blast. The acoustic torpedo left the sloop dead in the water and listing to port. Yet within minutes,

Chanticleer's Asdic had regained contact and the forward guns were trained on the bubbling, churning water where the depth-charges had detonated.

For the British sloop, firing a split-second after Henke, gave as good as she got. Henke, in fact, never knew he had scored a hit, as the detonation occurred almost simultaneously with that of a depth-charge just outside the aft section of *U–515's* hull. The area hardest hit was the engine room spaces aft, where the force of the explosion blasted the 2,440-pound weight of the air compressor off its moorings. Sea water began pouring in through the exhaust valves as Henke dived to a depth of 185 meters (over 600 ft.).

As usual in submerging, all hands moved forward to add weight to the bow and accelerate the dive. Carl Möller, coming from the electrical engine room, observed the beginning of a fire in the diesel engines. Möller immediately extinguished the flames and remained at the station to prevent its recurrence until help arrived. For his action in saving the boat and crew from certain loss, Möller earned the German Cross in Gold (a decoration between the Iron Cross First Class and the Knight's Cross of the Iron Cross).

Even at their great depth the Germans were not safe. HMS *Crane*, standing by her wounded sister-ship, tracked her underwater target with Asdic and hydrophones. Over the next three hours *Crane* made seven attacks, each with ten well-laid depth-charges at depths of up to 550 feet. When contact was lost, *Crane* remained by *Chanticleer* until the rescue tug from the convoy arrived to take the damaged ship in tow to the Azores. Below them, *U–515* twisted and turned to evade the attacks while crewmen worked frantically to plug the leaks and make the most essential repairs. The damage and labor depleted the submarine's air supply which could not have lasted more than two hours when the hydrophone operator at last indicated that the escorts had moved off.

Henke surfaced at 2102 hours to mark the end of an engagement whose results were obscured in the fog of war. The acoustic torpedo, whose effectiveness BdU so consistently overestimated, in this case accomplished more than was believed, as Henke had no idea of the damage he had inflicted. He reported "two T-5 misses" the next day to BdU. Towed to Horta in the Azores, the British sloop never sailed again and was recommissioned as depot ship *Lusitania II*. For their part, *Chanticleer* and *Crane* calculated one U-Boat as "probably destroyed" and a second shaken up; the U-Boat Assessment Committee reduced the claim to one submarine "probably slightly damaged."

U–515 in fact suffered the worst damage she had experienced in the war. Mahnken inventoried the total: rips in the stern buoyancy tank and one of the main ballast and fuel oil tanks; two-thirds of all electrical battery cells cracked; the diesel exhaust valves and exterior intake valves damaged and retaining water; auxiliary cooling-water motor pump out of action; the main switchboard, forward hydroplane motor, and other auxiliary motors shaken up; upper deck fuel lines punctured and leaking; and a loosened pipeline to one or more regulating tanks. The submarine was down by the stern and required continual blowing of ballast tanks to remain surfaced. Leaving an obvious trail of oil, she possessed only a limited ability to submerge.[7]

First priority on surfacing required the long-delayed message to BdU on the convoy's position and course, albeit eight hours old; even then it had to be repeated four times before the correct version was acknowledged. Then Henke confronted his two engineering officers with the key question: What could be done about the damage to the boat?

Mahnken advised a return to base for proper repairs, as the damage proved worse than that suffered on any previous patrol. Altenburger, however, did not want to try to cross the hazardous Bay of Biscay in the boat's present condition. He offered to assume the responsibility of effecting repairs at sea. If some kind of safe anchorage could be found, perhaps in the Canary Islands, the ruptured tanks could be welded to make the craft more seaworthy.

Henke opted in favor of the junior engineer's view. The willingness to take risks and push on, of course, formed a part of Henke's character. More to the point, to attempt a return through a stretch dominated by Allied aircraft in the boat's current condition invited disaster, especially given the problems experienced with Wanze and Naxos as radar detectors. *U–515* could no longer participate in convoy operations, but if BdU approved a return to the familiar, less-heavily defended waters off Freetown and the Gulf of Guinea the boat might still inflict some damage.[8]

Four days and over 600 miles later, *U–515* slipped into a quiet cove on the southwestern corner of the island of La Palma, westernmost of the Canary Islands. Crewmen rigged a tarpaulin over the stern of the submarine and set to work welding the ripped tanks, while others effected repairs in the interior. The crew worked all through the night of 22–23 November, but could not complete the necessary welding. Taking no chances on discovery, Henke departed on the morning of 23 November and proceeded over 100 miles to another anchorage on the southern coast of the island of Hierro. Another night's welding accomplished as much as could be done. The main cracks were repaired, though the exhaust valves still flooded with every dive and the repaired ballast tank had to be blown clear of water every hour on the surface.

Thanks largely to the work of Altenburger, *U–515* was again operational. As she could not risk another depth-charge attack, the prudent course would have been to return home as quickly as possible. Henke, however, determined to push on. This was not only consistent with his character, but very likely a response to the disciplinary problems he faced at home as well. On 24 November he requested, and obtained, permission to operate in the area from Dakar to Takoradi on the west African coast. The remainder of the patrol would test Henke's ability to balance offensive patrolling against the precarious safety of his vessel and crew—in microcosm, the same dilemma confronting the U-Boat Command.[9]

It took five days to reach the waters off Dakar and Freetown, a long-time U-Boat operational area abandoned by Dönitz since late August because of the meager successes there. Henke, based on the intelligence supplied by *U–306* (Kaptlt. Claus von Trotha), looked for convoys departing Dakar on the thirtieth and first of each month; he saw nothing, probably because ULTRA intercepts of von Trotha's observations led to variations in convoy schedules. Henke abandoned the area and followed the coastline as far east as Lagos, Nigeria, in quest of targets, but encountered only constant air patrols and broiling heat. He noted, however, that while the air cover was strong, it also appeared inexperienced, and with seven lookouts sharing every bridge watch he could count on adequate warning of attack.[10]

Finally on the afternoon of 17 December, off the coast of Togo, *U–515's* lookouts spotted two aircraft flying in a pattern that suggested an escort for coastal traffic. As on his previous patrol in the area, Henke let the aircraft lead him to his prey. The boat submerged and headed for the direction indicated. Sure enough, when the submarine surfaced at dusk a lone steamer could be seen off the starboard bow, heading west.

Henke's persistence in searching for targets and precautions to avoid detection had paid off. The British freighter SS *Kingswood* (5,080 tons), en route from Lagos to Takoradi with a load of 7,400 tons of cotton and ground nuts, journeyed alone in accordance with the previous week's relaxation of convoying. As no information had been received regarding the presence of enemy submarines, *Kingswood's* captain did not even consider it necessary to zigzag.

U–515, after two submergings to avoid patrolling aircraft, positioned herself with her forward tubes aimed at the merchantman's port beam. At 2020 hours, two torpedoes with magnetic detonators sped away toward their target; sixty-one seconds later, one found its mark just forward of amidships. The explosion generated a violent spray of water that swamped the bridge and nearly drowned the captain. Listing heavily to port, the stricken vessel still managed to get off a distress call. Henke's radioman reported the message to the commander, who ordered another shot. This one detonated underneath *Kingswood's* ammunition locker for the forward four-inch gun with a spectacular blast. The crew abandoned ship, which sank within fifteen minutes.

Despite the freighter's quick and violent death, none of the forty-eight crewmen and artillerymen she carried lost their lives. As usual, the U-Boat proceeded among the lifeboats and inquired after the captain; when no one came forward, a survivor was briefly interrogated as to the ship's identity and cargo. Then the U-Boat slipped away in the darkness.[11]

Henke saw the results of his attack almost immediately. On 19 December he abandoned pursuit of two separate steamers due to strong air escorts and effective, high-speed zigzagging by the intended victims themselves. Late that evening, however, a large ship could be seen heading west. Though it also zigzagged, Henke established a favorable position for attack just as the hour struck midnight.

In fact, *U–515's* actions had already determined the course of her target. SS *Phemius*, a 7,406-ton British freighter loaded with 2,200 tons of military and general stores, had been scheduled to depart Takoradi for Lagos the previous day until the submarine scare delayed her by 24 hours. She finally began her journey at dawn on 19 December, but after traveling all day an Allied aircraft signaled her to return to Takoradi. *Phemius* dutifully complied, but she had only completed three hours of the return trip when Henke's first torpedo slammed into her starboard side just forward of the engine room.

The captain believed the wound fatal and ordered the crew of eighty-four (twenty Europeans, fifty-three Chinese, and eleven army and navy gunners) and thirty passengers to abandon ship. The radioman dispatched four distress calls—the monitoring of which prompted Henke to fire another torpedo into her only six minutes after the first. To test its effectiveness after the heavy depth-charging a month earlier, the German commander decided to use a T–5 torpedo. The *Zaunkönig* detonated with only slightly less effect than that which had shattered *Chanticleer's* stern. *Phemius's* midsection broke off and sank, the bow and stern remaining above water for nearly three hours before finally submerging.

When Henke again went in among the lifeboats to look for the captain, two Chinese crewmen scrambled aboard to try to surrender. Henke refused the offer with the observation that he must have a European, whereupon the senior radioman came forward to be taken prisoner. Twenty-three of the merchant ship's crew and passengers perished in the attack, most of whom had been sleeping on the hatch covers close to the location of the first explosion. The remainder were picked up seven hours later by a French corvette that had belatedly come out to escort *Phemius* on her return to Takoradi.[12]

Henke quickly realized he had stirred up a hornet's nest. Twice before dawn the U-Boat had to dive to evade probing aircraft, and the next afternoon the unmistakable sounds of depth-charges could be heard in the distance. The time had come to leave.

That night, to throw off his pursuers, Henke set off two of his antiradar decoys known as Aphrodite, the balloon with suspended aluminum strips that simulated the radar echoes of a U-Boat conning tower. These decoys had an immediate effect, drawing star shells over their positions as *U–515* sped off to the west. But Henke nearly undid what he had accomplished by reporting to BdU his claimed sinkings. The appearance of a warship within two hours convinced Henke that his position had been "fixed" by the transmission. Nevertheless, he eluded discovery and laid low off the Ivory Coast.[13]

On the afternoon of Christmas eve, lookouts sighted a large steamer at a distance of twelve miles on a southeasterly course, heading right toward their position. Small smoke trails also betrayed the presence of escorts as accompanying aircraft forced *U–515* to seek cover. By the fall of darkness these converging courses allowed Henke to try a surface attack. The clear presence of an escort forced him to hesitate: Both engineering officers confirmed that the submarine could not withstand another depth-charge attack. Henke therefore opted to launch a T–5 against the escort, then fire a spread against the steamer.

The motor ship *Dumana* (8,427 tons), escorted by the Royal Navy trawlers *Arran* and *Southern Pride*, departed Marshall, Liberia, on 23 December for Takoradi with 200 tons of military stores and 22 RAF maintenance personnel, in addition to her own crew of 138 and 9 artillerymen. Aware of the U-Boat danger, *Dumana* carefully maintained her proper position between her escorts, but the formation was not zigzagging and traveling at a speed of only eight knots.

At a range of 2,500 meters, Henke fired a *Zaunkönig* at the escort trailing *Dumana*. Not realizing that his target amounted only to a trawler, Henke set the torpedo's depth at five meters; as a result, the T–5 passed under its target and the trawler's crew sailed on oblivious to the fate they had been spared.

Despite the miss, Henke proceeded with his second attack. At 2137 hours, the three remaining forward tubes discharged their loads at a range of only 600 meters. Two struck home within 15 seconds.

No one aboard *Dumana* suspected anything until the explosions rocked the starboard side. The ship immediately began to list, which grew so marked that temporary structures on the deck slid overboard onto life-boats being lowered, killing many of the occupants. *Dumana* sank in just five minutes, taking thirty-nine of those aboard with her. None of the survivors ever saw their attacker, though *U–515* closed to within 200 meters to confirm the sinking. Henke then turned and moved away to the southwest, satisfied that his gray-white paint job had proven its worth in reducing the U-Boat conning tower's visibility.[14]

In one of the continuing paradoxes of modern war, the submarine and crew withdrew from their task of destruction to celebrate the coming of the Prince of Peace. Christmas day arrived as Henke put distance between himself and the scene of his last action. That evening Henke took the boat down to allow an undisturbed observation of the holiday. Crew member Hans Hahn remembers:

> The Christmas tree (brought from Lorient for the occasion) was lighted and the regular lights extinguished. The captain gave a brief Christmas speech, then came the main meal: soup, roasted chicken (from tin cans), potatoes, and a mixed salad. Afterwards came strawberries with cream, followed by the singing of Christmas songs and the playing of records. Small gifts were exchanged, and to top it all off everyone received punch and chocolate. Throughout the festivities, the watches were relieved so all could participate.

The most welcome development that day, however, came with Henke's announcement that *U–515* was heading home.[15]

The cause for this decision lay in the still-precarious condition of the boat. After a month, the welded seam on the buoyancy tank had begun to leak again, and more so with each passing day. When it became obvious that further welding would be necessary, Henke steered for the Cape Verde Islands. On New Year's Eve, the submarine limped into a quiet, obscure cove on the island of Santiago to repeat the welding repairs. The crew celebrated the arrival of 1944 only with tarpaulin-muffled flashlights and torches. In three hours, the job was done and *U–515* glided unobtrusively back out to sea.

A major problem remained, however, with the batteries. Patched up after the heavy depth-charging in November, the constant need for surface recharging posed few difficulties in an area where Henke could keep the boat surfaced for much of each twenty-four-hour period. The omnipresent Allied air patrols over the Bay of Biscay, however, rendered any extended stays on the surface impossible, especially given the limited range of the Naxos search-receiver and the poor reception on the Wanze. Allied aircraft convincingly demonstrated this condition on 10 January, when *U–515* could surface for only four brief periods—for sixteen, fourteen, fifteen, and sixty-two minutes, respectively—before being driven under.

After the last submerging at 1840 hours, the exhausted condition of the batteries produced another ordeal. Unable to surface, the submarine crawled through the shallow waters off the northern Spanish coast all through the next day as the batteries ran down. At 1600 hours on 11 January the batteries gave out, the electrical engines lost power, and *U–515* came to rest on the floor of the coastal basin. Already submerged for twenty-two hours, the crew endured another three nerve-wracking hours in stagnant air before dusk's arrival gave them their only chance to surface. Had a patrol plane sighted them then, their only choice would have been to fight it out at poor odds. But their luck held, and the batteries at last were recharged as the crew gulped down fresh, cold air. As on his previous patrols, Henke then followed the Spanish coast until he reached a position for a straight dash to Lorient.

At last, on the morning of 14 January lookouts sighted two minesweepers sent out to escort the U-Boat into port. Still the danger had not passed as two British fighter-bombers attacked forty-five minutes after their escorts met them. All three German vessels returned fire until the planes broke off the action. At 1800 hours, *U–515* tied up at her berth in Lorient.[16]

In terms of tonnage sunk or prolonged endurance, *U–515*'s fifth patrol did not match her earlier accomplishments. Yet the growing Allied supremacy in the Battle of the Atlantic rendered this cruise's achievements the most remarkable in her career. To repair the level of damage sustained, maintain the patrol, sink enemy shipping, and survive to return home in early 1944 demonstrated far greater skill and competence than sinking unescorted merchantmen in 1942. Though not nominated for any decoration after this patrol, Henke displayed more leadership here than on any previous mission, tempering his natural aggressiveness with a cool realization of his vessel's limited capabilities. He also recognized the outstanding performance of his subordinates and crew, no less than five of whom received the coveted German Cross in Gold for their actions on this patrol: Chief Engineer Mahnken and his understudy, Altenburger; *Obersteuermann* (First Mate) Paul Wilde; *Oberbootsmannsmaat* (Boatswain's Mate, 2d Class) Hermann Kaspers; and Carl Möller, finally promoted to *Obermaschinistenmaat* (machinist's mate, 2d class).[17]

But in the end, it would not be enough.

NOTES

1. On flak armament, see KTB BdU, 1 December 1943, T1022/4067/PG 30336, and Henke's suggestions (Henke family papers); on radar detection gear, see Robert C. Stern, *Type VII U-Boats* (Annapolis, MD: Naval Institute Press, 1991), 124–26.

2. Author's interviews with Günther Altenburger in Kiel, 2 September 1989, and in Steinhude, 25 May 1991; personnel data in *U–515* crew list.

3. *U–515* KTB; "*U–515* Final Interrogation Report" (14–15), RG 38, NA; and Eberhard Rössler, *Die Torpedos der deutschen U-Boote* (Herford: Koehler, 1984), 116–22. The term *Flächenabsuchender* (shallow-searching) *Torpedo* sometimes used for 'FAT' (e.g., Stern, *Type VII*, 84–86) appears erroneous.

4. KTB BdU, 13 November 1943, T1022/3980/PG 30334; Jak P. Mallmann Showell, *U-Boat Command and the Battle of the Atlantic* (Lewiston, NY: Vanwell, 1989), 173–75. For a discussion of Dönitz's steadfast belief in continuing the U-Boat campaign, see Jochen Brennecke, *Die Wende im U-Boot Krieg. Ursachen und Folgen 1939–1943* (Herford: Koehler, 1984), 284–90.

5. *U–515* KTB; KTB BdU, 14 November 1943, T–1022/3980/PG 30334.

6. *U–515* KTB; Peter Cremer, *U-Boat Commander* (Annapolis, MD: Naval Institute Press, 1984), 154–59.

7. Accounts of the action are from *U–515* KTB; U-Boat Assessment Committee, "Précis of Attacks by H. M. Ships *Chanticleer* and *Crane*, 18 November 1943," copy furnished by the Ministry of Defence, London; account of HMS *Chanticleer* furnished by Mr. Ernie North, Portsmouth, UK, in letters of 12 May 1988 and 23 November 1992; author's interview with Carl Möller, Hamburg, 30 August 1989; Henke message of 19 November 1943, SRGN no. 26498, RG 457, NA; and "*U–515* Final Interrogation Report," RG 38, NA. The German Cross in Gold is described in Gordon Williamson, *Aces of the Reich* (London: Arms and Armour, 1989), 18–19.

8. *U–515* KTB; "*U–515* Final Interrogation Report" and *U–515* preliminary interrogations (Altenburger, 13 May 1944), RG 38, NA.

9. *U–515* KTB; "*U–515* Final Interrogation Report," RG 38, NA; copies of

intercepted messages of 24 November 1943, SRGN nos. 26758, 26761, 26771, RG 457, NA.

10. *U–515* KTB; Henke's experiences in the area recorded in BdU's message to *U–123* (Kaptlt. Horst von Schroeter) of 24 January 1944, intercepted and decrypted as SRGN no. 30860, RG 457, NA.

11. *U–515* KTB; Shipping Casualties Section/Trade Division, "SS *Kingswood*: Report of an Interview with the Master-Captain F. H. Parmee," 14 March 1944, file ADM 199/2146 (XC 009488), PRO.

12. *U–515* KTB; Shipping Casualties Section/Trade Division, "Report of an Interview with the Master, Captain T. A. Kent, SS *Phemius*," 9 March 1944, file ADM 199/2146 (XC 009488), PRO.

13. *U–515* KTB; Henke's message, later repeated, was both fixed and decrypted (SRGN nos. 28186–187, RG 457, NA).

14. *U–515* KTB; Shipping Casualties Section/Trade Division, "Report of an Interview with the Master, Captain Otto West, M. V. *Dumana*," 21 January 1944, file ADM/2146 (XC 009488), PRO; on Aphrodite, see Stern, *Type VII*, 132–33.

15. *U–515* KTB; letter of Hans Hahn to author, 1 November 1991.

16. *U–515* KTB; "*U–515* Final Interrogation Report," RG 38, NA.

17. The announcements of these decorations appeared in *Marineverordnungsblatt*, issues of 15 March, 15 April, and 15 July 1944.

16

The Lost War

His recent experiences on patrol, the ever-dwindling number of familiar faces in Lorient, and his brushes with Nazi authorities had all taken their toll on Werner Henke. This was most evident to Peter "Ali" Cremer at a chance meeting of the two commanders in Paris, during Henke's stopover en route to debriefing in Berlin. The two U-Boat captains with the longest continuous service in the Atlantic discussed the recent convoy action that had nearly killed them both. In happier days, the two had shared the company of young French and émigré Russian women in the Café Scheherezade; now they sat soberly in the Hotel Claridge discussing the tactics of survival.

In exchanging observations on the increased efficiency of Allied sonar and depth-charging measures, Cremer noted the contrast between the usually happy and gregarious Henke and the much more serious colleague now sitting across from him. Though the two agreed on the need for more variation in evasive tactics while submerged, "we felt our prospects for success were nil."[1]

In truth, neither suspected the true severity of the situation. When Henke presented his mission report in Berlin, his recommendations for U-Boats in the Gold Coast area were immediately radioed to *U–123* (Kaptlt. Horst von Schroeter), the next submarine dispatched to the area. Allied signal intelligence just as quickly intercepted and decrypted the message. The intelligence contributed to changes in procedures in the area so that *U–123* returned home empty-handed in late April 1944.[2]

Cremer's observations on Henke's subdued nature, however, proved temporary. When confronted by overbearing authority figures, his defiant character reasserted itself. Altenburger, who accompanied Henke to Berlin, later recalled the following incident in the capital:

> We boarded a streetcar that was packed full of passengers. One very large fellow, apparently a bigshot in the SA or SS, happened to step on Henke's foot. Henke said, "You could excuse yourself." The Party official instead began scolding him. So Henke knocked him to the floor, in front of all those Berliners—who howled, just howled with laughter!

Of course, the incident brought in its wake another critical report to Dönitz and more trouble for Henke. Pending his return from his next patrol, Henke would likely face additional disciplinary action.[3]

The most significant event for Henke during this interval was his marriage, on 14 March 1944, to Anita Plangl, the 32-year-old widow of a well-to-do mill owner. Henke had known the woman for some years, but their romantic relationship apparently developed only during his leave in the Tyrol in late January. A whirlwind courtship on the ski slopes of the Vorarlberg led to a small wedding in Hamburg, barely two weeks before Henke's scheduled departure on his next patrol. Henke pulled whatever strings he could to have her accompany him on a final stopover in Berlin, four days in Paris, and finally to the officer's quarters outside Lorient the night before he left on his last patrol.

Precisely what lay behind this rush to marriage can never be known. Entirely consistent with Henke's impetuous nature, and hardly an act of pessimism, it may even reflect Henke's concern for the future and a postwar Germany with less need for navy officers.[4]

U–515 and her crew also experienced a number of changes during the ten-week layover in port. A major turnover occurred among the ship's officers. Altenburger assumed the duties of chief engineer as Mahnken retired to a shore post. Heinrich Niemeyer headed to commanders' school at Danzig prepatory to receiving his own command, U–547; replacing him as first watch officer was Oblt. Karl Benz. The affable Dr. Jörg Jensen came over from U–801 to replace Priewe as ship's surgeon.

Eleven new crewmen boarded U–515 for her sixth patrol. Among those they replaced were Paul Wilde, chief navigator; Hermann Kaspers, who left his brother Helmut on board to "look after things"; and Carl Möller. All departed with the warm congratulations of the captain who had so long delayed their promotions and transfers. Even with personnel changes, the crew retained a wealth of combat experience, with nineteen men having served aboard the submarine since commissioning and fifteen others for at least three patrols.

Once again, technicians installed new armament and equipment aboard the submarine. On the lower platform of the conning tower, the twin-mount 20mm was replaced by an automatic 37mm gun, whose rapid-fire punch against aircraft had proven itself in combat trials. An improved version of Naxos replaced the older variant from the previous patrol.

More ceremony accompanied the arrival of the *Hohentwiel* apparatus, a true radar set that allowed the tracking of aircraft at a range of 15–20 kilometers and also acted as a radar search receiver for transmissions from Allied sets. As the first boat in Lorient fitted with the gear, *U–515* also encountered some of its early problems: a cumbersome mattresslike aerial, for example, whose movement interfered with that of personnel on the bridge and which proved difficult to retract. During a dry-run exercise outside of port, the aerial did not properly line up with its housing when it was lowered and suffered severe damage.[5]

U–515 did not receive, however, the latest and most basic improvement in U-Boat technology. The *Schnorchel* (anglicised as snorkel) was a tube that could be raised from a submerged submarine to the surface, allowing fresh air to enter the boat. This relatively simple improvisation marked a tremendous advance, for it allowed a U-Boat to recharge its batteries and operate its diesel engines underwater. The snorkel offered the possibility of converting an obsolescent submersible craft into a true submarine, capable of operating for extended periods below the surface. Earliest models of the snorkel, however, experienced numerous teething difficulties, among them a limitation on a U-Boat's top underwater speed to little better than its usual speed with electric motors.

Was Henke, as the senior and most successful Type IXC commander in France, offered a snorkel for *U–515*? Without documentation, the question cannot be examined, only raised. Five other IXC boats in Lorient, however, began the necessary conversion work for the snorkel installation during the period January–March 1944, though in each case the conversion work required two to three months' work. Why neither Henke nor Peter Cremer, the most experienced Type VIIC commander, received the snorkel is unclear. It is possible, of course, that Henke did receive the offer, and rejected it because of the delay and uncertainties involved.

As the crew made their final preparations for departure, a number were surprised and upset to see their commander bring his new bride aboard. Beyond a violation of flotilla procedures, it transgressed the ancient superstition of a woman bringing bad luck to a vessel. This received seeming confirmation when the rudder motor broke down, delaying departure for twenty-four hours.[6]

At last, on the afternoon of 30 March 1944, *U–515* and her sixty officers and crewmen left Lorient in the company of some patrol boats. According to one account, well-wishers on the dock threw flowers onto the U-Boat's deck for good luck; Henke had a crewman toss them unceremoniously over the side.[7]

That same day, another and much stronger force sortied from the harbor of Casablanca, roughly a thousand miles to the south. U.S. Navy Task Group 21.12, consisting of the escort aircraft carrier *Guadalcanal* and four destroyer escorts—*Flaherty*, *Chatelain*, *Pillsbury*, and *Pope*—represented the latest and most effective tactical organization in the Atlantic campaign: the hunter-killer group.

Since early June 1943, task forces built around small escort carriers in the central Atlantic had been freed from close convoy escort duty to pursue U-Boats wherever they could be found. The "baby flat-tops" scored their first great successes in the summer of 1943, when they were guided—without being so informed—by the latest ULTRA intelligence to several U-Boat refueling rendezvous, where they virtually annihilated the submarine supply tanker fleet. The task groups now shuttled between Norfolk and Casablanca, the carriers' planes scouting the ocean surface to a range of 100 miles on either side and perhaps 150 miles ahead of the formation. Their principal targets were the long-range U-Boats en route to operations off the coast of West Africa, Capetown, or the Indian Ocean.

The USS *Guadalcanal*, known as the "Can Do" under its commander, Captain Daniel V. Gallery, joined these operations in January 1944 and quickly claimed *U-544* (Korv.kapt. Willi Mattke). Gallery proposed to add another innovation to the hunter-killer teams, round-the-clock searching by aircraft to catch submarines surfaced by night, but bad weather hampered efforts to implement such a measure for the remainder of that cruise and the first part of the next. As he departed North African waters at the end of March, Gallery looked forward to favorable weather and sea conditions to prove his point.[8]

Henke received no intelligence or briefing regarding these groups, because the U-Boats that had encountered them had been sunk and no other sources of intelligence had produced the information. His own operational orders, not yet shared with the crew, called for a return to the Gold Coast operations area—BdU obviously counted on Henke's familiarity with the shipping and defensive conditions there to produce some results and further tie down Allied units. Without adequate intelligence, no one realized that *U–515*'s course would lead her straight into the path of a hunter-killer task force.

The outbound trip proved fairly uneventful as Henke retraced his previous route south to the Spanish coast and along the coastline west to Cape Finisterre before steering southwest into the open sea. The submarine surfaced for only four to five hours each night to recharge batteries, leaving behind occasional Aphrodite radar decoys to throw off air patrols. Airplanes were sighted several times, but the submarine always successfully dived without drawing attention. Henke pursued a steamer briefly on the afternoon of 7 April, but abandoned pursuit when the merchantman revealed herself as a neutral ship.

A disagreement arose between Henke and Altenburger as to whether *U–515* was trailing oil. The new chief engineer believed that an untraceable leak had developed in the forward bunker, leaving behind a discernible trace. In contrast to his views on repairing the boat during the previous patrol, Altenburger would not accept responsibility for continuing the patrol. Henke overruled him, proposing simply to exhaust all the fuel in the suspect bunker first to eliminate the leak as quickly as possible.

Henke remained sensitive, however, to concealing his position. When his radioman confirmed that the *Hohentwiel* was emitting radiation—the same harmless energy waves so consistently and mistakenly blamed for betraying U-Boat locations to Allied radar—Henke dropped its use. He radioed only once to BdU, to transmit the standard signal to indicate a successful passage of the Bay of Biscay.[9]

In fact, Henke's message and those sent by BdU to him, including departure orders radioed to Henke while still in Lorient, had all been intercepted and decrypted by Allied intelligence. But with the time required to put such information to operational use, ULTRA would play no role in the events about to unfold.[10]

Aboard *Guadalcanal*, the evening of 8 April offered Gallery the perfect conditions to attempt his night-flying experiment: a full moon, clear sky, and calm sea. At a position over 700 miles west of Gibraltar, the escort carrier launched four Avenger aircraft at 1800 hours, Greenwich mean time, to sweep the area 60 miles ahead and 100 miles on either side of the formation. The planes were due back at 2215, but at their first check-in the pilots reported deteriorating flying conditions, so Gallery scrubbed plans for a midnight flight. One plane reported a radar contact, but when no further report arrived, Gallery assumed nothing of consequence had developed.

But when the planes returned, the pilot reporting the contact specified that he had seen a submarine about sixty-four miles to the northwest. The U-Boat had dived before he could attack, and his radio report had not been coherently relayed. An eager Gallery determined to go after the target in spite of worsening weather. To allow the U-Boat time to resurface, he decided to wait one hour before sending out two planes to search.

Gallery's plan worked perfectly. Flying low through the low clouds and light fog that had set in, one of the two Avengers launched at 2315 spotted a submarine in just over an hour. The pilot dropped two depth bombs and in return received fire from the U-Boat's 37mm gun before the submarine again submerged. A sonobuoy released by the plane failed to pick up any propeller noises, but by now the task force was only forty miles away and closing fast.

On *U–515*, the aircraft sightings provoked no special concern, even though they were recognized as carrier aircraft. Henke rejected a suggestion to reverse course to shake off pursuit and maintained his southwesterly direction. At a depth of 100 meters, the hydrophones detected no sounds of approaching warships. Henke began to reconsider his intention to stay submerged until nightfall the next day.

A curious situation developed during the night. In the belief they had encountered the submarine attacked earlier, destroyer escort USS *Pope* of the task force's screen pursued a radar and sound contact to the north. In fact they had found another outbound U-Boat, *U–68* (Kaptlt. Albert Lauzemis), which managed temporarily to escape (she was sunk thirty hours later by *Guadalcanal*'s aircraft further south) while holding Gallery's attention. The task force's track now carried them north and west of Henke's position, so that the adversaries exchanged relative positions from the time of first contact.

Thus, at dawn on Easter Sunday, 9 April 1944, both commanders had slightly misjudged their situations. Henke thought he had shaken off pursuit, but did not realize he was not yet out of danger. Gallery believed he still had a submarine cornered—a claim maintained in his postwar writings—when he had actually lost contact with both U-Boats he had attacked. The distance between German and American, however, continued to narrow.

In the depths, Henke considered his options. The aircraft sightings the previous night had interrupted the battery recharging necessary for underwater operations. He lacked the snorkel that would have allowed him to recharge underwater. He could remain submerged all day and surface that evening, but if forced under again he would have no reserve power. There had been no sign of pursuit for hours, no propeller noises on the hydrophones. If he could surface and recharge now, he would build up the reserves needed for the submarine to have freedom to maneuver above or below the waves.

At Henke's command, *U–515* rose to periscope depth. A look through the sky periscope revealed a clear horizon and favorable cloud cover for spotting aircraft. The commander made his decision and gave the order: *"Auftauchen!"* ("surface!").

The U-Boat's chronometer read 0845, two hours ahead of the time kept aboard the American ships, as *U–515* broached the surface. Lookouts crowded the bridge and flak crews manned their guns as the batteries began recharging. For forty-five minutes, the sky and sea remained clear, and Henke's calculated risk appeared to have paid off.

But at 0930, lookouts sighted several ships' masts off the port quarter. Henke summoned *Matrosenobergefreiter* (Seaman, 1st class) Josef Wanzke, who possessed the best eyes among the crew, to the bridge. Wanzke studied the dim shapes on the northwest horizon through the binoculars for a minute, then announced: "Warships, including an aircraft carrier."

Before Henke could take any action, a plane dove out of the clouds on the starboard quarter. The 37mm gun jammed, but the two twin-mount 20mm pieces opened fire at the attacker. The aircraft's depth bombs fell short as the Avenger banked away. Henke immediately ordered a crash dive.

Aboard *Guadalcanal*, Lt.(jg) D. W. Brooks's report of sighting and attacking a submarine arrived at 0738 Greenwich mean time. The U-Boat, thought to be damaged in the last attack, lay only fifteen miles away from the carrier, and while submerged could be easily overtaken. Gallery ordered *Flaherty*, *Pillsbury*, and additional planes to the site of the attack, identified by green-dye markers dropped by Brooks. It took the destroyers less than forty minutes to reach the position. Gallery radioed: "OK, hop to it Big Boy. Bring us some prisoners."

At 0812 *Pillsbury*'s sonar made contact at a range of 2100 yards, soon verified by hydrophone. With *Flaherty* in support, *Pillsbury* launched a Hedgehog attack which produced one underwater explosion close by. A second attack quickly followed, this time resulting in a deep detonation that brought yellow plywood and fragments of insulation to the surface. In the churning aftermath of the attack, however, contact was lost.

Some aboard *U–515* felt that when Henke knew of a carrier's presence, he fell victim to "hunter's disease" and intended to attack. That he rejected a suggestion to stay at a shallow depth and use his T–5 torpedoes against his pursuers, however, disproves this. Instead Henke ordered a descent to 200 meters to ride out the awaited storm of depth-charges.

The half-hour wait for the attacking destroyers to arrive drove home to many crewmen how helpless their craft's limited underwater speed left them. Soon propeller noises could be heard, but the most unnerving experience came with *Pillsbury*'s sonar locking onto the U-Boat's hull: The sound resembled that of a circular buzz saw cutting into the steel around them, with the entire boat seeming to vibrate. They thought the explosion that followed resulted from a well-laid depth-charge, unaware how closely a hedgehog projectile had come to killing them all. The plummeting bomb must have struck *U–515* a glancing blow, causing only minor damage; had it landed squarely on the hull and exploded, the U-Boat would have all but disintegrated under the dense water pressure surrounding her.

Instead, Henke dove deeper to 240 meters (nearly 800 ft.). Several sonar decoys—canisters containing a compound of calcium and zinc that produced a mass of underwater bubbles, simulating the echo of a submarine—were released from the stern to mislead the destroyers' sonar probes. This appeared to succeed: The receding propeller noises signaled the Americans' departure. One hour passed, then two, and some of the crew began to hope they had escaped.

Above them, *Chatelain* joined *Pillsbury* and *Flaherty* in a search pattern that took the destroyers further west and away from Henke. *Guadalcanal* kept planes in the air on continual lookout, but for her immediate protection against U-Boat attack summoned the last destroyer, *Pope*, from the north. The latter had spent the morning trying to regain contact with the submarine attacked the previous night, but *U–68* had long since departed. Now *Pope* took up position 2,000 yards directly ahead of the escort carrier, steering southeast.

At 1133, *Pope* established an underwater sound contact only 700 yards away on her starboard beam. The destroyer briefly lost the contact, then regained it at 1152. Sonar operators definitely classified the echo as a submarine. Between 1157 and 1205 *Pope* launched two Hedgehog attacks, but with even less result than *Pillsbury* had achieved earlier. *Pope*'s captain, Lt. Cdr. Edwin H. Headland, considered that his prey was too deep for Hedgehog attacks and prepared to launch depth-charges at deep settings. The first pattern of eleven charges, set to 600 feet, dropped into the water at 1214.

When he heard the destroyer's noises overhead, Altenburger probably cursed Henke for not turning back to repair the oil leak: The chief engineer erroneously believed their pursuers had spotted the oil trail and followed it to their location. The first series of depth-charges detonated close by, but caused no damage. Twenty minutes later, however, a second pattern came closer, and *U–515* sustained her first serious damage. The blasts severed a lubrication-oil pipe and punctured a hole the size of a man's thumb through the pressure hull in the stern torpedo compartment. At the boat's depth, the water shot in like a jet, though Altenburger maintained trim by pumping the regulating tanks. But in the control room, the force of the explosions knocked out the depth gauges, further limiting Henke's freedom of maneuver.

For his third attack run, Lieutenant Commander Headland slowed his speed to ten knots and obtained a solid "read" on his underwater target. The two vessels were facing each other as *Pope*'s run began, but Henke began a slow, tight turn to starboard as the destroyer closed. The turn had just been completed when thirteen depth-charges dropped directly over *U–515*'s position.

Two or three charges struck the U-Boat's aft deck and rolled off before detonating. The explosions ripped open one of the ballast tanks and burst a pipeline leading in from an outboard fuel bunker. More water, now mixed with fuel oil, rushed into the aft torpedo room. The added weight dragged the U-Boat's stern down by over twenty degrees, a list that rendered the main suction pump incapable of pumping the water out. Trim tanks no longer sufficed to right the vessel, so crewmen continually ran forward to counterbalance the weight of sea water aft.

At last, Altenburger succeeded in plugging the principal leaks. The exhausted chief engineer advised Henke that they could not absorb further damage; Henke merely replied that to facilitate repairs he had already come to a shallower, and more vulnerable, depth. The only real hope was that the Americans would lose contact or run out of depth-charges.

Neither happened. *Pope* had enough weaponry remaining that Headland did not want to share the glory of the kill. When *Chatelain* moved up in support, the attacking destroyer signaled her to keep away: "Head westward, and don't do anything until we finish." After the devastating attack at 1307 hours, *Pope* made additional runs at 1320, 1343, and 1357. The last pattern initiated *U–515*'s final agony.

The seven depth-charges detonated close enough to the U-Boat's stern to jar loose Altenburger's improvised plugs, and water and oil again streamed in. All that could be done now was to abandon the compartment and secure the watertight hatch to the electric motor room, but the rising water found a broken box bolt and began to enter the engine room space necessary for underwater power. Now listing more than thirty degrees by the stern, almost the entire crew jammed into the forward compartments as *Fünf-fünfzehn* started to sink.

To regain an even keel, Henke increased speed, blew the main ballast tank, a⁻d f'nally emptied each of the aft fuel bunkers of their contents. At last, at a depth approaching 200 meters, these measures corrected the list. Now, however, a new problem arose, as free water moved forward into the rest of the submarine and the expansion of air in the rising aft part of the boat increased the heaviness of the bow and caused the entire submarine to begin to rise. Where she had been descending with her stern down, *U–515* was now ascending with her stern raised.

The state of the crew matched the battered condition of their vessel. Seven hours of ceaseless strain had taken a severe psychological and physical toll. Radioman Günther Virnau, who had not experienced a severe depth-bombing before, broke under the pressure and had to be knocked unconscious; a crewman laid him in a bunk in the petty officers' quarters.

Henke and Altenburger conferred as the boat rose toward the surface. When efforts to vent the blown fuel bunkers and slow the ascent failed, the chief engineer bluntly stated, "That's it." The boat, it seemed, had taken matters into her own hands. With the bow down by forty-five degrees, *U–515* was coming up.

Yet Henke refused to abandon the slight chance that they might yet escape. As they neared the surface, Henke asked his navigator for the course and distance to the Portuguese island of Madeira, the closest spot of land. If their tormentors had given up and departed, and if the engines could still be coaxed into action, Henke likely intended to head there and intern himself and his crew.

But the American destroyers had not left. Sonar contact had been lost as *U–515* rose rapidly from the depths, but *Chatelain* briefly regained contact and prepared to finally make her own attack of the day. The chronometer on the destroyer's bridge read 1504 as the commanding officer issued the order to fire depth-charges.

At that moment, a geyser of water rose just seventy-five yards off the *Chatelain*'s starboard beam. As the white foam subsided, the stern of a submarine emerged and fell back into the water, dragging the conning tower and deck of a U-Boat to the surface behind it. The submarine surfaced so rapidly that two of the just-released depth-charges crashed onto her foredeck and rolled off into the sea.

Henke opened the hatch in the conning tower and stepped onto the bridge. The sight of a destroyer less than 100 meters away shattered the last hope of escape. A quick glance around revealed three other destroyers, an aircraft carrier, and planes in the air converging on his position. They had surfaced in the middle of a task force. Only one order could be given.

"Alle Mann aus dem Boot!"—"All hands, abandon ship!"

At almost the same moment, the U.S. commander of the four destroyers issued his own order: "Sub! Sub is on the surface. Sink him. SINK HIM. Shoot everything you've got!"

Chatelain obliged, turning sharply to starboard to cross the U-Boat's bow with all weapons brought to bear. Three three-inch guns and several 40mm and 20mm flak pieces opened a withering fire at a range of only 150 yards. The German crewmen coming out of the conning tower, believed to be running to man their own guns, were cut down as they emerged: Even after the engagement, the U.S. action reports asserted that the U-Boat returned fire. The only thought in the minds of *U–515*'s crew, however, was to get off.

Those who followed Henke out the conning tower suffered the heaviest losses. One three-inch shell struck the base of the lower platform of the bridge, igniting the hydrogen bottles stored there for filling the Aphrodite balloons. The resulting fire in turn detonated much of the 37mm ammunition for the flak gun just as several sailors stepped onto the platform. The conning tower also drew the attention of the Avenger aircraft that attacked just after *Chatelain* opened fire: Four rockets struck there almost simultaneously with the destroyer's shells.

Many crewmen still huddled in the U-Boat's forward compartments never heard the order to abandon ship but their location allowed them to exit through the forward hatches and avoid the heaviest fire. The chance to escape could not overcome the psychological effects suffered by some during their long ordeal. One young sailor shot himself with a signal pistol rather than try to escape, and at least one man refused to leave the boat's interior. Radioman Virnau still lay unconscious in the petty officers' compartment when a shell landed there, killing him instantly.

For the rest, leaping overboard and swimming away brought no guarantee of survival. Two Wildcat fighter planes from *Guadalcanal* continued to dive and strafe the target, killing several crewmen; others, exhausted by their trial, were overcome by the sea. Altenburger, among the last to leave, dived into the sea without his lifejacket. One of the machinists in the water shared his with the chief, each with an arm looped through one of the sleeves. A burst from a strafing plane severed the jacket through the middle, though miraculously neither man was hit.

How long the firing lasted, how long the U-Boat stayed afloat, cannot be said with certainty because of disagreements in the U.S. Navy records. *Chatelain*, according to her action report prepared after the event, opened fire at 1505, ceased fire four minutes later, and watched *U–515* sink at 1512. Yet the same destroyer's logbook states that "sub sunk at 1516 still under fire from *Chatelain*; 1517 ceased firing." Neither Henke nor his crewmen had the opportunity to note precise chronologies, but most paused in the water to turn and look back at their vessel, their home for the last two years.

A white plume of smoke vented from the wreckage of the lower platform of the conning tower, but above the water line the submarine showed little of the damage that had doomed her. The boat's bow, however, disappeared even as they watched. As the water gradually overtook and extinguished the fire, the conning tower in its distinctive light-gray paint slid beneath the waves. At the last, the stern raised up and plunged into the depths. *U–515* sank at 3:12 P.M., Greenwich mean time, on Easter Sunday 1944, at position 34 degrees, 35 minutes N, 19 degrees, 18 minutes W.

Sixteen men of her complement died with her. The first watch officer, *Oberleutnant* Karl Benz, disappeared after he went into the water. *Oberfähnrich* Paul Dohrmann was killed by machine-gun fire from one of the strafing aircraft. The oldest and most experienced of the fourteen petty officers and enlisted men lost, twenty-seven-year-old *Obermaschinist* Hans Bruhs, had served aboard *U–515* since commissioning; he died on the lower bridge platform. Of the remaining casualties, two others had been present since the beginning on *U–515*; seven had made three to five patrols with Henke; and for three crewmen, their first voyage proved to be their last. Except for Bruhs, only one of the crewmen lost had attained the age of twenty-three. Five were nineteen.

The forty-four survivors, many wounded by bullets or shrapnel, struggled toward the American warships. Many, exhausted by their exertions, had to be pulled up the ropes onto the decks of the destroyer escorts. USS *Pillsbury* proceeded to the sinking site and recovered eight gallons of sample oil for technical intelligence. The battle was over.[11]

Henke and four of his crewmen found themselves aboard USS *Chatelain*. Almost immediately, Henke received an invitation to the ward room from the captain, Lt. Cdr. James L. Foley. Henke greeted Foley with a protest against the Americans' excessive fire: "You didn't have to kill so many of my men, we would have surrendered." When Foley's executive officer asked him which side he thought would win the war, Henke surprised his hosts with the response, in perfect English, "You have already won it."[12]

For all but one of the survivors of *U–515*, the ordeal had ended. For Werner Henke, the final phase had just begun.

NOTES

1. Peter Cremer, interview with author in Hamburg (Aumühle), 3 September 1989; and Peter Cremer, *U-Boat Commander* (Annapolis, MD: Naval Institute Press, 1984), 165–66.

2. See the detailed message of BdU to *U–123*, 24 January 1944, SRGN nos. 30856–857, 30860, RG 457, NA; and the KTB BdU, 30 March 1944, T1022/4065/PG 30343.

3. Interview with Günther Altenburger, Lübbenau, 13 May 1992.

4. Data taken from Henke's personnel record; Hans Herlin, *Verdammter Atlantik. Schicksale deutscher U-Boot-Fahrer* (Munich: Wilhelm Heyne Verlag, 1982), 134–35; and letter of Albrecht Henke to author, 10 December 1989. The former Frau Henke's physical condition precluded interviews or correspondence. The conclusions suggested are entirely my own.

5. "*U–515* Final Interrogation Report," RG 38, NA; *U–515* crew lists, U-Boot-Archiv; author's interview with Carl Möller, Hamburg, 30 August 1989; and Jak P. Mallmann Showell, *U-Boat Command and the Battle of the Atlantic* (Lewiston, NY: Vanwell, 1989), 173, 187.

6. On the snorkel, see Eberhard Rössler, *The U-Boat. The Evolution and Technical History of German Submarines* (Annapolis, MD: Naval Institute Press, 1981), 198–204; Fritz Köhl and Axel Niestle, *Vom Original zum Modell: Uboottyp IXC* (Koblenz: Bernard & Graefe Verlag, 1990), 30; and Cremer, *Commander*, 180–85. Data on Frau Henke's visit from interview with Günther Altenburger, Kiel, 2 September 1989, and *U–515* preliminary interrogations (Altenburger, 9 May 1944), RG 38, NA.

7. Herlin, *Verdammter*, 135–36, who places the departure on 29 March; both the POW interrogations and the KTB BdU, however, fix the date on 30 March.

8. See William T. Y'Blood, *Hunter-Killer: U.S. Escort Carriers in the Battle of the Atlantic* (Annapolis, MD: Naval Institute Press, 1983), 49ff.; Daniel V. Gallery, "Nor Dark of Night," *USNIP*, 95, 4 (April 1969), 85–90, and Gallery's more anecdotal *U–505* (New York: Paperback Library, 1967), 224–32.

9. "*U–515* Final Interrogation Report" and preliminary interrogations, RG 38, NA; Henke's destination is provided in the KTB BdU, 18 April 1944 (T1022/4065/PG 30345).

10. Decrypted translations of *U–515* and BdU messages are located in "COM-INCH File: Rough Notes on Daily U-Boat Positions and Activities, January-December 1944," SRMN–034, 665–74, RG 457, NA.

11. For sources on the engagement: On the American side, see the Action Report of Commander, Task Group 21.12, "Report of Sinking of *U–515* and *U–68* on 9–10 April 1944" (with appendices), 26 April 1944 (OpArchives); supplemented by the logs of the various ships involved (Records of the Bureau of Naval Personnel, RG 24, NA). On the German side, see the preliminary and final interrogations of *U–515*'s survivors (RG 38, NA); accounts of the U-Boat's loss by Hans Schultz and Ernst Heimann, on file in the U-Boot-Archiv, Cuxhaven; author's interview with Günther Altenburger, Kiel, 2 September 1989; and the account in Herlin, *Verdammter*, 136–52, based on interviews with survivors.

12. Cdr. Dawson Molyneaus (ret.), "The Sinking of U-Boat 515," *DESA News*, September-October 1988, 7–8.

17

A Little Hanky-Panky

Henke did not remain long aboard the *Chatelain*. Less than two hours after *U–515* sank, the destroyer escort came alongside the *Guadalcanal* and transferred her prisoners via a breeches' buoy. After a physical search and medical examination, Henke was led away to the ship's brig while armed guards escorted the four ratings to separate quarters. Later that evening, most of the remaining survivors transferred aboard from the *Pope*; Altenburger and Jensen joined Henke in the brig.

Task group commander Gallery followed standard navy procedure in dividing his prisoners according to rank, to limit communications among officers, noncommissioned officers, and enlisted men, and thus facilitate later interrogation. The three groups did not communicate with each other for the remainder of the voyage. Many crewmen did not realize for two days that their captain was aboard.

Gallery devoted little immediate attention to his "guests," as the navy preferred to leave interrogations to its stateside specialists. Gallery did press Henke for information about other submarines in the immediate vicinity, but the U-Boat commander refused. It made little difference, as Henke lacked the knowledge more quickly obtained by *Guadalcanal*'s own aircraft. During the night of 9–10 April, the carrier's planes caught *U–68* again and *U–214* (Kaptlt. Rupprecht Stock) on the surface. The latter escaped without damage, but *U–68*'s good luck from the previous night deserted her: She was sunk with the loss of all hands save one, who joined four wounded comrades from *U–515* in *Guadalcanal*'s sick bay.[1]

Finally the task force moved away from the U-Boat passage routes and steered for Norfolk. The voyage required seventeen days from the date of *U–515*'s sinking, but the German survivors—denied mutual contact, confined to their quarters except for brief exercise periods—knew neither their course, destination, nor ultimate disposition. This disorientation would play a part in the drama that began the day after Henke arrived.

The U-Boat captain asked to see Gallery concerning his incarceration. Described by his captor as "formal, respectful, and correct," Henke again protested the killing of his men in the water, and asked that he be removed from the ship's prison and quartered in an officer's stateroom, in accordance with the terms of the Geneva Convention. Gallery replied that the crowded conditions aboard did not permit such accommodations. If the Germans disliked their conditions, he added, perhaps they could be surrendered to British authority in Gibraltar during the next refueling stop.

The last point amounted to pure bluff. The task force was heading away from Gibraltar, and Gallery had no intention of handing over the tangible evidence of his success to anyone. According to Gallery's postwar account, this proposal immediately silenced Henke. The information Gallery provided to ONI in May 1944, however, offers a different view: "(Henke's) reaction was immediate. He stated that he would under no circumstances be taken prisoner by the British and that he would dispose of himself first."

Several days later, Gallery's chief master at arms asked to see him about Henke. In the course of regularly serving food to the German officer, the chief had engaged Henke in friendly conversation and gained his confidence. Henke apparently let slip the story of the *Ceramic* broadcast and the alleged British interest in trying him as a war criminal.[2]

It was Henke's first serious mistake.

Daniel Gallery was an imaginative and innovative commander whose achievements are not dimmed by his own postwar exaggerations. His successful experiment with night flying became standard practice for escort carriers in the Atlantic, though a number of carriers in the Pacific had flown night missions before him. His observations on the circumstances of *U–515*'s sinking, confirmed by Henke's own statements, led to the daring and successful capture of *U–505* in June 1944, though the U.S. Navy had long since provided guidelines on the possible salvage of a sinking submarine by a boarding party. When Gallery discovered Henke's supposed vulnerability to British jurisdiction, he immediately sought to exploit it for military advantage. In his words, "we worked a little hanky-panky."[3]

On 15 April, Gallery had his radioman produce a false message—using an authentic form and appropriate markings—with a request for Henke and his crew to be turned over to British authorities, but leaving the decision to Gallery's discretion. He then summoned Henke to the bridge—with charts of Gibraltar prominently on display—and handed the "dispatch" to his captive. Gallery reported Henke's immediate reaction as dejection, followed by resignation.

Then Gallery made his pitch. With the discretion given him by the "dispatch," Gallery could bring Henke and his men back to the United States—if Henke "would make it worth his while." At that, Gallery produced a prepared statement that read (in English only): "I, Kapitan Lieutenant [sic] Henke, hereby promise on my honor as a German officer that, if I and my crew are imprisoned in the United States instead of in England, I will answer questions truthfully when I am interrogated."

After reading the document, Henke looked at Gallery and said, "Captain, you know I can't sign that."

Gallery replied unequivocally that the Germans' passage to the United States depended upon Henke's signing the document. After a pause, Henke asked: "What would you do in my position?" The American—doubtless informed of Henke's earlier remark to the *Chatelain*'s executive officer—replied, "If I were convinced my country had lost the war, and I could help my crew by signing, I would sign." Some minutes passed in silence; the moment reminded Gallery of a scene in a movie. At last, Henke picked up a pen and signed. Gallery and his executive officer also signed as witnesses, and Henke returned to his cell.[4]

Werner Henke had made his second, and much greater, mistake. To this point his conduct in combat and captivity had been faultless, except for divulging to Gallery's chief his reluctance to become a British prisoner. Even that mattered only if Henke allowed it to influence his actions. That is precisely what happened.

By signing any kind of concession, Henke irrevocably compromised himself. Almost certainly he had no intention of honoring his statement, as he subsequently refused to cooperate with his captors. He had to expect, however, to face the consequences for such a course. In any case, he failed to recognize that the *Ceramic* broadcast had already placed him squarely in the public arena of psychological warfare, and now he had voluntarily handed his enemies a weapon to use against him.

Henke's seeking to avoid extradition while intending not to honor his statement reveals the same self-deception and egotism that led to his near dismissal from the service over three years earlier. He should have been all the more aware that his record of disciplinary problems and encounters with Nazi party representatives left him particularly vulnerable within Germany, should the use of his name again become a propaganda issue.

Ironically, the confrontation between Gallery and Henke rested upon a thoroughly confused understanding of the radio broadcast that had named Werner Henke as "War Criminal no. 1" in the first place. Neither man realized that a *British* broadcast had never been made. The voice that charged Henke with war crimes, it will be recalled, belonged to the U.S. Navy's own "Commander Lee Norden," a fictional identity with the authentic credentials of the Office of Naval Intelligence's Special Warfare Branch. Because of *Ceramic*'s British registry, the broadcast's origin became a matter of assumption and its true author simply neglected. Henke had paradoxically compromised himself to assure that he remained in the hands of those who had promised to prosecute him.

Gallery summoned the spokesman of the petty officer survivors, Heinrich Lamprecht, to persuade his comrades to also agree to talk in exchange for a guarantee of American captivity. The forty petty officers and enlisted men did sign an agreement dated 16 April to "answer truthfully all questions about U-Boat operations and equipment," though the German-language text contained so many grammatical errors that the Germans might have subsequently disavowed their concurrence on the basis of "confusion." Nevertheless, Gallery obtained what he wanted.[5]

Altenburger knew nothing of Henke's signed agreement, but the continuing drop in his captain's morale concerned him. Returning from one of his daily interrogation sessions with Gallery, Henke acknowledged to his chief engineer that the Americans were greatly pressuring him. Altenburger reminded Henke, "We are German officers, we are still at war, we cannot cooperate." Altenburger in part still held Henke responsible for not turning back after the oil leak was discovered.

On 26 April, the task group returned to its home base of Norfolk, Virginia. Between 8:00 P.M. and midnight that night, *U–515*'s crewmen filed down the gangplank into captivity. The blindfolds they wore prevented even a glimpse of the sea that had defined their world for so long. Werner Henke would never see it again.[6]

For the next six days the prisoners remained at Camp Allen, a processing facility at Norfolk's naval operating base. A personnel data card was prepared for each, with photographs, fingerprints, and biographical information. Henke acquired a new identity as Prisoner no. 5G-450-NA. No one was interrogated during this period, but all were evaluated for their potential intelligence value. Finally on 2 May, all of *U–515*'s survivors fit to travel (two remained in hospital) boarded trucks for new destinations. Officially, the prisoners now belonged to the U.S. Army, the permanent authority for POWs on American soil; in fact, they remained "available for further interrogation" by the specialists of Op-16-Z, the Special Activities Branch of the Office of Naval Intelligence.[7]

American intelligence of U-Boat warfare involved a labyrinth of organizations that shared a common goal, but which knew little of each other's precise contributions. The interception and decryption of U-Boat radio signals by the "Secret Room" of the Commander-in-Chief (COM-INCH) Combat Intelligence, Atlantic Section, for example, remained unknown to all but a privileged few at the highest levels. For all their intelligence expertise, the personnel of Op-16-Z did not know about ULTRA and the gold mine of intelligence it provided.

Thus, the paradox developed that Op-16-Z interrogated captured U-Boat crewmen for information already available from a more timely and reliable source. Yet ULTRA intelligence could not be overly used in operations, lest the Germans suspect that their codes had been compromised. Therefore, any information obtained by more conventional means—especially captured documents and interrogations—allowed a greater dissemination and operational use of such intelligence, and further insulated ULTRA from possible discovery.[8]

Under Cdr. John L. Riheldaffer, Op-16-Z had acquired extensive experience in interrogating over 700 captured German submariners by the end of 1943. With the assistance of army intelligence, the unit operated a special and highly classified interrogation center at Fort Hunt, located seventeen miles south of Washington, DC, near Mount Vernon. The recently expanded POW facilities there featured self-contained quarters "bugged" with hidden microphones, allowing prisoners to be isolated or intentionally paired as desired. Together with the extensive intelligence supplied by their British counterparts, Op-16-Z possessed an excellent picture of the U-Boat service.

On the subject of Werner Henke, Op-16-Z knew the truth behind the *Ceramic* broadcast, as its own liaison officer to the Special Warfare Branch read the speech as "Commander Norden." The ULTRA intelligence office apparently confirmed for Op-16-Z (without disclosing its source) the true version of the incident, as indicated by a May 1944 special collection of the intercepted December 1942 messages between *U–515* and BdU in the ULTRA intercept files. As early as August 1943, Op-16-Z had compiled a biographical sketch of Henke: Based upon POW statements, the report included his reputation as a strict disciplinarian, the dates of his decorations, his AWOL incident and punishment earlier in the war, and even the recovery of the butter cases during a previous patrol.[9]

For twenty-five *U–515* crewmen, the trucks they boarded on 2 May carried them to Fort George G. Meade in the neighboring state of Maryland. The next day they resumed their long journey to Papago Park, Arizona, where the U.S. Army maintained one of its principal camps for German Navy POWs. Those destined for Fort Hunt arrived in two groups, ten crewmen arriving there at 1:30 A.M. on the morning of 3 May while Henke, his officers, and the remaining six men followed that afternoon. None realized that the humorless officers in army uniform awaiting them were all Op-16-Z interrogators.[10]

For the petty officers and enlisted men, the interrogations followed a routine whose worth had been demonstrated many times. American officers overwhelmed their captives with a wealth of already accumulated knowledge of U-Boat commanders, weapons, and equipment, probing only for the needed confirmation or detail that the prisoners did not realize constituted the true object of interest. Their room conversations with comrades were recorded and studied for additional data.

In the end, *U–515*'s men told no more and no less than the average U-Boat POWs for the 1944–45 period. The most valued intelligence concerned the *Hohentwiel* radar equipment and its technical characteristics, disseminated throughout ONI. Op-16-Z's own postwar assessment of intelligence coups through interrogation of U-Boat survivors does not mention *U–515*, though *U–172* and *U–1229* are singled out for the valuable intelligence their survivors provided regarding torpedo types and the "Schnorchel" device, respectively. Nearly all the crewmen departed Fort Hunt between 11 and 18 May for brief stays at the holding enclosure at Fort Meade before moving on to Papago Park or another POW camp.[11]

More varied treatment, however, awaited the German officers. Altenburger, who remained at Fort Hunt for more than two weeks, experienced a wide range of tactics to solicit his cooperation. Sometimes he was treated as a comrade; once his captors took him on a guided tour of Washington, DC, for an afternoon and evening. Other days he remained in solitary confinement. Once denied water for most of a day, Altenburger then received a bottle of whiskey to quench his thirst: When brought in for questioning a couple of hours later, the intoxicated engineer yielded only "jokes and a lot of nonsense."

In particular, Op-16-Z sought information on radar-detection gear and new torpedo types—topics outside the general responsibility of a U-Boat chief engineer. A "stool pigeon" in the dress of a German officer once joined him in his cell, but he proved easy to unmask. Altenburger was never beaten or physically threatened, though interrogators offered vague threats about bombing raids against his home in Dresden. Finally, on 23 May *U–515*'s chief engineer departed Fort Hunt to begin twenty-one months of captivity in various U.S. camps. As his guards led him away, he wondered what had become of Henke, whom he had not seen since their arrival at the camp.[12]

Navy records provide only a skeleton of documentation concerning Henke's stay at Fort Hunt. Between 4 and 11 May, Henke was formally interrogated only five times, the longest lasting an hour and forty minutes, two requiring only twenty-five minutes each. For the first four days, Henke shared a cell with his first officer, Hans Schultz, still recuperating from a broken arm. Schultz later described the room as fair-sized but barren except for two beds, two chairs and a table; a window covered with wire mesh permitted some natural light to filter in. The two barely spoke, realizing that hidden microphones recorded every word. When Schultz's wound showed signs of infection, he was removed to the hospital. Henke spent the last four days in his cell alone.

The subject of Henke's interrogations doubtless ranged over a variety of topics—equipment, weapons systems, tactics, morale. His captors may have pressured him to make broadcasts or sign his name to propaganda leaflets. Ironically, Henke's final interrogator on 11 May was Lt. Cdr. Ralph G. Albrecht, who as "Commander Lee Norden" had labeled Henke as "War Criminal no. 1." No transcript of their discussion, nor of any of his navy interrogations, survives.[13]

Henke doubtless confronted tactics similar to those experienced by Altenburger. In one ploy, a civilian employee of Op-16-Z disguised as a member of the Royal Canadian Mounted Police interrupted a Henke interrogation, asking for the U-Boat captain's extradition to Canada for trial in Britain. Yet no evidence suggests that he was beaten or physically mistreated. The two reported instances of such behavior occurred only in April and May 1945, culminating in the suicide of one U-Boat captain and an official navy court of inquiry into the matter.[14]

Regardless of tactics or pressures used against him, however, Henke refused to talk. Probably recognizing the serious error he had made aboard the *Guadalcanal*, he resisted all efforts to obtain information or cooperation. In a letter summarizing Henke's case, Op-16-Z's commander described Henke's written agreement to cooperate but noted that "when brought to interrogation, the prisoner had a complete change of heart and steadfastly refused to answer any questions whatever, and it has been impossible to alter this determination."[15]

On 12 May, the navy abandoned further questioning and released him to army intelligence at Fort Hunt, with a recommendation for eventual transfer to the U-Boat POW camp at Papago Park, Arizona. The army, who moved their prisoner to a different part of the compound, interrogated Henke two days later on general morale questions; this is the only interrogation whose record has survived. Here Henke did offer his views, though he insisted his remarks should not be used for propaganda. Though he maintained the justness of Germany's cause and refused to concede supremacy in Allied weapons, Henke displayed an analytical insight toward the war and National Socialism.

"It may be judged that the prisoner does not favor Hitler as the right leader for Germany," noted the interrogation summary. "It would be hard to say who would be a good successor. He must be a man who has seen the world and is a good diplomat. . . . Present day conditions show that Nazism is not the right solution of the German problem." When asked how Hitler came to power, Henke replied: "(T)hrough unemployment, hunger, and a lost war. . . . Germany did not have only two big parties, but many parties, each of which thought it could build up the country. One cannot manage on that basis. Dissatisfaction led to the Nazi movement."

On the aerial bombardment of German cities, Henke unhesitatingly described it as a *Schweinerei* (filthy business) that, like the Allies' demand for unconditional surrender, only increased the people's spirit of resistance. As to his own inclinations, "he expresses his hatred of war, his desire for a peaceful life."[16]

At Fort Hunt, Henke appears to have recovered the morale and spirit he had lost aboard *Guadalcanal*. He knew he was due for promotion to the rank of *Korvettenkapitän* (Lieutenant Commander) with effect on 1 June, though he already assumed that rank for himself in his dealings with American authorities in May. His letter to his mother on 7 May revealed his concerns for his family and the future:

> I am doing well, my treatment and the food are both good, so please don't worry. You may write me as often as you wish. . . . Please transfer my

bank account to Anita but take out RM500 [about $125], to pay for your house maid. . . . Please also keep all my civilian things in good shape.

In a heavily censored letter to his mother and brother on 22 May, Henke again spoke of the future:

I hope the war will soon be over, in September it will be five years. What one misses is regular work, to which I am so accustomed. . . . Look after your own health, then everything will be all right. Say hello to all the neighbors for me. Did you receive my [three] other letters? Don't worry yourselves about me at all.[17]

Fate, however, had one more card to play.

Original navy plans called for Henke's transfer to Papago Park, the POW camp for unreconstructed U-Boat prisoners. As late as 20 May, the ONI officer at Papago Park planned to place Henke with such other "super Nazis" of the camp as Jürgen Wattenberg, former commander of *U–162*. Had this happened, Henke likely would have participated in the greatest mass escape of POWs in U.S. history, as Wattenberg and twenty-four other U-Boat prisoners tunneled their way out of Papago Park two days before Christmas, 1944.[18]

Yet Riheldaffer had already reconsidered. To send Henke to Papago Park would reunite him with most of his crew, to whom he could relate how he had defied the Americans and gotten away with it. The chief of Op-16-Z recounted his decision in a letter of 17 May to his Canadian counterpart, Cdr. C. H. Little:

It was finally decided that it would be a sign of weakness on our part to permit the prisoner to refuse to talk, after having signed the agreement, *without carrying through some form of "punishment."* He might also have made serious trouble for his crew in any camp or caused serious trouble in whatever camp he was assigned to as soon as the knowledge of his actions became known.

I therefore requested Captain Wynne [head of the British Admiralty Delegation in Washington, DC] to send the despatch . . . [so] that we could "turn him over to the British" for internment wherever they saw fit! Actually, there is little to be gained from him and the real benefit is in having him definitely separated from his crew so that *the crew may presume he has been severely punished in some way.* (emphasis added)

In the letter Riheldaffer recapitulated the story of the *Ceramic*, the subsequent radio broadcast, and Gallery's "hanky-panky" at sea. Of particular note are Riheldaffer's comments on Henke's actions and character:

> He was actually under the impression he would be tried and executed in England for the alleged shelling of survivors. Actually, the whole tale is fictitious and, so far as we know, he acted quite properly in sinking the *Ceramic*. . . . We believe that he later learned the truth about the broadcast and . . . lost his fear of any reprisals against him. Except for the single slip of signing the original statement he had conducted himself perfectly and is, apparently, a strong character and a good officer.[19]

Riheldaffer's reasoning contained one flaw. Henke had not learned the truth about the broadcast, and still believed in the threat of a war crimes trial whose outcome had been predetermined. Where Riheldaffer conceived of transfer to Canada as "punishment" in itself, Henke would interpret it as a death sentence.

Thus on 20 May the British Admiralty Delegation formally requested Henke's shipment to Canada. Army intelligence, unaware of the machinations behind the move, duly complied and began making the necessary travel arrangements. In early June the army completed their prisoner's travel itinerary. On the afternoon of Monday, 19 June, he would depart Baltimore's Pennsylvania Station aboard the "Montrealer" train for St. Albans, Vermont, where Canadian representatives would assume custody the next morning.[20]

Werner Henke probably began to sense something in early June. The interrogations no longer carried any urgency, yet he had heard nothing about a transfer to a regular POW camp. The average stay of German POWs at Fort Hunt during this period amounted to less than eight days; Henke had been there six weeks. He remained alone and isolated, except for brief exchanges with Hans Kastrup, lone survivor of *U–68*, and later with Fritz Kuert, survivor of the German blockade runner *Doggerbank*. The latter, the last countryman with whom Henke spoke, later recalled that the U-Boat captain never mentioned anything regarding escape.[21]

On 15 June, however, Henke must have learned of his planned transfer to Canada. Army intelligence officers, unaware of the background and significance of the move, doubtless informed Henke in the context of a move to an interim location—the holding enclosure at Fort Meade, Maryland—probably the next day, 16 June.

In Werner Henke's mind, the trip he would begin could only end on the scaffold. Daniel Gallery had presented him with a stark option two months earlier: talk, or be turned over to the British. He had not talked; therefore, he would be extradited for a "show" trial and likely execution. If his life was already over, however, perhaps there was a third choice.

As he had refused to talk, so too could he refuse to play the role written for him. In a final act of defiance, he could decide his own fate and deny the Allies their anticipated propaganda victory. He had made his determination; he needed only the opportunity.

At 6:00 P.M. on the warm, humid evening of Thursday, 15 June, he stepped from his quarters to begin his daily hour of exercise in the adjacent narrow yard. For fifty-five minutes, he followed his usual routine. With only five minutes left before his guard came to return him to his cell, Werner Henke stopped in his tracks, turned, and sprinted for the barbed-wire fence at the end of the enclosure.

To the last, he recognized no one as master of his actions but himself.

NOTES

1. Action Report, Commander Task Group 21.12, 26 April 1944, OpArchives.

2. See Daniel V. Gallery, *Clear The Decks* (New York: William Morrow and Company, 1951), 196–99; and Gallery, *U-505* (New York: Paperback Library, 1967), 236–40. The quotation is taken from the letter of Cdr. John H. Riheldaffer (head of Op-16-Z) to Cdr. C. H. Little, 17 May 1944, Op-16-Z day files ("ONI-Ottawa, 1–5–43 to ——"), RG 38, NA.

3. Cf. Gallery's "Nor Dark of Night," *USNIP*, vol. 95, no. 4 (April 1969), 85–90 (and source for "hanky-panky"); and the letter of Cdr. James H. Trousdale, *USNIP*, vol. 95, no. 9 (September 1969), 105–6; and Gallery, *U-505*, 247–50; and the report issued by commander-in-chief, U.S. Fleet, "Characteristics of Enemy Submarines" (22 January 1943), 3–7 to 3–9, copy in Document and Library Collection, U.S. Army Air Forces, RG 18, NA.

4. Quoted statements are consistent in both of Gallery's versions (*Clear*, 199–203 [including a facsimile of the faked "message"], and *U-505*, 240–42); the signed statement is located in the *U-515* preliminary interrogations, RG 38, NA.

5. The crew's statement is also located among *U-515* preliminary interrogations, RG 38, NA; Hans Herlin, *Verdammter Atlantik. Schicksale deutscher U-Boot-Fahrer* (Munich: Wilhelm Heyne Verlag, 1982), 154–56, denies any crew agreement on the basis of interviews, but the signatures are genuine, as verified by the POW personnel forms signed on arrival in Norfolk.

6. Altenburger interview, Kiel, 2 September 1989; log of *Guadalcanal*, 26 April 1944, RG 24, NA.

7. Headquarters, Fifth Naval District to Provost Marshal General, War Department, "German Prisoners of War-Request for Transfer of Custody," 2 May 1944, COMINCH Formerly Secret 1944 file A16–2(3)/EF30, RG 80, NA.

8. "Functions of the 'Secret Room' (F–211) of COMINCH Combat Intelligence, Atlantic Section, Anti-Submarine Warfare, WWII," Study SRMN–038, RG

457, NA; Ladislas Farago, *The Tenth Fleet* (New York: Paperback Library, 1964), 201–12; interview with Captain (ret.) Wyman H. Packard (former U.S. Navy intelligence officer), Washington Navy Yard, 15 February 1990.

9. ULTRA copies of intercepts located in "COMINCH File of Memoranda concerning U-Boat Tracking Room Operations, January 1943–June 1945" (182), SRMN–032, RG 457, NA; Op-16-Z memorandum no. 939 for Op-16-W, "Werner Henke Klt.," 19 August 1943, in Op-16-Z subject files (memoranda for Op-16-W, July-December 1943), RG 38, NA; Fort Hunt described in folder "CPM Branch," G–2 Division (MIS-Y Branch) records, RG 165, NA.

10. War Department G–2 Division memorandum, "Transfer of German Naval Prisoners of War," 2 May 1944, POW Operations Division formerly classified decimal file 253.91, RG 389, NA; Altenburger interview, 2 September 1989 (the chief engineer did not realize he had not left U.S. Navy custody); and Fort Hunt logs of Op-16-Z, Op-16-Z subject files, RG 38, NA.

11. Preliminary and final interrogation reports, *U–515*; Op-16-Z spot item no. 269, "Hohentwiel Fu.M.G. (Radar)," 10 May 1944, all in Op-16-Z files, RG 38, NA; Op-16-Z history in "U.S. Naval Administration in World War II: Office of Naval Intelligence" (mss., n.d.), OpArchives; transfers of *U–515* crewmen regularly noted in correspondence of the POW Operations Division, classified decimal file 253.91, RG 389, NA.

12. Altenburger interview, 2 September 1989; PMGO memorandum of 23 May 1944, POW Operations Division file 253.91, RG 389, NA.

13. Data taken from Fort Hunt logs and berthing lists, Op-16-Z subject files, RG 38, NA; Schultz's account in Herlin, *Verdammter*, 170.

14. Farago, *Tenth Fleet*, 150, for the Henke story; on the incidents involving U-Boat captains Friedrich Steinhoff (*U–873*) and Paul Just (*U–546*), see Just's memoirs, *Vom Seeflieger zum Uboot-Fahrer. Feindflüge und Feindfahrten 1939–1945* (Stuttgart: Motorbuch, 1979), 192–204; and the summary report of the Navy investigation, "Irregularities Connected with the Handling of Surrendered German Submarines and Prisoners of War at the Navy Yard, Portsmouth, NH," 19 June 1945, in A16–2(3)/EF30, 1945 Secret SecNav CNO correspondence files, RG 80, NA.

15. Riheldaffer to Little, 17 May 1944, RG 38, NA.

16. "Report on Interrogation of P/W HENKE, Hans (sic), Korvettenkapitän," 14 May 1944, 201 POW files, G–2 Division (MIS-Y Branch), RG 165, NA.

17. Henke's personnel file dates his promotion as 1 June 1944, although the paperwork was not completed before his death and was apparently never confirmed; this and the letters of 7 and 22 May 1944 are in the Henke family papers.

18. On Henke's planned transfer, Lt. Cmdr. V. R. Taylor to Riheldaffer, 20 May 1944, file "Taylor, VR, Incoming Letters 1943–45," Op-16-Z administrative files, RG 38, NA; on the escape, see John Hammond Moore's excellent *The Faustball Tunnel: German POWs in America and Their Great Escape* (New York: Random House, 1978).

19. Riheldaffer to Little, 17 May 1944.

20. See the four memoranda regarding Henke's transfer, 20 May–9 June 1944, in POW Operations Division class. file 253.91 General (Ft. Hunt), RG 389, NA.

21. "CPM Branch" report, 53, RG 165, NA; Herlin, *Verdammter*, 177.

Conclusion

Even in death, Werner Henke remained a thorn in the side of the Allies. The shooting death of an inmate on the perimeter of a secret installation might have proven troublesome in view of the close proximity of private homes. At least one local resident heard the gunfire and ran upstairs to her bedroom window to see Henke's body caught on the wire. But neither she nor any of Fort Hunt's civilian neighbors ever inquired about what went on in the camp.[1]

Nevertheless, even acknowledging the shooting would compromise the center's secrecy. Army Colonel John L. Walker, commanding officer at Fort Hunt, therefore ordered Henke's body transported immediately to Fort Meade, forty miles to the north. Thereafter, all official records, including the formal response in November 1944 to German inquiries, testified to Henke's death at Fort Meade. Henke's interment there furthered the deception. The only documentary proof that Henke never left Fort Hunt is found in the absence of his name from the record of POW transfers assiduously maintained by the Army Provost Marshal General's Office.[2]

If U.S. authorities preserved Fort Hunt's secrecy, the explanation "shot while trying to escape" never satisfied his family or others who knew Henke well. News of the shooting soon spread among U-Boat POWs scattered around the country. By the end of the war, captured submariners likened the suspicious circumstances of Henke's death to an anecdote told them by African-Americans. A white sheriff discovers the body of a black man in the street, notes the twelve bullet holes in the corpse, and concludes, "Damn, another suicide."[3]

Yet as we have seen, Henke's death involved less conspiracy than tricks, misunderstanding, and irony. American officers played on Henke's fears of transfer to British authority without ever considering their prisoner's logical, and even threatened, response. The decision to send Henke to Canada reflected the perceived need for some kind of "punishment," but for appearance rather than effect. For his part, Henke—a man who shrank from no confrontation with higher authority—allowed himself to be destroyed by a shadow. Armed with the truth of the *Ceramic* incident, aware that the sole survivor was safe in German captivity and available for any defense, Henke uncharacteristically chose not to fight at all.

The ironies surrounding Henke's death are particularly compelling. As noted earlier, both Henke and his captors overlooked the fact that the "war criminal" broadcast had been issued by the Americans, not the British. And had Henke yielded to Op-16-Z's pressure to cooperate, any intelligence he would have divulged would have been far less significant than what the Allies already possessed through ULTRA.

Most ironic, Henke fell victim to a propaganda legacy of World War I, the image of the cold-blooded, professional U-Boat commander who routinely committed war crimes. This poster portrait contrasted sharply with the reality of Werner Henke's character: temperamental, cosmopolitan, and as humane in his conduct as the nature of unrestricted submarine warfare allowed. Five of the vessels he sank suffered no casualties among their crews; four other ships lost only one man each in their sinkings (see appendix 2).

As we have seen, Henke remained an outsider in the German Navy officer corps throughout his ten-year career. He did not enter the navy as a life-long ambition, but as a professional opportunity. His family background and education differed from that of most of his comrades. He was impetuous, independent, and outgoing in a service that valued reserve, discipline, and reflection. Moreover, Henke's age, civilian career, extensive travel, and receptivity to such new and foreign influences as Cole Porter and jazz gave him a breadth of perspective not common among his fellow officers.

Yet at the moment of his death, the lone wolf returned to the pack. Henke's end ultimately reconciled his idiosyncratic personality with navy tradition. Suicide did not figure in Henke's makeup, but defiance did. When he learned of his imminent departure for Canada, Henke considered himself a dead man. In his eyes, to force the Americans to kill him in the act of escape represented both a gesture of defiance and his only choice.

The same gesture can be seen on several occasions in modern German naval history. The High Seas Fleet's mass scuttling in Scapa Flow in 1919, the scuttling of the *Admiral Graf Spee* outside Montevideo harbor and the suicide of her captain in 1939, the final battles of battleships *Bismarck* and *Scharnhorst* "to the last shell," even Dönitz's continuation of the U-Boat campaign after May 1943, all represented a tradition of "heroic death" when hope of victory was gone. As Erich Raeder had written of the overwhelming odds against his surface forces in 1939, the only course left them was "to show they know how to die with dignity"—and they had.

Such a tradition meshed all too well with the policies of National Socialism. Adolf Hitler's dedication to expansion and conquest dominated the last ten years of Henke's life. The latter's entry into the navy directly resulted from Hitler's expansion of the armed forces to prepare for the eventual conflict his policies guaranteed. The need for trained officers in the desperate struggle kept Henke at the front when his transgressions threatened to end his career. His success as a submarine commander, a destroyer of the merchant ships that had earlier supplied his livelihood, brought him fame and recognition that culminated in a personal decoration from Hitler himself. And fittingly, *U–515*'s fate— surrounded and destroyed by superior numbers and technology—foreshadowed that of Nazi Germany.

But though his career served and reflected National Socialism, Henke's character could not be reconciled to the ideals that ruled the Third Reich. As noted, *U–515*'s crew enjoyed listening to the same jazz and Cole Porter music at sea for which German youths were arrested and sent to concentration camps at home. Henke's battle with the *Gauleiter* and Gestapo of Innsbruck demonstrated his loyalty to friends over ideology, just as his constant disciplinary problems reflected a rebellious independence. Henke's combat successes served the goals of his regime, but they also shielded Henke and his men in their own subversion of those goals.

Thus developed the paradox that Werner Henke ably served, and was amply rewarded by, a system antithetical to many of his own beliefs. Firmly rooted in the German past, Henke embodied key elements of Germany's future: adaptable to change, open to new ideas and influences, unimpressed by symbols of authority. If National Socialism signified Germany's tortured and bloody transition to the modern era, it was Henke's fate to pay a part of that terrible price.

On 18 July 1944, Dönitz issued a eulogy for Henke throughout the U-

Boat service. "We have lost one of our best," lamented the navy commander in chief. "In sorrow we dip our flags to this iron-hard, brave warrior, the example to his inspired crew, and our good comrade." Earlier, a British radio propaganda broadcast reported Henke as missing in action, adding: "There was always something very honorable and upstanding about Werner Henke. . . . We can only hope that Henke was saved and taken prisoner. Such men will still be needed later."[4]

For once, German and Allied broadcasts were both correct.

NOTES

1. Interview with Mary Scheeler, *Mount Vernon Gazette*, 27 February 1992. The same article also describes the wholesale destruction of records at the fort at war's end.

2. Review of correspondence in POW Operations Division classified decimal files 253.91 (General) and 253.91 (Ft. Hunt), May–June 1944, RG 389, NA; the November 1944 correspondence is cited in the Prologue.

3. Albrecht Henke interviews, 18–19 September 1987; Wolfgang Hirschfeld, *Das letzte Boot: Atlantik Farewell* (Munich: Universitas, 1989), 207–8.

4. Dönitz, "Tagesbefehl an die Ubootwaffe," 18 July 1944, in Henke family papers; *Soldatensender Calais* broadcast of 3 June 1944, in Op-16-W subject file "Broadcasts," RG 38, NA.

Appendix 1

The Place of Henke in the U-Boat War

In contrast to the natural elements that shaped its character, the Battle of the Atlantic was measured in the headquarters of both sides with graphs, charts, and numbers. Calculations of production and loss rates, enemy losses, and projections of future trends converted blasted ships and dead men into colored lines and figures on paper. Yet this was the only way that the progress of the campaign could be traced at the highest levels, and the numbers were not meaningless. Additional evaluation of these numbers today can provide a better understanding of the longest battle of all in World War II.

A statistical review of Werner Henke and U–515's record illustrates both the unique history of that submarine and the overall conduct of the U-Boat war.

A convention of U-Boat literature features a listing of the most successful commanders to establish their relative performance. The usual ranking simply follows the total amount of merchant tonnage sunk. This omits such critical factors as enemy warships sunk or damaged, the period in the war when the merchant vessels were sunk, and the performance of missions outside the tonnage war. The last is particularly significant for the 1943–45 period, when even Dönitz conceded the prime mission as tying down the maximum number of enemy forces. There can be little doubt that Henke's fifth patrol, when he sank only three vessels but returned safely in spite of heavy damage, represented a greater accomplishment than the relatively easy sinkings of the first patrol.

The listing of "top" U-Boat aces that follows (see Table A.1) differs from previous rankings in two aspects. First, the tonnage derives from

Table A.1
Top U-Boat Aces of World War II

Name	Tonnage Sunk	Pct. Sunk After 1 Sept. 1942
Otto Kretschmer	257,451 (+1 destroyer)	0%
Wolfgang Lüth	228,917 (+1 submarine)	45.3%
Erich Topp	181,754 (+1 destroyer)	0%
Heinrich Lehmann-Willenbrock	177,965	0%
Viktor Schütze	174,459	0%
Herbert Schultze	173,475	0%
Günther Prien	172,153 (+1 battleship)	0%
Heinrich Liebe	170,996	0%
Karl-F. Merten	165,294	31.1%
Heinrich Bleichrodt	158,420 (+1 sloop)	15.1%
Joachim Schepke	156,941	0%
Georg Lassen	152,953	58.9%
Carl Emmermann	147,585	72.4%
Werner Henke	142,636	100%

Source: Compiled from data in Rohwer, *Axis Submarine Successes*. Where merchant ships were sunk by two U-Boats, tonnage was equally divided between the claimants.

Dr. Jürgen Rohwer's most recent research, which reduces many of the tonnage figures from earlier assessments. The table further adjusts for sinkings in which two or more submarines participated. Thus, Henke receives credit for only one-half of the 6,034 tons of freighter *Antinous*, as *U–512* completed her sinking. Second, the table places this data in the context of tonnage sunk after 1 September 1942, after which Allied supremacy in the Battle of the Atlantic began to assert itself.

The totals of these fourteen aces gain in significance when seen as part of the overall U-Boat effort. The 2,461,000 tons of shipping sunk represents nearly 17 percent of all Allied merchant vessels (14,675,800 tons) sent to the bottom by all German, Japanese, and Italian submarines during World War II. Incredibly, these fourteen commanders sank nearly one-fifth of all Allied merchant ships lost to submarines during the war. By contrast, a grand total of only 131 U-Boats managed to sink or damage six or more vessels during the war; another 190 U-Boats sank or damaged one to five ships. The remaining 850 German submarines—nearly 75 percent of all those commissioned during the war—failed to damage even a single Allied vessel.[1]

Wartime claims and credits of merchant tonnage sunk naturally exceeded the actual totals by varying degrees. As a modification to Table A.1, let us also consider claimed sinkings by some of the top U-Boat aces against their actual totals (see Table A.2).

Henke's accuracy in claimed sinkings, sufficiently remarkable to draw postwar praise by Dönitz,[2] is significant for two reasons. First, it demonstrates that he did not exaggerate his victories. More importantly, such precision reflects the character of solo long-range operations against relatively weakly defended areas. Most of Henke's sinkings represented unescorted single ships, where the identities and exact tonnage could be quickly ascertained by interrogation of survivors. Many of Lüth's and Lassen's victims fell into the same category.

Operations against convoys, on the other hand, handicapped an accurate identification and tonnage of vessels sunk. It is worth recalling

Table A.2
Examples of Claimed versus Actual Sinkings

Name	Claimed Tonnage	Actual Tonnage	Difference (Pct.)
Lüth	268,322	228,917	17.2%
Prien	202,000	172,153	17.3%
Kretschmer	313,611	257,451	21.8%
Lassen	205,000	152,953	34.0%
Schepke	233,971	156,941	49.1%
Henke	162,000	142,636	13.6%

Source: Herzog and Shomaekers, *Ritter der Tiefe*, and Rohwer, *Axis Submarine Successes*.

that Henke's most exaggerated claims occurred in his attack upon Convoy TS 37 in May 1943, when the confusion of battle led him to claim nine ships instead of the actual seven. Actions against surface warships proved violent, chaotic affairs, as Henke's experiences demonstrate. It is not surprising that commanders who operated primarily against heavily defended convoys should believe they inflicted more damage than they did.

The American submarine effort in the Pacific reinforces this view. Total wartime claims of four thousand Japanese vessels totalling 10 million tons sunk were reduced by postwar analysis to 1,314 vessels and 5.3 million tons. Such assessments adjusted the claims of the leading American ace, Dick O'Kane, from 31 ships and 227,800 tons to 24 ships and 93,824 tons sunk.[3]

The U-Boats' success against independent merchant ships underscores the vulnerability of these vessels to submarine attack. Postwar analysis indicates that the sinking of independents constituted the most effective means of sinking Allied tonnage. A review of the 19 most successful patrols of the war—including Henke's third cruise—reveals that 885,000 of the 1,114,000 total tons sunk during these operations represented independent ships.[4] Werner Henke and *U–515* formed an integral part of the most efficient German submarine operations of the war.

Henke's success also sheds some light on the role of ULTRA intelligence and "lone wolf" operations of long-range U-Boats. Beginning with *U–515*'s second patrol, dozens of messages exchanged between Henke and BdU were intercepted and read by Allied intelligence, yet these had no tactical significance for Henke's operations. First, Henke's solo activities required far less radio communication than wolf-pack boats attacking a convoy. Second, the Allies could only make sparing operational use of signal intelligence for offensive purposes—as in the destruction of the "milk-cow" tankers in June–August 1943—lest Dönitz realize that his codes had been compromised. Therefore radar, radio direction-finding, and visual sighting remained the principal means by which *U–515* was detected.

Yet ULTRA did limit *U–515*'s contribution to the submarine war. When Henke and his comrades radioed their sightings of convoys, the latter were rerouted to evade their pursuers. Whenever Henke reported on conditions in an operational area, and passed along his hard-earned lessons in Allied defensive measures and practices, the eavesdropping enemy knew precisely what to change before the next U-Boat arrived.

Conversely, Henke wasted valuable time searching in vain for shipping patterns and traffic routes altered on the basis of ULTRA intercepts. Finally, the intercepts yielded a great amount of technical intelligence on the latest German radar detectors and torpedoes.[5]

Table A.3 provides an overview of the U-Boat war in the Atlantic. The three dates selected combine appropriate stages of the Battle of the Atlantic with key dates in Henke's submarine career. The first date, 20 August 1940, is an arbitrary selection based on the opening of Lorient as an operational base, Hitler's declaration of unrestricted submarine warfare (17 August), and the approximate midpoint of Henke's U-Boat officer training. The second date, 12 August 1942, marks *U–515*'s departure on her first patrol at the height of the campaign. The final date, 9 April 1944, when *U–515* was sunk, illustrates the extent of Allied dominance in 1944.

The "Total U-Boats" in the table reflects only those submarines at sea in the Atlantic for those dates, as recorded in the BdU war diary; the "U-Boats Lost on Patrol" indicates those boats that did not return from these patrols. The tonnage-sinking rates (tons sunk per U-Boat per day at sea) follows BdU's own formula, representing the daily average for the month indicated.

As can be seen, the U-Boat forces at the beginning of the campaign were few in number and limited to obsolescent models of considerable age, yet they accomplished the highest sinking rates and suffered the fewest losses. In part this testified to the outstanding training and experience of the U-Boat captains of the time (six of the top twelve aces noted above commanded their own submarines by October 1939). Above all, however, it reflected the poor state of Allied defenses.

By August 1942, the U-Boat arm had both greatly expanded and considerably upgraded its forces. Newly constructed submarines of the latest designs comprised the bulk of the fleet. Yet, while U-Boats claimed over 587,000 tons in August 1942, the relative sinking rate declined significantly from that of two years earlier while German losses increased. Allied defensive measures had more than kept pace with submarine developments, especially when it is remembered that German communications intelligence and cryptographic security enjoyed the advantage over the Allies at this time.[6]

In April 1944, Dönitz's forces still maintained a sizable strength but their defeat had already been sealed. Despite the presence of some newer models, over two-thirds of the submarines represented classes in use

Table A.3
The U-Boat War, 1940–44

		20 August 1940	12 August 1942	9 April 1944
TOTAL U-BOATS		27*	89	60
U-BOAT TYPES	II C	7		
	VII A	6		
	VII B	8	1	
	VII C		48	28
	VII C/41		2	
	VII D		2	2
	VII F			1
	IX A	3	1	
	IX B	2	2	1
	IX C		28	9
	IX C/40			12
	IX D			6
	X B		1	
	XIV		4	1
U-BOAT AGES (YRS)				
	0-1	9	55	17
	1-2	12	31	26
	+2	6	3	17
TONNAGE–SINKING RATE (Tons sunk per U-Boat per day)		715	220	36
U-BOATS LOST ON PATROL		1	9	18
	Pct.	3%	10%	30%
COMMANDING OFFICERS' AVERAGE AGE		30.4	30.9	28.7

*One boat, U-A, did not belong to any category, but was built for Turkey and never delivered.

Source: KTB BdU; Gröner, *Die deutschen Kriegsschiffe*, Vol. 3; Lohmann and Hildebrand, *Die deutsche Kriegsmarine*, Vol. 3; and Tarrant, *U-Boat Offensive*.

twenty months earlier, and the proportion of boats over two years old was actually greater than that of August 1940. Sinkings of merchant ships declined to negligible amounts, while losses rose to horrific totals.

The average age of U-Boat commanding officers also merits attention. Though the average declines for the final period, it is not a drastic drop. A more systematic review of the ages of *Kommandanten* of 304 newly commissioned U-Boats throughout 1944 reveals an average age of 26 years, 8 months; 129 commanders fell below the age of 25. (Henke, aged 33 in August 1942, was only one month shy of 35 in April 1944.)

More to the point, perhaps, are the findings of British intelligence in December 1943 regarding the average operational experience of submarine captains: Nearly half possessed only six months or less of experience in command, and for 30 percent of the total the figure amounted to only three months. Henke by contrast belonged to the eight percent with 16 or more months of experience.[7]

The operational history of *U-515* itself encapsulates much of the history of the Atlantic campaign. The essential data for the submarine's six war cruises is reproduced in Table A.4.

The easy successes of the first patrol came against relatively light Allied defenses off Trinidad and Tobago. Never again would Henke and his crew experience such relative success and such little risk. A comparison between the third and fifth patrols is revealing, as both occurred in the same operational area off the West African coast. The relative increase (roughly 37%) in the number of "air alarms" (submergings due to sightings or radar-impulse detection of aircraft) illustrates the increased air protection for this distant area over the seven-month interval between Henke's appearances.

Yet this merely underscores Henke's ability to avoid depth-bombings on the fifth patrol, when his vessel was too badly damaged to risk additional wounds. That he still managed to sink ships and make his presence felt without unduly exposing his command constitutes a remarkable achievement, far surpassing his single-night savaging of a lightly protected convoy.

Also noteworthy in Table A.4 are the travel rates achieved by *U-515*, consistently maintained throughout her career in spite of the constant growth of Allied air power. Without a basis for comparison with other Type IXC boats, no firm conclusions can be drawn, but Henke's ability to keep on the move probably contributed significantly to the boat's long career.

A final factor in evaluating Henke and his crew concerns torpedo

Table A.4
U–515's Operational Patrols

PATROL NO.	DATES	DAYS AT SEA	MERCHANT SHIPS SUNK	TONNAGE	TONS/DAY AT SEA	DISTANCES SURF./SUB. (TOTAL)	TRAVEL RATES/DAY (SURF./SUB.)	NO. AIR ALARMS	NO. DEPTH-BOMBINGS
1	Aug. - Oct. 1942	64	10	52,807	825.1	9,481/ 425.5 (10,266.5)	153.8/ 6.6	11	2
2	Nov. 1942 - Jan. 1943	61	1	18,713	306.8	7,721/ 807 (8,528)	126.6/ 13.2	17	10
3	Feb. - June 1943	124	10	58,456	471.4	18,915.5/ 1,467.5 (20,383)	152.5/ 11.8	43	10
4	Aug. - Sep. 1943	15	0	-----	-----	1,761/ 311 (2,072)	117.4/ 20.7	4	1
5	Nov. 1943- Jan. 1944	66	3	20,913	316.9	8,601/ 1,061	130.3/ 16.1	36	1
6	Mar. - Apr. 1944	10	-----	-----	-----	ca. 1,400 Total	ca. 140.0	(Sunk)	(Sunk)

Source: KTB *U–515;* Rohwer, *Axis Submarine Successes.*

accuracy, recorded in Table A.5. The table also notes the varieties in warhead types on each patrol in the Kriegsmarine's desperate race to improve its weapons technology.

In contrast to many other aspects of a submarine's performance, torpedo marksmanship reflected the captain's individual ability. He supervised surface torpedo firings carried out by the first watch officer, and conducted all submerged firings himself. Henke's overall record of 50 hits in 70 shots (71.4%), and six of nine submerged firings (66.7%) indicates a key ingredient in *U–515*'s success: Henke was an excellent shot. Most of these firings occurred at ranges of 600 to 1,000 meters, but he achieved some hits at distances of 1,500 meters. Much of this can probably be attributed to his experience as a merchant marine officer: A familiarity with ship sizes, drafts, and speeds facilitated his work in calculating firing angles, ranges, and torpedo depths.

How does his performance compare with other U-Boat commanders? Again no firm answer can be given until a systematic review of available records provides the necessary data. Some indication, however, is given in fragmentary monthly statistics maintained by the U-Boat Command.

Grave problems with defective torpedoes dogged German submarines throughout the early war period, and remained a source of concern for the rest of the war. The torpedoes with which Henke began his career could be detonated either by contact with the target's hull or by the proximity of the hull's magnetic field, but the unreliability of the latter precluded their use until the introduction of the Pi–2 detonator. Even with this handicap, German submariners during the period September–October 1940 maintained a torpedo accuracy rate of 62.5 percent (173 hits of 277 fired, excluding duds). But by October–November 1942, the time of Henke's first patrol, the general accuracy rate had declined to 53.4 percent with duds, only 48.5 percent without. By the period May–July 1943, when Dönitz abandoned the struggle against the North Atlantic convoys, the figures declined again to 45.3 and 43.3 percent, respectively.[8]

Thus Henke's marksmanship far exceeded the average. Together with his facility for movement, his balancing of boldness with judgment, his seamanship, and a capacity for a unique brand of leadership that overcame his crew's legitimate grievances, Werner Henke deserved his place as one of the outstanding submarine commanders of the war. Supported by a superb veteran crew, generally permitted to operate in areas suited to his boat's capabilities, and often blessed with good fortune, Henke

Table A.5
Torpedo Attacks by *U–515*

PATROL NO.	DATES	ATTACKS			TORPEDOES FIRED/HIT			WARHEAD TYPES
		SURF.	SUB.	TOTAL	SURF.	SUB.	TOTAL	
1	Aug.-Oct. 1942	9	3	12	13/18	5/5	18/23	Contact
2	Nov. 1942-Jan. 1943	4	0	4	10/17	----	10/17	Contact
3	Feb.-June 1943	5	1	6	15/17	0/2	15/19	Contact, Magnetic
4	Aug.-Sep. 1943	----	----	----	----	----	----	Contact, Magnetic, Acoustic
5	Nov. 1943-Jan. 1944	4	1	5	6/9	1/2	7/11	Contact, Magnetic, Acoustic, FAT
6	Mar.-Apr. 1944	----	----	----	----	----	----	Contact, Magnetic, Acoustic, FAT
TOTALS		22	5	27	44/61	6/9	50/70*	

*Includes two duds known to have struck targets.

Source: *U–515* KTB; *Schussmeldungen*, Bibliothek für Zeitgeschichte, Stuttgart; *U–515* Final Interrogation Report, Op-16-Z files, RG 38, NA.

and the men of *U–515* accomplished more than anyone had a right to expect.

But in the end, it only delayed the inevitable. The final proof of Henke's ability lies in the survival of most of his crew, the only victory left to the men of the U-Boat service.

NOTES

1. Many boats, of course, were training submarines or did not become operational before Germany surrendered, but between 550 and 600 combat U-Boats failed to make a successful attack. See Jak P. Mallmann Showell, *U-Boats Under the Swastika*, 2nd ed. (Annapolis, MD: Naval Institute Press, 1987), 16–18; and V. E. Tarrant, *The U-Boat Offensive 1914–1945* (Annapolis, MD: Naval Institute Press, 1989), 151, for a discussion of differing figures of tonnage sunk.

2. Karl Dönitz, *Memoirs: Ten Years and Twenty Days* (Annapolis, MD: Naval Institute Press, 1990), 338.

3. Clay Blair, Jr., *Silent Victory: The U.S. Submarine War Against Japan* (New York: Bantam Books, 1976), 877–78.

4. See Bodo Herzog and Günter Schomaekers, *Ritter der Tiefe-Graue Wölfe* (Wels, Austria: Welsermühl München-Wels, 1976), 308–9.

5. See "A Preliminary Analysis of the Role of Decryption Intelligence in the Operational Phase of the Battle of the Atlantic," U.S. Navy OEG Report #66 (August 1951), Study no. SRH–367, RG 457, NA.

6. See Patrick Beesly, *Very Special Intelligence: The Story of the Admiralty's Operational Intelligence Centre 1939–1945* (Garden City, NY: Doubleday & Company, 1978), 116–22, 153–54.

7. Rolf Güth and Jochen Brennecke, "Hier irrte Michael Salewski: Das Trauma von 'Kinderkreuzzug' der U-Boote," *Schiff und Zeit* 28 (1989), 45; Beesly, *Very Special*, 210.

8. Data for September–October 1940 incorporated with general assessments of U-Boat sinkings in BdU files, PG 30956 (T–1022/3403); subsequent data from monthly "Torpedolageberichte" in files PG 33349 and 33351 (T–1022/2097). See also Eberhard Rössler, *Die Torpedos der deutschen U-Boote* (Herford: Koehler, 1984), 84–94, 100–101.

Appendix 2

Sinkings by *U–515*

Listed below, in chronological order, are the ships sunk or permanently disabled by *U–515* during her twenty months of operations during the war. Provided for each vessel are the date(s) of sinking, type of ship, name, tonnage, nationality or registry, position, number of crewmen and passengers, and number of lives lost (sources for data provided in text).

12 September 1942: Motor tanker *Stanvac Melbourne* (10,013 tons, Panamanian), 10°30′N, 60°20′W; 49 crew, 1 lost.

12 September 1942: Motor tanker *Woensdrecht* (4,668 tons, Dutch), 10°27′N, 60°17′W; 37 crew and 35 survivors of another sunken vessel, 1 lost.

13 September 1942: Steamer *Ocean Vanguard* (7,174 tons, British), 10°43′N, 60°11′W; 51 crew, 11 killed or missing.

13 September 1942: Freighter *Nimba* (1,854 tons, Panamanian), 10°41′N, 60°24′W; 31 crew and passengers, 19 lost.

14 September 1942: Steamer *Harborough* (5,415 tons, British), 10°03′N, 60°20′W; 49 crew, 2 lost.

15 September 1942: Motorship *Sörholt* (4,801 tons, Norwegian), 10°45′N, 60°00′W; 38 crew, 7 lost.

16 September 1942: Freighter *Mae* (5,607 tons, U.S.A.), 08°03′N, 58°13′W; 34 crew, 1 lost.

20 September 1942: Steamer *Reedpool* (4,838 tons, British), 00°58′N, 57°34′W; 41 crew and 16 survivors of another sunken vessel, 6 lost.

23 September 1942: Freighter *Lindvangen* (2,412 tons, Norwegian), 09°20′N, 60°10′W; 23 crew, 15 killed or missing.

23 September 1942: Freighter *Antinous* (6,034 tons, U.S.A.), 08°58′N, 59°33′W (ship abandoned and taken in tow, sunk the next day by *U–512*); 48 crew, no losses.

11–12 November 1942: Destroyer depot ship HMS *Hecla* (10,850 tons, British warship), 35°43′N, 09°54′W; 847 officers and other ranks, 279 lost.

7–8 December 1942: Passenger liner and troopship *Ceramic* (18,713 tons, British), 40°30′N, 40°20′W; 278 crew and 378 passengers, all but one lost in sinking and subsequent storm; survivor taken prisoner.

4 March 1943: Motor ship *California Star* (8,300 tons, British), 42°32′N, 37°20′W; 70 crew and 4 passengers, 50 killed, missing, or died of wounds; 1 survivor taken prisoner.

9 April 1943: Motor ship *Bamako* (2,357 tons, French), 14°57′N, 17°15′W; 37 crew and passengers; 20 lost.

30 April–1 May 1943: Motor ship *Corabella* (5,682 tons, Canadian), 07°15′N, 13°49′W; 48 crew, 9 killed or missing.

30 April–1 May 1943: Steamer *Bandar Shahpour* (5,236 tons, British), 07°15′N, 13°49′W; 70 crew and passengers, 1 lost.

30 April–1 May 1943: Motor ship *Kota Tjandi* (7,295 tons, Dutch), 07°15′N, 13°49′W; 77 crew and passengers, 6 lost.

30 April–1 May 1943: Freighter *Nagina* (6,551 tons, British), 07°19′N, 13°50′W; 115 crew and passengers, 2 lost.

1 May 1943: Freighter *Mokambo* (4,996 tons, Belgian), 07°58′N, 14°14′W; 58 crew and passengers, no casualties.

1 May 1943: Steamer *City of Singapore* (6,555 tons, British), 07°55′N, 14°16′W; 97 crew and passengers, no casualties.

1 May 1943: Freighter *Clan Macpherson* (6,940 tons, British), 08°04′N, 14°12′W (ship abandoned twice and drifted 10 miles before sinking); 140 crew, 4 lost.

9 May 1943: Motor ship *Corneville* (4,544 tons, Norwegian), 04°50′N, 01°10′W; 41 crew, no casualties.

18 November 1943: Sloop HMS *Chanticleer* (1,350 tons, British warship), 40°06′N, 19°48′W (ship towed to safety but never sailed again); 192 officers and other ranks, 31 killed.

17 December 1943: Freighter *Kingswood* (5,080 tons, British), 05°57′N, 01°43′E; 55 crew, no casualties.

19 December 1944: Freighter *Phemius* (7,406 tons, British), 05°01′N, 00°47′E; 84 crew and 30 passengers, 23 killed or missing, 1 taken prisoner.

20 December 1943: Motor ship *Dumana* (8,427 tons, British), 04°27′N, 06°58′W; 147 crew and 22 RAF passengers, 39 killed or missing.

Selected Bibliography

PRIMARY SOURCES

National Archives, Washington, DC

Record Group 242, National Archives Collection of Seized Enemy Records, 1942–
Microcopy T–1022: German Navy
Microcopy T–175: Reichsführer-SS and Chief of the German Police

Record Group 38, Records of the Office of the Chief of Naval Operations (CNO)
Office files of Op-16-Z
Office files of Op-16-W

Record Group 165, Records of War Department General and Special Staffs
G–2 (Intelligence) Division

Record Group 457, Records of the National Security Agency
SRGN Collection of U-Boat Communications Intercepts

Record Group 389, Records of the Office of the Provost Marshal General
Prisoner of War (POW) Operations Division

Record Group 80, General Records of the Department of the Navy
General Correspondence of the Secretary of the Navy

Record Group 24, Records of the Naval Bureau of Personnel
Deck logs of U.S. warships

Record Group 262, Records of the Foreign Broadcast Intercept Service
Intercepted Broadcasts of Radio Berlin

Operational Archives (OpArchives), Washington Navy Yard

Action Reports
Records of the Tenth Fleet
World War II Command Files

Public Record Office (PRO) Kew, U.K.

Records of the Admiralty (ADM 199)

Stiftung Traditionsarchiv Unterseeboote, Cuxhaven

Collected historical materials and photographs

Wehrgeschichtliches Ausbildungszentrum, Marineschule Mürwik

Historical materials relating to Crew 33

Bibliothek für Zeitgeschichte, Stuttgart

Schussmeldungen (torpedo-firing reports) for *U–515*

Henke Family Papers, Lüneburg

Werner Henke's personal papers, service record, photographs

Chicago Museum of Science and Industry

Donated U.S. Navy materials relating to *U–505*

INTERVIEWS AND CORRESPONDENCE

The following family members, associates, and crewmen of *U–515* provided information concerning Werner Henke and his command in the form of interviews (I) and/or correspondence (C) during the period 1987–92: Albrecht Henke (I/C); Karl-Friedrich Merten (I/C); Wilhelm Müller-Arnecke (I/C); Peter Cremer (I); Reinhard Hardegen (I); the late Heinrich Niemeyer (C); Günther Altenburger (I); Carl Möller (I/C); Hans Hahn (I/C); the late Günter Eckert (I); Hermann Brandt (I); Herbert Bölke (I); Werner Rasche (I); Hermann Kaspers (I); Günter Schoppmann (C); and Eduard Voigt (I).

GERMAN NAVY AND GOVERNMENT PUBLICATIONS

Marineverordnungsblatt, 15 March–15 July 1944.
M.Dv. Nr. 416/3, Torpedo-Schiessvorschrift für U-Boote, Heft 3: Feuerleitung auf U-Booten. Berlin: Oberkommando der Kriegsmarine, 1943.
Rangliste der Deutschen Kriegsmarine (M.Dv. Nr. 293), 1935–42. Berlin: E. S. Mittler & Sohn, 1935–42.
Statistisches Reichsamt. *Statistisches Jahrbuch für das Deutsche Reich 1939–40*. Berlin: Statistisches Reichsamt, 1940.

The U-Boat Commander's Handbook (U.S. Navy translation of *Marine-Druckvorschrift [M.Dv.]* No. 906, 1943 ed.). Intro. by E. J. Coates. Gettysburg, PA: Thomas Publications, 1989.

SECONDARY SOURCES: BOOKS

Alden, John D. *The Fleet Submarine in the U.S. Navy: A Design and Construction History*. Annapolis, MD: Naval Institute Press, 1979.

Angolia, John R. *On the Field of Honor: A History of the Knight's Cross Bearers*. 2 vols. San Jose, CA: Roger J. Bender, 1978–80.

Beesly, Patrick. *Very Special Intelligence: The Story of the Admiralty's Operational Intelligence Centre 1939–1945*. Garden City, NY: Doubleday & Company, 1978.

Bidlingmaier, Gerhard. *Einsatz der schweren Kriegsmarineeinheiten im ozeanischen Zufuhrkrieg*. Neckargemünd: Scharnhorst, 1963.

Bird, Keith W. *German Naval History: A Guide to the Literature*. New York: Garland, 1985.

Blair, Clay, Jr. *Silent Victory: The U.S. Submarine War Against Japan*. New York: Bantam Books, 1976.

Bonatz, Heinz. *Seekrieg im Äther. Die Leistungen der Marine-Funkaufklärung 1939–1945*. Herford: E. S. Mittler & Sohn, 1981.

Bowen, Frank C. *The Flag of the Southern Cross 1939–1945*. London: Shaw Savill & Albion Co., n.d.

Brennecke, Jochen. *Jäger-Gejagte: Deutsche U-Boote 1939–1945*. Munich: Wilhelm Heyne Verlag, 1986.

———. *Die Wende im U-Boot-Krieg. Ursachen und Folgen 1939–1943*. Herford: Koehler, 1984.

Buchheim, Lothar-Günther. *Das Boot*. Munich: R. Piper, 1976.

———. *Zu Tode Gesiegt: Der Untergang der U-Boote*. Munich: C. Bertelsmann Verlag, 1989.

Busch, F. O. *Akten des Seekrieges*. Berlin: Brunnen Verlag, 1940.

Busch, Harald. *So War der U-Boot-Krieg*. Bielefeld: Deutscher Heimat-Verlag, 1952.

Cameron, John, ed. *The "Peleus" Trial*. Vol. I of the War Crimes Trials series, ed. by Sir David Maxwell Fyfe. London: William Hodge and Co., Ltd., 1948.

Childers, Thomas. *The Nazi Voter: The Social Foundations of Fascism in Germany, 1919–1933*. Chapel Hill: University of North Carolina Press, 1983.

Clough, Ethlyn T., ed. *German Life*. Detroit: Bay View, 1913.

Costello, John, and Hughes, Terry. *The Battle of the Atlantic*. New York: Dial Press/James Wade, 1977.

Cremer, Peter, with Fritz Brustat-Naval. *U-Boat Commander*. Trans. by Lawrence Wilson. Annapolis, MD: Naval Institute Press, 1984.

Deutsches Marine Institut, ed. *Marineschule Mürwik*. Herford: E. S. Mittler & Sohn, 1985.

Dönitz, Karl. *Memoirs: Ten Years and Twenty Days*. Intro. and afterword by Jürgen

Rohwer, trans. by R. H. Stevens. Annapolis, MD: Naval Institute Press, 1990.

Dülffer, Jost. *Weimar, Hitler, und die Marine. Reichspolitik und Flottenbau 1920–1939.* Düsseldorf: Droste Verlag, 1973.

Elliott, Peter. *Allied Escort Ships of World War II: A Complete Survey.* Annapolis, MD: Naval Institute Press, 1977.

Farago, Ladislas. *Burn After Reading: The Espionage History of World War II.* New York: Walker and Company, 1961.

———. *The Tenth Fleet.* New York: Paperback Library, 1964.

Feining, Franz, and Prowe, Friedrich. *Thorn in alten Ansichten.* Zaltbommel/NL: Europäische Bibliothek, 1981.

Führer Conferences on Naval Affairs 1939–1945. Foreword by Jak P. Mallmann Showell. Annapolis, MD: Naval Institute Press, 1990.

Gallery, Daniel V. *Clear the Decks!* New York: William Morrow and Company, 1951.

———. *U–505.* New York: Paperback Library, 1967.

Gannon, Michael. *Operation Drumbeat. The Dramatic True Story of Germany's First U-Boat Attacks Along the American Coast in World War II.* New York: Harper & Row, 1990.

Gasaway, E. B. *Grey Wolf, Grey Sea.* New York: Ballantine Books, 1970.

Gröner, Erich. *Die deutschen Kriegsschiffe 1815–1945.* Cont. and ed. by Dieter Jung and Martin Maass. 6 vols. Koblenz: Bernard & Graefe Verlag, 1985–91.

Hagen, William W. *Germans, Poles, and Jews: The Nationality Conflict in the Prussian East, 1772–1914.* Chicago: University of Chicago, 1980.

Hamilton, Richard F. *Who Voted for Hitler?* Princeton: Princeton University Press, 1982.

Herlin, Hans. *Verdammter Atlantik. Schicksale deutscher U-Boot-Fahrer.* Munich: Wilhelm Heyne Verlag, 1982.

Herzog, Bodo, and Schomaekers, Günter. *Ritter der Tiefe-Graue Wölfe. Die erfolgreichsten U-Boot-Kommandanten der Welt.* Wels, Austria: Welsermühl München-Wels, 1976.

Hessler, Günter. *The U-Boat War in the Atlantic 1939–1945.* Published under the auspices of the Ministry of Defence. London: Her Majesty's Stationery Office, 1989.

Heuer, Reinhold. *Siebenhundert Jahre Thorn 1231–1931.* Danzig: W. F. Burau, 1931.

Hinsley, F. H., et al. *British Intelligence in the Second World War.* 5 vols. in 6 pts. New York: Cambridge University Press, 1979–81. London: Her Majesty's Stationery Office, 1979–90.

Hirschfeld, Wolfgang. *Das letzte Boot: Atlantik Farewell.* Munich: Universitas, 1989.

Hocking, Charles, ed. *Dictionary of Disasters at Sea During the Age of Steam.* London: Lloyd's Register of Shipping, 1969.

Högel, Georg. *Embleme, Wappen, Malings deutscher U-Boote 1939–1945.* Herford: Koehler, 1987.

Irving, David. *Hitler's War.* New York: Viking Press, 1977.

Jähnig, Bernhart, and Letkemann, Peter. *Thorn: Königin der Weichsel 1231–1981.* Göttingen: Vandenhoeck & Ruprecht, 1981.

Kahn, David. *Seizing the Enigma: The Race to Break the German U-Boat Codes, 1939–1943.* Boston: Houghton Mifflin, 1991.

Keel, Daniel, ed. *Das Ringelnatz Lesebuch.* Zürich: Diogenes, 1984.

Köhl, Fritz, and Niestle, Axel. *Vom Original zum Modell: Uboottyp IXC. Eine Bild- und Plandokumentation.* Koblenz: Bernard & Graefe Verlag, 1990.

Koppes, Clayton R., and Black, Gregory D. *Hollywood Goes to War: How Politics, Profits, and Propaganda Shaped World War II Movies.* Los Angeles: University of California Press, 1987.

Kurowski, Franz. *Die Träger des Ritterkreuzes des Eisernen Kreuzes der U-Bootwaffe 1939–1945.* Bad Nauheim: Podzun 1987.

Lohmann, Walter, and Hildebrand, Hans H. *Die Deutsche Kriegsmarine 1939–1945: Gliederung-Einsatz-Stellenbesetzung.* 3 vols. Bad Nauheim: Podzun-Verlag, 1956–64.

Mallmann Showell, Jak P. *U-Boat Command and the Battle of the Atlantic.* Lewiston, NY: Vanwell, 1989.

———. *U-Boats Under the Swastika.* 2nd ed. Annapolis, MD: Naval Institute Press, 1987.

McLachlan, Donald. *Room 39: Naval Intelligence in Action 1939–1945.* London: Weidenfeld and Nicolson, 1968.

Middlebrook, Martin. *Convoy.* New York: William Morrow and Company, 1976.

Middlebrook, Martin, and Everitt, Chris. *The Bomber Command War Diaries. An Operational Reference Book, 1939–1945.* London: Viking, 1985.

Militärgeschichtliches Forschungsamt, ed. *Das Deutsche Reich und der Zweite Weltkrieg.* 6 vols. to date. Stuttgart: Deutsche Verlags-Anstalt, 1979–90.

Moore, Capt. Arthur R. *A Careless Word . . . A Needless Sinking.* Kings Point, NY: American Merchant Marine Museum, 1983.

Moore, John Hammond. *The Faustball Tunnel: German POWs in America and Their Great Escape.* New York: Random House, 1978.

Morison, Samuel Eliot. *The Atlantic Battle Won, May 1943–May 1945.* vol. X of *History of United States Naval Operations in World War II.* Boston: Little, Brown and Company, 1975.

———. *The Battle of the Atlantic 1939–1943.* vol. I of *History of United States Naval Operations in World War II.* Boston: Little, Brown and Company, 1975.

Neitzel, Sönke. *Die deutschen Ubootbunker und Bunkerwerften.* Koblenz: Bernard & Graefe Verlag, 1991.

Noakes, Jeremy. *The Nazi Party in Lower Saxony 1921–33.* Oxford: Oxford University Press, 1971.

Peter, Karl. *Acht Glas (Ende der Wache). Erinnerungen eines Offiziers der Crew 38.* Reutlingen: Preussischer Militär-Verlag, 1989.

Poolman, Kenneth. *The Sea Hunters.* London: Sphere Books, 1982.

Price, Alfred. *Aircraft versus Submarine: The Evolution of the Anti-Submarine Aircraft 1912 to 1972.* Annapolis, MD: Naval Institute Press, 1973.

Prien, Günther. *Mein Weg nach Scapa Flow.* Berlin: Deutscher Verlag, 1940.

Ritter, Gerhard A., with Martin Niehuss. *Wahlgeschichtliches Arbeitsbuch: Materialen zur Statistik des Kaiserreichs 1871–1918.* Munich: C. H. Beck, 1980.

Rogmann, Heinz. *Die Bevölkerungsentwicklung im preussischen Osten in den letzten hundert Jahren.* Berlin: Volk und Reich, 1937.

Rohwer, Jürgen. *Axis Submarine Successes 1939–1945*. Intro. material trans. by
    John A. Broadwin. Annapolis, MD: Naval Institute Press, 1983.
————. *The Critical Convoy Battles of March 1943*. Trans. by Derek Masters. An-
    napolis, MD: Naval Institute Press, 1977.
Rohwer, Jürgen, and Hümmelchen, Gerd. *Chronology of the War at Sea 1939–
    1945*. Trans. by Derek Masters. 2 vols. New York: Arco Publishing, 1972–
    74.
Roskill, Stephen W. *The War at Sea 1939–1945*. 3 vols. in 4 pts. London: Her
    Majesty's Stationery Office, 1954–61.
Rössler, Eberhard. *Die Sonaranlagen der deutschen U-Boote*. Herford: Koehler, 1991.
————. *Die Torpedos der deutschen U-Boote*. Herford: Koehler, 1984.
————. *The U-Boat. The Evolution and Technical History of German Submarines*.
    Trans. by Harold Erenberg. Annapolis, MD: Naval Institute Press, 1981.
Rust, Eric C. *Naval Officers Under Hitler: The Story of Crew 34*. New York: Praeger,
    1991.
Salewski, Michael. *Die deutsche Seekriegsleitung 1935–1945*. 3 vols. Frankfurt/M.
    and Munich: Bernard & Graefe Verlag, 1970–75.
————. *Von der Wirklichkeit des Krieges: Analysen und Kontroversen zu Buchheims
    'Boot.'* Munich: Deutscher Taschenbuch, 1976.
Schultz, Willi. *Linienschiff Schleswig-Holstein*. Herford: Koehler, 1991.
Smith, Bradley F. *Reaching Judgment at Nuremburg*. New York: Basic Books, Inc.,
    1977.
Stern, Robert C. *Type VII U-boats*. Annapolis, MD: Naval Institute Press, 1991.
Stjernfelt, Bertil, and Böhme, Klaus-Richard. *Westerplatte 1939*. Freiburg: Rom-
    bach Verlag, 1979.
Tarrant, V. E. *The U-Boat Offensive 1914–1945*. Annapolis, MD: Naval Institute
    Press, 1989.
Thomas, Charles S. *The German Navy in the Nazi Era*. Annapolis, MD: Naval
    Institute Press, 1990.
Topp, Erich. *Fackeln über dem Atlantik. Lebensbericht eines U-Boot-Kommandanten*.
    Herford: E. S. Mittler & Sohn, 1990.
van der Vat, Dan. *The Atlantic Campaign: World War II's Great Struggle at Sea*.
    New York: Harper & Row, 1988.
Vause, Jordan. *U-Boat Ace: The Story of Wolfgang Lüth*. Annapolis, MD: Naval
    Institute Press, 1990.
Werner, Herbert. *Iron Coffins: A Personal Account of the German U-Boat Battles of
    World War II*. New York: Holt, Rinehart & Winston, 1969.
Williamson, Gordon. *Aces of the Reich*. London: Arms and Armour, 1989.
Y'Blood, William T. *Hunter-Killer: U.S. Escort Carriers in the Battle of the Atlantic*.
    Annapolis, MD: Naval Institute Press, 1983.
Young, John M. *Britain's Sea War: A Diary of Ship Losses 1939–1945*. Wellingbor-
    ough: Patrick Stephens, 1989.

SECONDARY SOURCES: ARTICLES

Alman, Karl (Franz Kurowski). "Kapitänleutnant Werner Henke." *Der Landser-
    Ritterkreuzträger Nr. 2*, no. 680 (1971), 11–85.

Baumgart, Winfried. "Zur Ansprache Hitlers vor den Führern der Wehrmacht am 22. August 1939." *Vierteljahreshefte für Zeitgeschichte* 16, no. 2 (April 1968), 120–49.

Daugherty, William E. "Commander Norden and the German Admirals." In William E. Daugherty and Morris Janowitz, eds., *A Psychological Warfare Casebook*. Baltimore: Johns Hopkins University Press, 1958, 494–97.

Gallery, Daniel V. "Nor Dark of Night." *United States Naval Institute Proceedings* 95, no. 4 (April 1969), 85–90.

Güth, Rolf, and Brennecke, Jochen. "Hier irrte Michael Salewski: Das Trauma vom 'Kinderkreuzzug' der U-Boote." *Schiff und Zeit*, no. 28 (1989), 43–47.

Hoch, Gottfried. "Zur Problematik der Menschenführung im Kriege." In *Die Deutsche Marine: Historisches Selbstverständnis und Standortbestimmung*, comp. by Deutsches Marine Institut/Deutsche Marine Akademie (Herford: E. S. Mittler & Sohn, 1983), 191–216.

Molyneaus, Capt. Dawson (ret.). "The Sinking of U-Boat 515." *DESA News*, (September–October 1988), 7–8.

Mulligan, Timothy P. "German U-boat Crews in World War II: Sociology of an Elite." *Journal of Military History*, 56, no. 2 (April 1992), 261–81.

Pierburg, Franz. "Thorn—wie es um 1910 war." In Horst Ernst Krüger, ed., *Thorn—Stadt und Land. Geschichte, Geschichten, Namen, Erinnerungen, 1231–1981*. Lüneburg: privately published, 1981, 17–25.

Reinhardt, Uta. "Lüneburg zwischen Ersten Weltkrieg und Drittem Reich." *Niedersächsisches Jahrbuch für Landesgeschichte*, Bd. 54 (1982), 95–127.

Rössler, Eberhard. "Die deutsche U-Bootausbildung und ihre Vorbereitung 1925–1945." *Marine-Rundschau*, 68, no. 8 (1971), 453–66.

Salewski, Michael. "Das Offizierkorps der Reichs- und Kriegsmarine." In Hanns H. Hoffmann, ed., *Das deutsche Offizierkorps 1860–1960*. Boppard/R.: Harald Boldt, 1980, 211–29.

Schimpf, Axel. "Der Einsatz von Kriegsmarineeinheiten im Rahmen der Verwicklungen des spanischen Bürgerkrieges 1936 bis 1939." In Deutsches Marine Institut, ed., *Der Einsatz von Seestreitkräften im Dienst der auswärtigen Politik*. Herford: E. S. Mittler & Sohn, 1983, 76–103.

Thomas, C.R.W. "Making Naval Officers in Germany." *United States Naval Institute Proceedings*, vol. 64, no. 1 (January 1938), 39–56.

Trenkel, Hermann. "Die Thorner Schulstrasse." *Westpreussen-Jahrbuch 1958*, 93–98.

Walle, Heinrich. "Individual Loyalty and Resistance in the German Military: The Case of Sub-Lieutenant Oskar Kusch." In Francis R. Nicosia and Lawrence D. Stokes, eds., *Germans Against Nazism: Nonconformity, Opposition and Resistance in the Third Reich. Essays in Honour of Peter Hoffmann*. New York; Oxford: Berg, 1991, 323–50.

Wells, Robert D. "Persuading the U-Boats." *United States Naval Institute Proceedings*, 90, no. 12 (December 1964), 53–59.

Wiedersheim, III, Lt. Cdr. William A. "Officer Personnel Selection in the German Navy, 1925–1945." *United States Naval Institute Proceedings*, 73, no. 4 (April 1947), 445–49.

UNPUBLISHED MATERIALS

Haddon, Gordon W. "The Loss of the *Ceramic*." Hampshire, England, November 1989 (copy of the U-Boot-Archiv, Cuxhaven).

Merten, Karl-Friedrich. "Traum und Wirklichkeit eines Berufes. Lebenserinnerungen" (Merten papers).

Operations Evaluation Group (OEG) Report 51, "Anti-Submarine Warfare in World War II, Part 2: Anti-Submarine Measures and Their Effectiveness," n.d. (ca. 1946), Office of Scientific Research and Development.

Peter, Karl. "Der Fall des Oberleutnants zur See Kusch. 'Wider besseres Wissen zum Tode verurteilt'—Stimmt das?" 1985 (copy in the U-Boot-Archiv, Cuxhaven).

Schaefer, Jobst. "Die Ernährung des U-Bootsfahrers im Kriege." Inaugural dissertation for the Medical Department, Christian-Albrechts-Universität Kiel, 1943.

Index

Names of ships are italicized. Ranks for officers are the highest achieved in service.

About the Author

TIMOTHY P. MULLIGAN is an archivist specializing in captured German and World War II era U.S. military and naval records. He edited the volume *Wolf Packs* in the Time-Life series *The Third Reich* (1989), and wrote the book, *The Politics of Illusion and Empire* (Praeger, 1988).